INDIGENIZING JAPAN

INDIGENIZING JAPAN

Ainu Past, Present, and Future

JOE E. WATKINS

THE UNIVERSITY OF
ARIZONA PRESS
TUCSON

The University of Arizona Press
www.uapress.arizona.edu

We respectfully acknowledge the University of Arizona is on the land and territories of Indigenous peoples. Today, Arizona is home to twenty-two federally recognized tribes, with Tucson being home to the O'odham and the Yaqui. The University strives to build sustainable relationships with sovereign Native Nations and Indigenous communities through education offerings, partnerships, and community service.

ISBN-13: 978-0-8165-5598-7 (hardcover)
ISBN-13: 978-0-8165-5597-0 (paperback)
ISBN-13: 978-0-8165-5599-4 (ebook)

Cover design by Leigh McDonald
Cover art by Koji Yuki
Typeset by Sara Thaxton in 10.5/14 Warnock Pro with Helvetica Neue LT Std and Iva WF

All photographs are by the author unless otherwise noted.

Library of Congress Cataloging-in-Publication Data
Names: Watkins, Joe, 1951– author
Title: Indigenizing Japan : Ainu past, present, and future / Joe E. Watkins.
Description: [Tucson] : University of Arizona Press, 2025. | Includes bibliographical
    references and index.
Identifiers: LCCN 2025004372 (print) | LCCN 2025004373 (ebook) | ISBN 9780816555987
    hardcover | ISBN 9780816555970 paperback | ISBN 9780816555994 ebook
Subjects: LCSH: Ainu—Japan—Hokkaido—Social conditions | Ainu—Japan—Hokkaido—
    Government relations | Ainu—Cultural assimilation—Japan—Hokkaido | Japan—Ethnic
    relations
Classification: LCC DS832 .W357 2025 (print) | LCC DS832 (ebook) | DDC
    305.894/60524—dc23/eng/20250807
LC record available at https://lccn.loc.gov/2025004372
LC ebook record available at https://lccn.loc.gov/2025004373

Printed in the United States of America
♾ This paper meets the requirements of ANSI/NISO Z39.48-1992 (Permanence of Paper).

CONTENTS

List of Illustrations   *vii*

Acknowledgments   *xi*

Introduction   3

1. Who Are the Ainu?   11

2. Biological and Genetic Origins   35

3. Archaeology of the Japanese "Mainland" (Honshu-Shikoku-Kyushu)   49

4. The Archaeology of Hokkaido and the Ainu   77

5. History of Japanese Colonization and Assimilation of the Ainu   91

6. Assimilating the Indigenous: Other Colonial Policies of Assimilation   109

7. Organizing and "Becoming" Indigenous   135

8. Nationalizing the Past and Homogenizing the Present   157

9. Contemporary Ainu and Their Issues   171

10. Looking Back and Moving Forward   195

References   *211*

Index   *229*

ILLUSTRATIONS

Figures

1. The Ainu Porotokotan Museum in Shiraoi, 2007   4
2. Map of Japan   16
3. Peopling of the Japanese archipelago   45
4. Landmasses during the Late Pleistocene showing
    Paleo-Honshu Island and Paleo-Sakhalin-Hokkaido-
    Kuril Peninsula   50
5. *Dogū* from Hakodate Jomon Culture Center   59
6. Lacquered bowl from the Korekawa Site, Aomori
    Prefect, Honshu   60
7. Fire-flame pottery jar, Tokyo National Museum   62
8. Reconstructed long house at Sannai Maruyama,
    Aomori City, Honshu   65
9. Archaeological remnants of Early Yayoi rice paddies,
    Sunazawa Site, Hirosaki City, Aomori Prefect, Honshu 70
10. Chronology of Hokkaido archaeological cultures   78
11. The Kiusu Earthworks Burial Circles Site, Chitose
    City, Hokkaido   82
12. Jichinyama stone circle, Otaru, Hokkaido   82
13. Chronology comparison between Honshu
    and Hokkaido   84

14. Reconstructed Okhotsk pit structure, Hokuto Site
    near Kushiro, Hokkaido   86
15. Postage stamps issued by the Japanese government
    celebrating the 2021 UNESCO World Heritage
    Convention Designation of Jomon Prehistoric Sites
    in Northern Japan   159
16. *Inaw* carved by Koji Yuki and used in a ceremony
    at the beginning of a field session at Utoro, Hokkaido   164
17. Kato photographs bear skull bones at the Ikushina-Kita
    Kaigan Site, Shari   165
18. Koji Yuki and colleagues preparing for a ceremony
    at the Ikushina-Kita Kaigan Site, Shari   166
19. Upopoy Memorial Site, Shiraoi, Hokkaido   178
20. The late Ryukichi Ogawa, a major leader of the
    repatriation movement in Sapporo   179
21. National Ainu Museum in Upopoy   185
22. Entryway to Lake Akan's Ainu Village   185
23. Assembled Ainu dancers and non-Ainu participants
    at the Shakushain Festival   188
24. Kamuynomi held at an archaeological site on the
    Hokkaido University campus   189
25. Altar of the Raporo Ainu Nation Kamuynomi   190
26. Nibutani Ainu Community Asircepnomi (First
    Salmon Ceremony)   192
27. The author and Carol Ellick dressed in Ainu finery   193
28. Reconstructed tower at Sannai Maruyama Site, Aomori
    City, Honshu   199

Tables

1. Monthly temperature ranges and precipitation in
   Sapporo and Tokyo, Japan   18
2. Jomon chronology, with climate, economy, settlement,
   and population information   56
3. Yayoi chronology, with subsistence and settlement
   pattern information   68

4. Important dates of Ainu and Japanese government
   interaction 105
5. Important dates of American Indian and American
   government interaction 111
6. Important dates of First Nations and Canadian
   government interaction 118
7. Important dates of Australian Aboriginal and
   Australian government interaction 122
8. Important dates of Māori and Aotearoa New Zealand
   government interaction 126
9. FRPAC's five basic policies and relevant major activities
   in promoting Ainu culture 145

ACKNOWLEDGMENTS

This research would not have been possible without the help of many people over the course of the years since I first visited Hokkaido and became aware of the situation of the Ainu. Dr. Hirofumi Kato, who first invited my wife and me to participate in the "Ainu Culture Promotion Law: Its Past, Present and Future" symposium at Hokkaido University in Sapporo, Japan, in December 2007, has become a friend as well as a colleague. His translation of many conversations from Japanese to English and back again kept me from trying to rely on handheld devices that would have made misunderstandings common. Dr. Teruki Tsunemoto has been involved in helping me better understand the nuances of the Japanese legal system as it pertains to things Ainu and has become a friend as well. Other members of the Center for Auni and Indigenous Studies at Hokkaido University have offered tremendous help throughout this process as well, and the book is better thanks to their assistance.

The year I spent as visiting professor at the Global Station for Indigenous Studies and Cultural Diversity at Hokkaido University in 2022–23 is what has made this project possible, since it gave me the time to focus on finalizing my ideas and this text. Ms. Sumie Hirose, Ms. Natsumi Hoshi, and Ms. Mayu Hirota ran the office expertly and helped me navigate the Japanese systems involved in day-to-day life in Sapporo, and I thank them continuously for their help. I especially thank Amanda Gomes for helping me with various translations from Japanese to English.

Most of all, however, I thank my wife, Carol Ellick, for supporting me throughout the project—from its inception to the innumerable discussions of its possibilities—and for her support as I floundered in a sea of Japanese culture shock. This book would have been impossible without her continued support.

INDIGENIZING JAPAN

Introduction

In December 2007, my wife, Carol Ellick, and I traveled from Albuquerque, New Mexico, to Sapporo, Japan, at the request of Professor Hirofumi Kato of Hokkaido University. We were invited to participate in a symposium titled "The Ainu Culture Promotion Law: Its Past, Present and Future," held at the Center for Ainu and Indigenous Studies on the Hokkaido University campus. My presentation provided basic information on the various methods and criteria used by American Indian tribes to determine tribal membership, and Carol presented on various processes of public education and outreach within archaeology. The next morning, the symposium participants took a bus trip to the Ainu Museum Porotokotan near Shiraoi (see figure 1).

As the group was treated to a tour of the reconstructed Ainu village, we listened to Ainu songs, watched Ainu dancers, and enjoyed an Ainu meal of fish soup, millet, and local greens. I fed cookies to the two captive black bears, who eagerly gobbled them up. After a tour of the museum, we went to Nibutani to tour the Ainu Museum there. Then we all got back on the bus for the trip to our evening lodging. The following morning, the bus dropped off Carol and me at the New Chitose airport, where we caught our plane back to the United States. We couldn't stay any longer, but we were told they'd be inviting us back. The entire trip lasted a jet-lagged four days, but it was the first of numerous trips to Hokkaido

FIGURE 1 The Ainu Porotokotan Museum in Shiraoi, 2007.

to work with the Center for Ainu and Indigenous Studies on its program
of developing Indigenous archaeology with and for the benefit of the
Ainu community.

Throughout my visits to Hokkaido, I have been privileged to meet
Ainu artisans in Nibutani; Ainu performers at Utoro and Lake Akan;
Ainu leaders and politicians in Sapporo, Biratori, Chitose, and Teshikaga;
and Ainu people of all walks of life throughout the island. In 2008, we
were honored to be invited to participate in the Shakushain Memorial
Festival in a hilltop park in Shizunai, offering sake in the hopes of positive
futures at the enormous statue of Shakushain. There we again ate Ainu
food, listened to Ainu songs, and watched Ainu dancers—finally participating in the last few public dances. As an American Indian in Japan, I
was as much a curiosity to the Japanese and the Ainu as the Ainu have
been across the generations. The singing and dance groups reveled in the
fact that they were Ainu, and they all enjoyed the celebratory day.

This book is the product of more than fifteen years of thought, pro-
crastination, and germination of ideas and relationships. It has been slow

to develop, but that has been okay. My issue had always been that there is so much to say about the Ainu from an outsider's perspective. For those who are not familiar with the Ainu—either personally or professionally—there is a lot to unpack. The Ainu are a part of modern Japan as well as its archaeology and history, whether Japanese archaeologists and historians readily acknowledge that. The Ainu have been a part of Japanese history since the eighth century, even though Japanese historians have attempted to write them out of it for quite a while. Recent genetic studies continue to proclaim that the Ainu and the mainland Japanese are genetically different. This "forest" of scientific studies and disciplines initially blinded me to the idea that it wasn't necessary for me to write a compendium of every thought that somehow might involve the Ainu—archaeologically, historically, genetically, or any other aspect of the scientific enterprise that deigns to work on Ainu issues.

Ultimately, it became obvious that it wasn't possible to create a book that included everything there is to know about the Ainu. My role, as I see it, is to write enough about the Ainu for a general audience to provide background on the various aspects that have been used by authors and researchers to report on the Ainu as Japan's Indigenous population. To this end I have looked at numerous specialized studies that offer information about specific aspects of the Ainu and have tried to generalize or summarize those studies so that interested readers will know where to continue searching should they be so inclined. The "Further Readings" section in each chapter will provide readers and researchers with some idea of those articles and references that would be good places to start.

Because this book is intended as a general reader for multiple audiences, I have tended to rely on some sources more than others. In my research I have found that many recent works rely on the same sources and often repeat information commonly cited. While this may be seen as an overreliance on English-writers' viewpoints or perspectives, it is also based on the limited number and availability of (until recently) English publications on these issues. Even with the availability of translation programs such as Google Translate, Deepl, and ChatGPT, the amount of time involved in trying to read up-to-date papers on Ainu topics is unimaginable for most researchers, me included. In addition, pay-to-view subscription services for many periodicals are unaffordable for many retired researchers.

Why me and why now? I am an American Indian anthropologist/ archaeologist. I have been "doing" anthropology/archaeology for more than fifty-five years, but I have always been a member of an Indigenous community. My perspective as an archaeologist has given me a better understanding of the ways that the deep time of the past continues to impact contemporary culture, and my perspective as an anthropologist has given me a better appreciation of cultural diversity. While my Indigeneity does not a priori give me insights into what it means to be Ainu (or any other group other than Choctaw), it does inform my perspectives on what it means to be a member of a colonized community that has experienced discrimination, economic and social disadvantages, and other things that made us "separate but equal" in the eyes of the government and our surrounding majority populations. I also pride myself on my involvement with Indigenous archaeology, defined initially by George P. Nicholas and Thomas D. Andrews (1997, 3n5) as "archaeology done with, for, and by Indigenous peoples." Although I am not writing about any of my own archaeological research in this volume—except how it has been influenced by Ainu colleagues who were at the archaeological sites—I find it necessary to at least approach the topic as a way of trying to tie the deep time of the Ainu with the threads of Japanese historical chronicles.

Ultimately, I made a cheat sheet that admonished me to keep working and posted it in my office at the Global Station for Indigenous Studies and Cultural Diversity at Hokkaido University, where I was a visiting professor from July 2022 to June 2023. It read:

FOCUS!
It's NOT a book on the archaeology of Japan!
It's NOT a book on the genetics of Japan!
It's NOT a book on the history of Japan!
It's NOT a book on Ainu history!
It's NOT an Ainu ethnography!
It's just got ALL of those things in it!

While I didn't take a physical copy of this admonition with me everywhere I went, I did carry it mentally and I recited it to myself every time I started down a pathway that threatened to derail my progress. The year I spent in Sapporo at Hokkaido University was a life-changing experience that allowed me to see what it feels like to be an outsider within what has been thought to be a homogenous culture. But, even so, I don't think I know how an Ainu person must feel every day. I could always go back to the United States if I felt too much of an outsider, but Ainu people can't do that—although it might be one of the reasons that many Ainu people have moved to larger cities where their anonymity can help them escape the stigma of being publicly known to be Ainu.

The time in Hokkaido gave me the opportunity to interact with Ainu from different towns and situations. Conversations were constrained by my lack of Japanese and the equal lack of English by most Ainu people, but the colleagues who translated our conversations were patient and helped ensure that there was enough context for all of us to understand the meanings of the statements and questions. The Ainu people were always very welcoming to me and helped me feel comfortable in their communities. I gave presentations to various community groups on topics of interest to them, especially in relation to American Indian issues and American Indian ways of exerting tribal sovereignty in the United States. The Ainu are VERY interested in finding ways to use examples of American Indian and other Indigenous groups to exert their Indigenous sovereignty within the recognizably limited Japanese system.

I came to learn that much of Ainu history is like American Indian histories in the United States—stories of colonization, policies of assimilation and culture decimation, social discrimination, and economic deprivation. I came to understand that the Ainu "had no history" outside of the dominant Japanese one. But, as in American Indian situations, Ainu culture has persisted. Many Ainu people "hid in plain sight" and kept on practicing their culture in private, away from governmental bureaucratic eyes; many others publicly continued their traditional ways, keeping their perspectives and traditions alive through their children and homes.

This book has been structured in a somewhat linear fashion as a way to provide the reader with a way of placing the Ainu within the Japanese society that has tried to subsume and assimilate them as a means of erasing their culture. It begins with a general discussion of the geography of Japan as a means of setting the physical context of the area. Following a discussion of the genetic studies that have been used to separate the mainland Japanese from the Ainu, the book offers information on the deepest histories available through archaeology to provide a background upon which to place later cultural manifestations that are reflected in archaeological deposits. Following that, the book looks at the cultural developments of the Japanese mainland and Hokkaido Island over time as groups of people became adapted to local environments and ecological zones and developed more fully as distinct cultures. The book then offers a general history of the Japanese–Ainu relationships and the attempts at assimilation that the Ainu underwent at the hands of the Japanese government. The final chapters offer information on contemporary Ainu issues and Ainu attempts to come to terms with those issues.

But this book is not just about the Ainu, and it is not intended just for those interested in Japanese studies. It is, in some ways, a bit of a generic history of Indigenous peoples worldwide. The struggles the Ainu have faced (and continue to face) as one of the newest officially recognized Indigenous groups in the global Indigenous community are not unique. The Ainu, like the Indigenous peoples of the United States, Canada, Australia, and New Zealand, have struggled to survive in the face of centuries of overwhelming governmental policies designed to convert them from their identity as separate peoples into Japanese commoners of the lowest societal order. Perhaps not surprisingly to American researchers, the Meiji government of the nineteenth century modeled its approaches to assimilate the Ainu on American policies toward American Indians.

As such, this book will serve as a case study for other Indigenous groups and researchers involved in those sorts of studies and enterprises. I hope it will be useful for Japanese readers who are currently unaware that the Ainu continue to exist and that the Japanese policies that were implemented were not enough to defeat the Ainu spirit. I am especially hopeful that Ainu people who read this book will find it of some use as they continue finding their way in the Indigenous world of which they are a new and growing part.

Of course, it is important to recognize that this manuscript is in no way the *final* word on the Ainu; it is merely *a* word, and there can't be a *final* word so long as the Ainu themselves continue to exist. It is my hope that there will be many Ainu researchers and authors who will find issue with what I'm presenting here to the extent that they *have* to write a volume describing how they see things and why they believe they continue to exist.

Things have evolved over time as the Japanese government has attempted to come to terms with the growing concepts of Indigenous within a global exercise of differences that have been suppressed over time. The Ainu, as a generalized population, have continued to become more aware of what it means to have survived colonization, assimilation, and attempted erasure.

This book is for the Ainu, in the hopes that the information here will help others better understand the Ainu journey through time and in contemporary Japan.

CHAPTER 1
· · · · · · · ·
Who Are the Ainu?

In August 2023, *JAPAN Forward*, an online magazine, published a three-part interview with Keiko Nakamura proposing to offer "the true history of Hokkaido" (Manning 2023). Nakamura, the author of *The Edo Shogunate's Northern Defense: How the Samurai Defended the "Japan Territory"* (2022), writes in an advertisement for her book that "the history of Hokkaido is now in danger, being dominated by the 'Ainu view of history'!" This view "has created a narrative that the exploitative Japanese divested the powerless Ainu of their land, Ezo [now Hokkaido]. And thus they must return it to them" (Manning 2023).

Nakamura's interview with the online magazine offers a Japanese version of history full of brightness and virtue, one that presents the Matsumae clan and other Japanese rulers and administrators as benevolent masters concerned only with trade and economic development. It is a one-sided story from the perspective of the Japanese majority and totally dismisses any negative aspects (or actually fails to present any such negative aspects at all).

This is, unfortunately, not the first attempt at rewriting the story of Ainu–Japanese historical interactions and the status of the Ainu as "the Indigenous people of Japan." Anthropologist ann-elise lewallen (2015, 9) writes, "Two Hokkaido politicians engaged in separate online attacks, questioning the veracity of the Ainu position as indigenous peoples and as a coherent ethnic community in 21st century Hokkaido."[1] She discusses how the "cyber hate speech incidents are troubling for the state of Ainu human rights" (9).

This ammunition was used by the Japanese *netto uyoku* (net far right) to add to and increase anti-Korean and anti-Chinese protests and rallies as a means of inciting and strengthening nationalism.[2] This was reaffirmed in 2019 when Mai Ishihara, an Ainu woman and professor at the Center for Ainu and Indigenous Studies at Hokkaido University, used that same cyber–hate speech incident as an example of how the voices (and visages) of the Ainu have been silenced, erased, or caricatured. She cited Yasuyuki Kaneko, one of the Hokkaido politicians involved in the exchange. She drew attention to his August 2014 tweet that "the Ainu *minzoku* ["ethnic group"; "nation"; "race"; "separate people"] no longer exist." Ishihara (2019, 613) criticized Kaneko's statement that "by identifying themselves as 'Ainu,' people benefit from government welfare, including low-interest housing loans, scholarships, and support for obtaining driving licenses, as well as subsidies to the Ainu Association of Hokkaidō" as inflaming distrust of Ainu people and the programs created for them by the Japanese government.

In 2008, the Japanese government recognized the Ainu as "the Indigenous people of Japan" through the June 6, "Resolution calling for the Recognition of the Ainu People as an Indigenous People of Japan" (lewallen 2008, 1). This was the culmination of a long struggle by the Ainu of Hokkaido and other parts of Japan to gain the recognition that they are different from the Wajin—the ethnic Japanese. The government's acknowledgment reinforces the Ainu contention that they were never fully assimilated despite more than one hundred years of attempts by the Japanese government to convert the Ainu into Japanese no different from everyone else in the archipelago. The acknowledgment followed on the heels of Japan's vote for the approval of the United Nations Declaration on the Rights of Indigenous Peoples (UNDRIP) in 2007. Yet, while the gov-

---

1. Anthropologist ann-elise lewallen prefers to use lowercase letters for her names rather than capitalizing them.

2. In this book, italics will be used for the first occurrence of general Japanese words but not thereafter. Japanese words common in English conversation such as "samurai" and "sushi" will not be italicized, nor will proper nouns.

ernment's official 2008 acknowledgment of the Ainu as Indigenous created an outward-facing step toward progress in Ainu rights, it "failed to lay the foundations for proper antidiscrimination legislation" (Cotterill 2011, 3).

More than a decade later, the Japanese government passed another law to further recognize the Ainu as an Indigenous people. In April 2019, the Act Promoting Measures to Achieve a Society in which the Pride of Ainu People is Respected was enacted, and it came into effect in May 2019. The act itself recognizes the Ainu people as an Indigenous people who have lived across the northern part of the Japanese archipelago, especially in Hokkaido. It aims to advance a wide range of measures and programs in a manner to increase regional, industrial, and tourism promotion, in addition to the previous welfare measures and cultural promotion program established by previous laws, resolutions, and policy measures.

The contemporary Ainu of Japan, regardless of whether they reside in cities like Sapporo or Asahikawa, smaller towns like Biratori or Obihiro, or in the larger cities of Honshu like Osaka and Tokyo, continue to live in a society that is not openly welcoming. Even though the government has officially declared that the Ainu are the "Indigenous population of Hokkaido," there are still those who do not see the Ainu as separate, let alone "separate but equal."

This is troubling to many who continue to believe in the Japanese concept of Nihonjinron (see Habu and Fawcett 1999)—the idea that Japan was (and still is) a homogenous culture with a common origin and that "we are all Jomon," referring to the early prehistoric culture that forms the basis of the cultures that follow in the Japanese archipelago. The inscription of Jomon Prehistoric Sites in Northern Japan onto the UNESCO World Cultural Heritage List on July 27, 2021, reintroduced this concept into Japan as a point of national pride (and local tourism marketing), in spite of the possibility that the Jomon (at least in Hokkaido) is ancestral Ainu. As Philip L. Kohl (1998, 240) writes: "Archaeological sites become national monuments [whose] artifacts are stored and displayed in national museums and constitute an invaluable part of the national patrimony." In Japan, this nationalization of the past has been part of an ongoing program to further homogenize the Japanese present, much as Japan has presented its "homogenous" culture.

Such use of archaeology for nationalistic endeavors is not new, nor is it confined to one region or another (see Arnold 1990; Fowler 1987;

Gustafsson and Karlsson 2012; Kohl 1998; Niklasson and Hølleland 2018; Sommer 2017; Trigger 1984). Ulrike Sommer (2017, 166) argues that "many statements about the national past are in reality political statements about the present and the future." Clare Fawcett (2009, 232) has indicated how the descriptive nature of Japanese archaeology "has led to archaeological results being incorporated into a discourse which molds a new national identity (and some would say a new nationalism) for Japan."

Additionally, Yasuyuki Yoshida and John Ertl (2016, 47) describe "how 'the Jomon' is incorporated into left-wing political ideologies and activism." Their ethnographic research shows how "the archaeology of the Jomon period manifests in Japan today through social activism that, while inspired by the archaeological past, effects change in the present" (48) and offers some understanding of public archaeology in Japan. They discuss three ways that archaeology has been involved in "not only acts to promote nationalism, but also has been a catalyst for progressive politics and pluralistic re-imaginings of Japanese people and society" (50). In closing, they note the importance of "ethnographically informed archaeology that seeks to . . . understand how people and culture are inspired, influenced, and transformed by archaeological knowledge and practices" (68).

Who Are the Ainu?

The question "Who are the Ainu?" can often lead to multiple answers. Ask Japanese people on the street, and chances are you will get a multitude of answers. Some will tell you that they were people who once lived in Hokkaido but are no longer around. Others will tell you that they are the primitive people of Japan who still exist in some areas but who are mostly assimilated. Others might offer the statement that "some of their best friends are Ainu" and that the Ainu are no different from any other Japanese person. One would probably receive similar responses on an American city street if passersby were asked about American Indians.

I can't say that I have always known about the Ainu, but I have known about them for some time. I am an American Indian and an archaeologist. I have always been interested in Japan's early archaeology, its early history, and the people who lived in Japan from as far back as 40,000 years ago (B.P. or Before Present [before 1950]) until the present. I'm not sure exactly when I first became aware of the Ainu—maybe it was the February 1967 *National Geographic* magazine article that described "the Vanishing Ainu" (Miyazawa and Hilger 1967)—but I can say that I was deeply impacted by the Smithsonian Institution's National Museum of Natural History's *Ainu: Spirit of a Northern People* exhibit in Washington, D.C., in 1999–2001 and the resultant catalog (W. Fitzhugh and Dubreuil 1999).

Why am I writing about the Ainu *now*—at this point in time? I care deeply about the situation the Ainu are currently facing and hope to be able to help them in some way. I have different perspectives than the local Japanese person who might be conducting research on the Ainu. As an American Indian, I have experienced discrimination similar to what Ainu people have told me they experience; as a non-Japanese person, I believe my perspective will be less colored by my cultural upbringing and the incomplete history I might have been taught in public school. As an Indigenous person, I also understand what it means to be outside the national narrative that places the colonizing culture at the forefront and the colonized culture some distance behind the arc of civilization.

Often, introductory paragraphs in books or articles about the Ainu indicate that they are an Indigenous people of Japan whose homelands include northern Honshu and Hokkaido, the Sakhalin peninsula, and the Kuril Islands. They are also tied inextricably to the past. A sidebar in a book on a famous Ainu artist, the late Bikky Sunazawa, describes them as "Japan's indigenous people, who lived in fishing, hunting, and gathering tribal groups for centuries" and as "one of the most enigmatic ethnic groups in the world" (Dubreuil 2004, xix–xxv). They are stereotypically described as "noted for their hirsute bodies, wavy hair and narrow heads" (Watanabe 1973, 1). Historical photographs often show Ainu men with heavy beards dressed in traditional clothing, while women are shown with large areas of tattoos around the mouth and lips. However, most contemporary Ainu individuals (with the exception, perhaps, of very young cultural activists) no longer choose to outwardly display facial tattoos or heavy beards, and they easily blend in with their ethnic Japanese counterparts.

Physical Geography of the Japanese Archipelago

Japan is an island nation with an area of approximately 146,000 square miles (ca. 378,138 square kilometers). It is situated in the northern Pacific in East Asia near the Korean peninsula, China, and Russia. It is an island nation made up of four main islands—from north to south, Hokkaido, Honshu, Shikoku, and Kyushu—and more than three thousand smaller islands, including Okinawa and other islands of the Ryukyu archipelago that extends far to the southwest of the main islands (see figure 2). The Sea of Japan separates Japan from the Asian mainland to the west. The Sea of Okhotsk is to the north of Hokkaido; Tsugaru Strait is to the south and separates Hokkaido from Honshu. The East China Sea is to

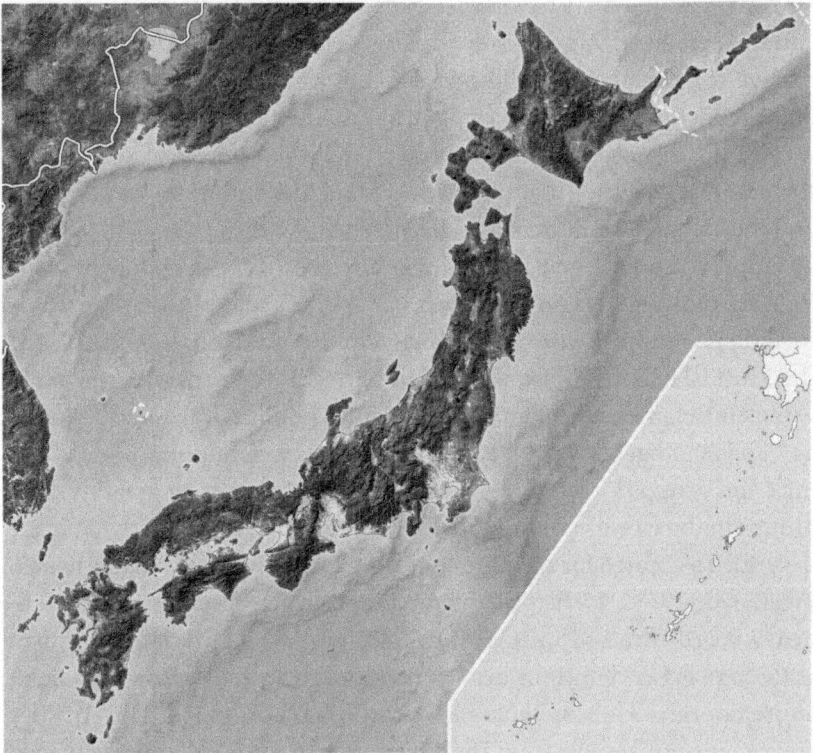

FIGURE 2 Map of Japan. This Wikipedia and Wikimedia Commons image is from the user Chris 73 and is freely available at http://commons.wikimedia.org/wiki /File:Sea_of_Japan_Map.png under the Creative Commons cc-by-sa 3.0 license.

the southeast of the Japanese mainland. These seas are extensions of the Pacific Ocean.

Geologically, Japan lies along the boundary between the Eurasian, North American, and Pacific Tectonic Plates. This is part of the area known as the "Ring of Fire" and is very active tectonically. The topography is mountainous and composed of numerous volcanos, including Japan's most famous, Mount Fujiyama, located about sixty miles southwest of Tokyo. Most of these volcanoes are dormant. As a result of these active tectonic plates, earthquakes are common throughout the islands. In March 2011, the Tohoku earthquake, centered about forty-five miles off the east coast of Honshu Island, triggered a catastrophic tsunami that hit Sendai and caused the Fukushima Daiichi Nuclear Disaster.

Most of Japan is in the temperate zone, apart from the subtropical southern island chains. There are four distinct seasons: winter (December through February), spring (March through May), summer (June through August), and autumn (September through November.) The average annual temperature is 59°F (15°C) with a winter range of 15°F to 61°F (−9°C to 16°C) and a summer range of 68°F to 82°F (20°C to 28°C). Humidity is high, ranging from 50 percent to 75 percent. Each of the major islands experiences distinct variations of weather (see table 1).

The peak rainy season is from May to October, with some regional variations. Yearly rainfall averages 39 to 98 inches (100 to 250 centimeters). Occasionally, seasonal typhoons bring heavy rains that can flood the plains along the coasts. In regions bordering the Sea of Japan, the winter monsoon, laden with snow, can be destructive. Snowfall is generally heavy along the western coast, where it covers the ground for almost four months.

Second in land area only to Honshu, Hokkaido is Japan's northernmost island and Japan's biggest prefecture, covering roughly 32,000 square miles (more than 83,000 square kilometers)—about 22 percent of Japan's land area.

Hokkaido is mountainous and composed of numerous volcanoes but interspersed with valleys and fertile plains that support agriculture, with the highest mountain being Mount Asahi at 7,513 feet (2,290 meters) above sea level. The volcanic activity has created numerous natural hot springs (*onsen*) that have been used for centuries; the volcanic activity

TABLE 1 Monthly temperature ranges and precipitation in Sapporo and Tokyo, Japan

	Sapporo		Tokyo	
	Temperature (Min–Max)	Precipitation	Temperature (Min–Max)	Precipitation
January	17 to 30°F −8.4 to −1.2°C	4.3 inches; 110 mm	36 to 50°F 2.1 to 10°C	2.4 inches; 60 mm
February	17 to 31°F −8.4 to 0.5°C	3.5 inches; 90 mm	37 to 51°F 2.6 to 10.8°C	2.2 inches; 55 mm
March	26 to 38°F −3.2 to 3.4°C	3.1 inches; 80 mm	42 to 57°F 5.4 to 13.9°C	4.5 inches; 115 mm
April	38 to 51°F 3.5 to 10.8°C	2.2 inches; 55 mm	51 to 66°F 10.4 to 19.1°C	5.3 inches; 135 mm
May	49 to 63°F 9.4 to 17°C	2.2 inches; 55 mm	60 to 74°F 15.3 to 23.5°C	5.5 inches; 140 mm
June	57 to 70°F 14 to 21.1°C	2.4 inches; 60 mm	66 to 79°F 19.2 to 26°C	6.7 inches; 170 mm
July	64 to 76°F 18 to 24.6°C	3.5 inches; 90 mm	74 to 86°F 23.1 to 30°C	6.1 inches; 155 mm
August	66 to 78°F 19 to 25.6°C	4.9 inches; 125 mm	76 to 89°F 24.3 to 31.4°C	6.1 inches; 155 mm
September	58 to 72°F 14.3 to 22.3°C	5.5 inches; 140 mm	70 to 82°F 20.8 to 27.6°C	8.9 inches; 225 mm
October	46 to 60°F 7.6 to 15.8°C	4.3 inches; 110 mm	59 to 72°F 15.3 to 22.2°C	9.3 inches; 235 mm
November	35 to 46°F 1.4 to 8°C	4.5 inches; 115 mm	49 to 63°F 9.6 to 17.1°C	3.7 inches; 95 mm
December	23 to 34°F −4.9 to 1.3°C	4.5 inches; 115 mm	40 to 54°F 4.5 to 12.4°C	2.4 inches; 60 mm
Year	41.4 to 54.3°F 5.3 to 12.4°C	45.1 inches; 1145 mm	55 to 68.7°F 12.8 to 20.4°C	63 inches; 1600 mm

Source: "Climate in Japan: Average Weather, Temperature, Rainfall, Sunshine," Climates to Travel, accessed November 30, 2024, https://www.climatestotravel.com/climate/japan.

is also responsible for large obsidian formations that have been used by Hokkaido inhabitants for thousands of years for their lithic raw material sources.

The regional capital of Sapporo is located at the same latitude as London, with Tokyo approximately five hundred miles to the southwest. As a result, the climates of Sapporo and Tokyo are very different. In Hokkaido, cold winds and heavy snow come from nearby Russia's Siberia (Vladivostok is 435 miles west), whereas snow is rare in Tokyo. On the contrary, typhoons are common in Honshu but rare in Hokkaido; few are worrisome because they weaken so much by the time they reach Hokkaido or veer on a more northeastern pathway toward Alaska.

A Brief History of the Ainu

The first recorded depiction of "others" is an eighth-century description of the "Eastern Barbarians" (Emishi) in the *Nihon Shoki*, Japan's second-oldest history book, as "hairy, non-human, flesh-eating savages" (Siddle 1996, 27). Over time, the depiction of those who came to be known as Ainu continued, enforcing this stereotype—the Wajin ("the people of Wa," or ethnic Japanese) were "civilized" and the Ainu were barbarians.

Archaeologists have discovered material evidence of economic interaction in the form of trade between the Ainu and the Wajin as early as the fourteenth century when metal and lacquerware become more common in archaeological complexes along the southern portion of Hokkaido. Interaction with the people of Honshu and those of Hokkaido subsequently increased, with trade from Honshu, China, and northeastern Asia becoming more evident in archaeological deposits associated with Ainu groups. By the fifteenth century, there were trading posts established on the Oshima Peninsula of Hokkaido for regularizing trade between "Ezo" (the name for Hokkaido at that time) and Honshu.

The relationships between Japanese and Ainu people were not always peaceful, however. Countless wars waged during the period from 1450 to 1550, leading to roughly one hundred years of instability and conflict that defined one of the most violent chapters of Japan's history. The nominal authority of society at this time was the shogun, the military commanders, but the *daimyo*—the heads of the powerful Wajin families and vassals to the shoguns—began to replace the shoguns as the true authority. However, there were also constant conflicts between clans because of the less-centralized form of ruling.

James Clavell's 1975 book *Shōgun* and the 1980 television miniseries by the same name were set at the end of this period and offered generalized information on the Japanese social and governance structures at this time period to Western audiences (me included). For many of us, it was the first inkling we had of this portion of Japan's history. In 2024, a new television series based on *Shōgun* was released that likely exposed many more non-Japanese people to this period of Japanese history and culture.

During the Tokugawa era (also known as the "Edo" Period), from 1603 to 1867, Wajin culture was codified by various regulations issued by the military government (*bakufu*) of the Tokugawa regime (Loy 2010, 46–50). This was the time when the influence of the shoguns weakened and samurai became unemployed *ronin*—masterless, wandering samurai. Local lords, more specifically the heads of the most powerful families, began to have a significant influence in their respective regions, eventually positioning themselves as the de facto rulers over the shoguns.

As the Tokugawa regime sought to shape a national social practice ("Japanese culture"), the Ainu were further separated from Japanese people. Contemporary accounts indicate that the Ainu were often depicted as "so different in appearance, custom and language that the idea of assimilation with the rest of Japan was initially unthinkable" (Loy 2010, 53). To fortify this segregation, the Ainu were not allowed to wear Wajin hairstyles, weren't permitted to wear Wajin-styled straw raincoats or sandals, and were not allowed to learn or speak Japanese.

At this time, the Ainu were considered important by their trading partners primarily for their trade and labor possibilities. The Matsumae clan established a series of trading zones (*bashos*) that were parceled out to senior retainers of the clan. Each basho had exclusive rights to trade with the Ainu communities of the island of Hokkaido within their assigned trading zone and to guarantee the security of Japanese interests there (J. Cornell 1964, 289; Siddle 1996, 43–45). Concomitant with the increased Matsumae control of trade with the Ainu was increased exploitation of Ainu resources and Ainu labor. As local resources decreased (or were harvested beyond sustainable levels), Ainu men became more reliant on working for the Japanese traders at the expense of hunting and gathering and other such economies within their home locations. Tensions between the Matsumae and local communities reached a peak in 1669 when a group of Ainu warriors under the leadership of the chieftain Shakushain advanced toward Matsumae Ezo (Howell 2005, 113–14). The

Ainu were defeated and Shakushain was soon after assassinated during peace negotiations.

Interaction between Wajin and the Ainu continued in a similar vein until the opening of trade between Japan and America, Britain, and the Netherlands in 1856. When the military took over control of Edo, the Edo government redoubled its efforts to force Ainu assimilation and encouraged agriculture as a means of making the colonization of Ainu lands a reality.

With the Meiji Restoration of 1868, the government divided the land throughout Japan into "prefectures" that functioned through bureaucratic structures originally developed by the daimyo (vassals of the shoguns). Ezo was renamed "Hokkaido" in 1869, and colonization became a major focus of the Meiji government. In addition to the purposeful colonization of Hokkaido by retired military men who were encouraged to become farmers by the Japanese government, the Japanese made a concerted attempt to join with the Western industrial nations. To accomplish this, the Japanese virtually replicated British, American, and colonial European Indigenous policies (see chapter 6 for more details) and applied them to bring their relationship with the Ainu under central governmental control. Assimilation measures, aimed at turning the Ainu into productive and localizable Japanese citizens, were enacted piecemeal in the first thirty years of the Meiji era, culminating in the 1899 Former Aborigines Act, which aggressively sought to alleviate the suffering of Ainu communities in Hokkaido through a mixture of assimilation and welfare policies.

In spite of this attempt to incorporate the Ainu into mainstream Japanese society, Japan continued to represent the Ainu as other-than-real Japanese when they displayed Ainu individuals at the 1903 Osaka Industrial Exposition and again in the 1904 St. Louis Exposition. The "primitive" Ainu acted as a backdrop for the "civilized" Japanese: images of the Ainu wearing traditional clothing were placed in contrast to Japanese houses and gardens, and their habitation structures were markedly different from the Japanese ones. Anthropologists Nancy J. Parezo and Don D. Fowler, in their book *Anthropology Goes to the Fair* (2007, 210–14), describe the Ainu experience as an exhibit of the primitive Japanese. Chris Bullfinch (2017, 7) notes that, to the Japanese, the 1904 Exposition "was the perfect opportunity, both scientifically and politically, for Japan to present its native people at the World's Fair, simultaneously distancing

themselves racially from their 'savages' and participating in the intellectual and cultural vogue of anthropology."

In 1930, the Japanese government began promoting its policies
through the Ainu Association of Hokkaido, a government organization
designed to provide funds to Ainu to help them successfully assimilate
into Japanese society (Loy 2010, 90). Much like the single-minded manner in which the American government treated American Indians, the
Japanese government generally considered the Ainu a single, culturally
homogenous group despite obvious differences in geographic location,
language dialects, and customs. Even after the founding of the Ainu Association, the Ainu did not consider themselves as having such an explicitly shared identity.

The Contemporary Ainu

It is difficult not to associate the Ainu with the culturally loaded Japanese
concepts of "barbarian," "rural," and "natural." Harder still is shaking off
the association that various external (and occasionally, internal) groups
impose as they try to reach an understanding of what it means to be Ainu
in a contemporary world.

Today's Ainu are multifaceted people. Many coexist as "Japanese" and
as "Ainu," and an unknown number either fail to publicly acknowledge
their Ainu heritage or do not know they are of Ainu descent. In 2007,
the Hokkaido government's Department of Environment and Lifestyle
reported 23,782 individuals who identified as Ainu in Hokkaido (as reported in Onai 2011, 3). The *Report on the 2008 Hokkaido Ainu Living
Conditions Survey* (Onai 2011) documented information obtained from
a survey conducted by an interdisciplinary team of researchers from the
Center for Ainu and Indigenous Studies of Hokkaido University.

The report found that nearly 70 percent of those who consider themselves to be Ainu lived in Iburi, Hidaka, and Ishikari subprefectures of
Hokkaido (Onai 2011, 121) and that 90 percent of those who responded
were born in Hokkaido. It pointed out that many people who responded
to the survey indicated mixed parentage with Wajin, with less than
20 percent of those who responded indicating that both parents were
Ainu. Interestingly, the report found that only about 10 percent of the

respondents felt that they were "constantly aware of their Ainu heritage," with an overall trend showing "reduced awareness of Ainu status" being conspicuous among those under thirty (Onai 2011, 122).

In terms of economics, the survey found that the Ainu respondents received lower annual incomes than non-Ainu—3.692 million yen versus 4.406 million yen for the average annual household income in Hokkaido (Onai 2011, 123). It also found that the ratio of those receiving public assistance was significantly higher among Ainu people than in Hokkaido as a whole, with 5.2 percent among Ainu and only 3.9 percent in Hokkaido (Onai 2011, 123).

Additionally, the survey pointed out differences between Ainu and general Hokkaido populations concerning education and educational attainment and health risk factors. The Ainu also had a stronger sense of inequality arising from their racial/ethnic background. Similar disparities exist between American Indians and non-Indian populations in the United States, with American Indian death rates and poverty higher than that of the general population and educational achievement lower (Centers for Disease Control and Prevention 2013).

The 2008 survey as summarized here presents a general picture of the Ainu of Hokkaido, but there are other pockets of Ainu living in Japan outside the island. Mark K. Watson (2010, 2014) provides a discussion of the difficulty of gaining a true picture of Ainu individuals living outside Hokkaido in cities like Tokyo. He writes that "as a result of the prefectural jurisdiction of social welfare budgets, *non*-Hokkaido Ainu are excluded from the Hokkaido Ainu Association's 'official' population statistic" (Watson 2010, 270). Using the results of two Tokyo government-funded surveys in 1974 and 1988, he posits that there are perhaps five thousand Ainu living in the area (2010, 270), which would amount to about 17 percent of the projected total Ainu population.

Watson's work highlights the difficulty of discussing a "typical" Ainu population in Japan. He indicates three issues that impact a more valid depiction of Ainu geographical and population localities (Watson 2014, 24–25n1): (1) the Hokkaido government's surveys have been sent only to those Ainu registered with the Hokkaido Ainu Association, (2) the geographical focus of the surveys has been limited to the prefecture of Hokkaido, and (3) the social stigma associated with "being Ainu" contributes to consistent undercounts. Watson's (2014, 64) description of the Tokyo Ainu as "a people without history" is based not only on the absence of a shared history of individual Ainu in the city but also on the idea that most histories—and indeed, most research on "the Ainu"—focus on those who live in Hokkaido at the expense of urban Ainu elsewhere.

Naohiro Nakamura (2015, 660–61) writes on the problems of identity politics in Japan, arguing that identity of the Ainu is inextricably linked to Hokkaido by governmental officials: "government and policy makers tend to miscount and misperceive urban Indigenous populations, which has recurrently resulted in 'statistical genocide,' meaning that the government uses these incorrect population counts to justify reduced funding for social programs." His review of the pros and cons of "self-identification to recognize Indigenous belonging" (663–64) provides a good synopsis of the issues that face not just the Ainu but Indigenous peoples worldwide: one problem with self-identification may lead to overreporting as "wannabes" try to appropriate Indigenous privileges such as targeted governmental programs. In terms of underreporting, people who choose not to identify with a minority or ethnic group to which they seemingly belong do so most often when the group is especially stigmatized and discriminated against. "The main problem in underreporting," notes Nakamura (2015, 664), "is that inaccuracies may affect the reliability of data and the credibility of surveys of stigmatized populations."

Is an Ainu any less Ainu because they have chosen to live in a different geographical locality than that which the government recognizes as their "home place"? In other places in the world, Indigenous peoples share the same issues when they move away from their homelands (for whatever reason) and become a part of the growing urban masses. Ainu people who live in the urban centers on Honshu struggle to maintain connections to one another and to maintain their identity. Kanako Uzawa (2018) writes about her life growing up in the Tokyo area and the needs of the urban Ainu living there and the gaps in social and economic levels of urban Ainu compared to non-Ainu people.

Contemporary Identity in a Multicultural World

It is evident that "Ainu" carries with it numerous definitions and stereotypes about what being a member of this group means. A person's feeling of being a part of a group (or, conversely, of being excluded from a group) is part of their identity. In a very basic way, everyone has multiple "identities"—sibling, child, adult, student, and so forth—and each of these "identities" contributes a portion to the overall picture of who we are. Identity encompasses any number of things such as memories, experiences, relationships, and values that create one's sense of self. It also encompasses political opinions, moral attitudes, and religious beliefs, all of which guide the choices one makes on a daily basis.

Identity can be created by the individual ("*I am* American Indian because . . ."), imposed on an individual by an outside person or organization ("*You are* an American Indian because . . ."), or refuted by the individual or the outside organization ("*You're not* an American Indian because . . ."). Identity can be accepted or refuted, and the strength of an individual's identity can vary over time and geography. To add even more complexity, identity may be totally internalized and not exhibited to others ("I am an American Indian, but I don't tell anyone").

Ethnicity can refer to "'race,' culture, geographic region, language/ dialect, religion, and sometimes economic or social position" (Leach, Brown, and Worden 2008, 760) and is most often used to cast identity upon others (or cast people as "others"), but even the defining characteristics may not be consistently applied by people. Individuals with parents of more than one ethnicity, for example, may exhibit outward appearances that influence the way observers consider their identity, whereas the individual may not identify with that ethnicity. I have worked with individuals with one American Indian parent who looked more like their non-Indian parent, and yet they considered themselves American Indian. And, in Japan, a relatively closed society with a dominant paradigm of homogeneity, biethnic individuals may be even more reticent to express a non-Japanese identity.

Social science researchers Sarasa Oikawa and Tomoko Yoshida (2007) offer a discussion of biethnic identity development in Japan. Their study included people who each had one Japanese and one non-Japanese parent. While none of study's participants were Ainu, the study is worthwhile and applicable to the issues the Ainu face in terms of identity development. They note that "those who differ in terms of lineage, culture, or nationality are considered less 'Japanese' or even 'non-Japanese'" (Oikawa and Yoshida 2007, 637). Their study indicates the role that outward appearance plays in the development of identity—those individuals who did not "look" Japanese were treated differently, while those who "looked" Japanese were able to fit into the homogenous society more easily. However, even those biethnic individuals who looked Japanese were treated differently once the fact that they were biethnic was discovered.

Oikawa and Yoshida found that the way the biethnic individuals of their focus groups preferred to be treated fell into three categories. They classified those individuals who wished to be considered for who they personally were as "Unique Me"; those who wanted to be associated with the prevalent stereotypes, most of them being positive, of biethnic individuals in Japan as "Model Biethnic"; and those who just desired to be like everyone else under a broader category of "Just let me be Japanese" (2007, 644–45).

No comparable study has been done among the Ainu, of whom there are many biethnic individuals (of mixed Ainu–Japanese parentage or ancestry) who do not exhibit the stereotypical outward appearances that most Japanese expect of Ainu individuals and who quietly go about their lives as "Japanese." These "hidden Ainu," as Ishihara (2019, 613) identifies them, are those who know they have Ainu ancestry, do not disclose their Ainu heritage, and choose to identify as "Japanese," not "Ainu." There are others, as Ishihara (2019, 613) notes, who are aware of their Ainu heritage "but do not know how to address this even if they want to talk about it." These "Silent Ainu" (Ishihara 2019) constitute a unique group identity of people who *know* they are Ainu but perhaps don't know how to *be* Ainu.

Defining Identity

As indicated in the previous section, there are various ways that identity can be defined. Aside from the internal decisions made by the individual, outsiders (nonkin, governmental officials, organizations, and so forth) occasionally get involved in determining who qualifies to publicly pronounce an identity. Often, these external groups are involved in trying to ensure that particular programs or benefits go to those whom they believe are entitled and not to individuals who are not.

In the United States, the designations "American Indian" or "Native American" (I use the terms interchangeably) have implications toward various classes of benefits and have been defined by the federal govern-

ment and by each one of the 574 separate tribal groups.[3] The federal
government does not confer American Indian identity on an individual
but instead relies on the various tribal groups to accept an individual's
application for membership in the tribe and to determine who is and who
is not a recognized tribal member.

American Indian tribes have various means of identifying the individuals who qualify to be members of the tribal group. Some tribes rely on
"tribal blood quantum"—a mythical percentage of "Indian blood" inherited from an Indian ancestor—while others only require an individual to
document direct familiar kinship to a known tribal member ("descendancy"). Tribes that use blood quantum as membership criteria generally
require a minimum amount of "Indian blood" (one-half, one-quarter, or
one-eighth), whereas those tribes that use descendancy are not shackled
by minimal amounts. The determination of "Indianness" can get complicated, especially as the generational distance from the original ancestor
widens or the details of family ancestry get blurred by time and circum-
stance. Also, the idea of blood relation is a cultural determination, one
that may be out of sync with biological connectedness if one is unaware
of who is part of the lineage due to the erasure of identity in the past.

The idea of "blood quantum" is not unheard of in Ainu studies either, as lewallen (2016, 51) writes: "During my stay in Ainu communities
(2004–2009), Ainu often explained their relationships to one another
and to outsiders through the idiom of blood, specifically the lack of Wajin (ethnic Japanese blood) and the possession of Ainu blood, or vice
versa." She notes the problems with using blood quantum to define who
is or isn't Ainu, writing "any economic or political initiatives that hinge
eligibility on the degree of heritable Ainu ancestry, quantified by blood
or genetic material, restrict Ainu ethnicity to a finite and exponentially
shrinking pool" (51).

Using ancestry for determining group membership is a bit easier, but
it nonetheless requires that an individual demonstrate through birth and
death records a direct familial relationship with an ancestor who is accepted as a tribal member. Using ancestry as a means of determining
rights to tribal membership allows for larger tribal membership, espe-

3. This number incudes 347 Native entities in the contiguous forty-eight states and
227 Native entities in Alaska.

cially as generations move further and further away from the original tribal group. Using the idea of tribal blood quantum, an individual who might be considered 1/126 Indian by blood would still be allowed to be a tribal member—essentially seven generations removed from their 100 percent Indian ancestor.

Taken in reverse, the "one-drop rule" (also known as hypodescent) operates on the concept that *any* degree of ancestry from a particular group takes precedence over all other types of ancestry.[4] In America, Black or African ancestry took precedence over any other ancestry for a time after the American Civil War of 1865, and many people considered individuals with even "one drop" of African blood to be nonwhite, regardless of how long ago their ancestor with the "questionable" blood lived. Most often, hypodescent was used to prevent specific groups of people from exercising rights (such as marriage and voting rights, in the case of African Americans). In Japan, a similar idea remains prominent: "anyone known to possess any Ainu or other minority blood . . . is assigned to that minority . . . by Japanese society" (lewallen 2016, 51).

More recently, with the popularity of personal DNA testing kits such as AncestryDNA, 23andMe, or MyHeritage, large numbers of individuals in the United States have found that they have "Native American" ancestry. While there are specific genetic markers and blood types that are more commonly found within tribal groups than within other groups, there is no single American Indian DNA. American Indian scholar Kim TallBear (2013, 523) notes that "indigenous governments use the common DNA parentage test, or DNA profile, simply in order to prove that a potential tribal or First Nation citizen is the biological offspring of a tribally enrolled parent." This is a "scientific" form of the ancestry method of determining tribal membership, but it is more than that. "Privileging genomics in the designation of a citizen and in broader identity constructions," TallBear notes, "is a value decision about which facts matter and which do not" (526).

A three-day symposium in Vancouver, British Columbia, in 2015 titled "DNA and Indigeneity: The Changing Role of Genetics in Indigenous Rights, Tribal Belonging, and Repatriation" was convened to

---

4. See "Hypodescent: The 'One-Drop' Rule," *Passing Beyond Passing* (blog), July 28, 2018, https://pages.vassar.edu/passingbeyondpassing/hypodescent-the-one-drop-rule/.

look at "potential drawbacks and ethical challenges associated with the many different uses of human genetics" (A. Walker, Egan, and Nicholas 2016, 2). The first session focused on the "promise and perils of using genomics to construct and interpret Indigenous identities," the second session looked at the "potential for genetic information to assist with the repatriation of human remains," and the third session examined the "problematic history of genetic research with Indigenous peoples before turning to the present to identify opportunities to work together." Combined, these sessions described and discussed the interaction between DNA and Indigeneity as well as the implications for genetics research on ancient DNA.

The next chapter will discuss "Ainu genetics" more specifically as a means of examining the different histories of the Wajin and the Ainu. I will also look at the roles this genetic difference plays (and has played) in the relationships between the Japanese government and the Ainu populations of Japan, Sakhalin, and the Kuril Islands. These all have implications for the acceptance of the Ainu as Japan's Indigenous population.

Authenticity

As part of the question of Indigenous identity of whatever sort, there is always a question of authenticity. By this I mean that someone who has an Indigenous identity may not seem any different from those around them, and this might lead others to question the individual's right to identify as Indigenous. As I was growing up as an American Indian boy, schoolmates often asked me, "Where's your pony?," "Do you live in a tipi?," or "Where's your headdress?" They thought I couldn't be "authentic" unless I exhibited the stereotypical items associated with American Indian cultures—more typically, North American Plains Indian culture as represented in movies. The late Ainu leader Shigeru Kayano, in his book *Our Land Was a Forest* (1994, 104–5), recounts similar experiences about encounters with non-Ainu people: "The lack of mainlander's knowledge concerning the Ainu [is startling]. Even schoolteachers observed 'Your Japanese is so good' or 'I see you wear the same things Japanese do.'"

Authenticity is more often a concern of outsiders who attribute specific characteristics to populations, but insiders of the group in question also use this concept in relation to people who are unknown to them but who claim group membership. As previously noted, Naohiro Nakamura (2015, 664) draws attention to the idea of "authenticity" by those who make a claim for Indigenous identity: while external regulators may accept "proof" of belonging of an individual, internal regulators may not. Often, "new" applicants or unknown individuals might require more than just "proof" to be accepted as a group member.

And even more broadly, external groups may not consider the ethnic group in question as "authentic" at all. Anthropologist Sidney C. H. Cheung (2003, 954) notes that some Japanese researchers no longer study the Ainu because "the increasing commercialization of Ainu culture through tourism . . . has made 'pure' Ainu culture and traditions more difficult to discern." This raises the question of whether it is the responsibility of an ethnic group to remain static and unchanging while the rest of the world continues to move forward, and whether progress is either possible or expected.

This becomes a concern when groups rely on tourism and its economic benefits. Individuals who participate in tourist enterprises often must portray themselves in a way that matches the tourists' preconceived ideas of the group—American Indians generally must have long hair to be considered authentic; Ainu must wear their traditional clothing and accoutrements so that they can be easily identified from a distance. Tourists often come to visit places in search of an authentic experience and believe that must include clothing, locations, languages, and other cultural stereotypes. This places the individual in a situation where he or she must choose how the quest for authenticity influences their true self.

More recently, the general Japanese population has become more aware of Ainu culture through a popular manga (comics or graphic novels originating from Japan) by Satoru Noda titled *The Golden Kamuy*. The manga is set in early twentieth-century Hokkaido after the Russo-Japanese war. Ex-soldier Saichi Sugimoto—nicknamed "Sugimoto the Immortal" for his death-defying acts in battle—seeks a fortune in order to fulfill a promise made to his best friend. Together with a young Ainu girl named Asirpa, the pair search for the hidden treasure accompanied by various other characters. Throughout the series, the author has interwoven a great deal of information about Ainu culture and has influenced his readers' ideas about the Ainu. Additionally, the 2020 film

Ainu Mosir (World of the Ainu), set in an Ainu tourist-reliant community of Hokkaido, offers international audiences a glimpse of Ainu tradition and contemporary life through the struggles of a fictional Ainu teenage boy.

Identity Politics

Naohiro Nakamura's (2015, 663) discussion of the ways that Tokyo Ainu identify themselves indicates a consistent problem that has been discussed as part of "identity politics" globally. "Identity politics" can be defined as "a wide range of political activity and theorizing founded in the shared experiences of injustice of members of certain social groups," or "a specific constituency marginalized within its larger context. Members of that constituency assert or reclaim ways of understanding their distinctiveness that challenge dominant characterizations, with the goal of greater self-determination" (Heyes 2024). Combining this with the concept of ethnicity, "ethnic identity politics frames ethnic identity as a tool used by the politically less powerful to oppose the status quo" (Leach, Brown, and Worden, 2008, 758).

Social geographer Audrey Kobayashi (2020, 153) writes about the problems that the use of identity politics can play for ethnic groups: "Most groups who assert rights on the basis of identity politics essentialize their identities as a basis for making political claims." This "essentialism" can lead to oversimplification of the ethnic group as well as the dominant group against which political action is taken. She discusses the ways that identity politics can lead to conflict in multicultural societies: those who argue that nations should "maintain a dominant cultural identity to which Others should adapt or assimilate," those who argue that multiculturalism is itself separatist and "prevents marginalized groups from accessing full equality rights enjoyed by members of the dominant group," and those who use the concept of multiculturalism "to transcend, rather than reinforce, notions of cultural separation" (A. Kobayashi 2020, 153).

Taken by itself, identity politics can create conflict where most of the population may not have seen it before. Ethnic groups often feel the need to bring the attention to the broader public and beyond just governmental policymakers, and identity politics is just one way of doing so. The quest for rights is not one for "special" rights but for "equal" rights that have been historically denied due to discrimination, stigmatization, and marginalization.

In Japan, the emergence of identity politics seems to have led to more formal delineation of the differences between the Wajin and the Ainu. These differences are also used by some groups to argue that the Ainu are not "good enough" to be considered "real" Japanese.

Indigeneity

The concept of Indigeneity is fraught with identity and politics and is often used to create a comparative structure between Indigenous people and the nation-state within which they reside. Paulette Steeves (2018) says, "Indigeneity cannot be discussed without a review of the colonial politics, policies, and practices that have historically worked to reinforce acculturation and the erasure of Indigenous identities and lifeways." Dominic O'Sullivan (2017, 16) posits that "Indigeneity is a developing theory of justice and political strategy used by indigenous peoples to craft their own terms of belonging to the nation state as 'first peoples.'"

Francesa Merlan (2009, 304) writes, "As a general concept, indigeneity is susceptible to arguments for greater or lesser inclusiveness, with a variety of possible (and often contested) implications." Social scientists Shanna Peltier and Jeffrey Ansloos (2021, 1) point out that "a person does not merely become Indigenous or develop an Indigenous identity through individual self-proclamation in endorsing an ancient relative."

Therefore, the concept of Indigeneity is one that continues to develop globally yet carries with it local and regional implications. As groups develop more formal internal structures, their social cohesion develops more fully as well. Even with the broad descriptors cited here, the idea of Indigeneity continues to develop as social groups more formally interact with their previous colonial governments.

In Japan, the concept of Indigeneity is playing out as various Ainu groups such as the Raporo Ainu Nation push the Japanese government to move beyond the mere ratification of the United Nation Declaration on the Rights of Indigenous Peoples and on to recognition that the Indigenous Ainu have rights that should be recognized and acted upon by the government.

Concluding Remarks

This chapter has been designed to provide a glimpse of the Ainu through a brief telling of their history within Japan as well as some basic information on various concepts relating to Indigenous groups, ethnic groups, and others within which the Ainu are situated. These concepts play important roles in helping understand the issues that have faced the Ainu as they seek their place within contemporary Japanese society. Ainu identity can be either openly displayed or subtly exhibited, and some people who are Ainu choose not to outwardly show their Ainu identity. This hesitancy derives from some of the discrimination the Ainu have suffered at the hands of the ethnic Japanese through the history of the relationships between the two peoples. Ainu relationships with the ethnic Japanese began when the Japanese first interacted with Ainu groups in the Tohoku region of eastern Honshu and the Oshima Peninsula of southern Hokkaido. The relationships developed out of a trading enterprise, but, over time, tensions led to open warfare. Forced by economic desperation, the Ainu became reliant on Wajin products and trade items for survival. After the reinstatement of the direct imperial rule by the Meiji Restoration in 1868, purposeful Japanese colonization of Hokkaido began. Since then, the colonialist assimilation policies of the Japanese government have contributed to Ainu issues as a minority population in Japan.

Further Reading

Readers who are unfamiliar with Japan and its general culture as a background should read books such as Joy Hendry's *Understanding Japanese Society* (2013) and any number of recent travel guides to Japan. Shigeru Kayano's *Our Land Was a Forest* (1994) provides a good background to one Ainu person's life in the mid-to-latter part of the twentieth century. Additionally, the 1999 catalog of the Smithsonian Institution's National Museum of Natural History's *Ainu: Spirit of a Northern People* exhibit by William Fitzhugh and Chisato O. Dubreuil is a great introduction to various aspects of Ainu life and materials.

Readers interested in the history of Ainu–Wajin relationships should consult Richard Siddle's 1996 work *Race, Resistance and the Ainu of Ja-*

pan and Brett Walker's 2001 *The Conquest of Ainu Lands: Ecology and Culture in Japanese Expansion, 1590–1800*. For contemporary Ainu issues, I suggest Mark K. Watson's 2014 volume *Japan's Ainu Minority in Tokyo: Diasporic Indigeneity and Urban Politics* and Christopher D. Loy's 2010 "The Ainu of Northern Japan: Indigeneity, Post-national Politics, Territoriality."

And, of course, I highly recommend Satoru Noda's 2014 *Golden Kamuy* as a fun way to learn about aspects of historical Ainu culture while getting a bit of Japanese history.

CHAPTER 2

· · · · · · · · · ·

Biological and Genetic Origins

This chapter provides a scientific version of the "origin" of the people today known as Ainu. Over the past century, comparisons based on physical and genetic differences between the Ainu and the Wajin (generally speaking) have been used by various scientists to create hypotheses that explain the origin of the Ainu within the broader general Japanese populations. Technological developments are enabling geneticists to collect and analyze DNA from ancient populations with greater frequency and accuracy, which, in turn, is leading to increased insights into and refinement of the population history of the Japanese archipelago and of the Ainu.

Few people acknowledge the contributions of the Ainu in the development of the Japanese population; the Ainu were generally considered by governmental officials and scientists either as a hindrance to the expansion and growth of the early Japanese empire or as a seemingly minor contributor to early Japanese populations. Anthropologist Mark Hudson (2014a, 121) has noted the scarcity of discussion or analysis of the Ainu as part of a larger Japanese story:

> When Ainu do appear in a national setting—for example in textbooks on
> ancient Japan—it is usually in one of two contexts: the debate over the
> biological origins of the Japanese people or the debate over the Emishi, a

population in northeast Japan who are mentioned in ancient texts as resist-
ing the expansion of the Japanese state and who may be related to the Ainu.

It's easy to understand the fascination that Japanese people might
have had with such populations whose outward appearances and culture
were seemingly different from their own and who occupied lands that
early Japanese cultures wanted, much in the same way that nineteenth-
century Americans in the eastern United States were fascinated by stories of American Indians and the frontier. In Japan, such interest seems
to have fueled the continued search for the origins of the "barbarians," to
continue to write them out of Japanese history, to serve the curiosity of
Japanese academics, or to serve as justification for Japanese politicians
to continue to ignore contemporary Ainu issues.

Historically, two groups have been identified that have been considered different from mainland Japanese populations—the Ryukyuan peoples in Okinawa and the southern portions of the archipelago, and the
Ainu in the northern portions of the archipelago. The Ryukyuan kingdom existed in the southern Ryukyu Islands until its conquest by Japanese forces in 1609, when it became a colony and subject of the Japanese
empire. The Ryukyuan people have continued to maintain their sense of
separateness from the mainland Japanese and continue to lobby for recognition as a self-sufficient population to regain self-governance outside
the Japanese sphere (see Abe 2023).

The origin of the Ainu has often been a topic of conversation with
anthropologists, both in Japan and abroad. One of the first Europeans
to work with and live among the Ainu, the missionary John Batchelor
([1901] 2006), stated: "That the Ainu inhabited Japan long anterior to
the Japanese is a well-known fact. . . . The old histories of Japan . . . tell
us that on coming to Japan the ancient Japanese often made war upon
the Ainu living at that time upon the mainland." As noted in the previous chapter, the earliest histories of Japan described the existence of
"barbarians" to the north who are presumed to be the ancestors of the
contemporary Ainu.

So, while there is early historical mention of people who are believed
to be Ainu, why are the Japanese so interested in Ainu origins? Is it a
scientific question that "needs" answering to fill in the broader human
history of development? Do the Ainu themselves wonder about their

origins to the extent that the scientific community does? What are the political implications (if any) that follow from the continued scientific questions about the origins of the Ainu and their differences from the "mainland Japanese"? Is it really a pressing scientific question, or is it simply a matter of curiosity?

The Indigenous peoples of North America in general do not share the same interests as archaeologists and anthropologists to find out the scientific origins of the first peoples to inhabit North America.[1] The politics of the study of the early peopling of North America has become much more involved within the past thirty years. Many tribal groups maintain that "we've always been here" and "we don't need science to tell us our history." Lakota lawyer and author Vine Deloria Jr. (1995, 84) draws attention to this point as well:

> By making us immigrants to North America they [scientists] are able to deny the fact that we were the full, complete, and total owners of this continent. They are able to see us simply as earlier interlopers and therefore throw back at us the accusation that we had simply found North America a little earlier than they had.

Indigenous archaeologist Paulette Steeves (2021) argues that the "real" history of North American occupation goes back to at least 130,000 years ago. She also argues that the aggressive defense of scientific hypotheses about early peopling of North America 14,000 years ago is "academic violence against Indigenous people" (CBC-Radio Canada 2022).

But it is important to emphasize that genetics does not equal culture! There is nothing about a person's genetic makeup that influences their culture. People learn their culture from the people around them and the stories, ideas, language, and belief systems they share. One can "learn" another culture regardless of whether one is genetically the same as all other members of that culture. As you read through articles on genetics or the archaeological cultures of the past, keep in mind that it is individuals that make up any and all cultures.

---

1. "Indigenous peoples of North America" refers to Native Americans / American Indians and Alaska Natives in the United States; and First Nations, Métis, and Inuit in Canada.

A Genetics Primer

Television shows take a great deal of liberty in presenting genetic data obtained from forensic tests and in amazingly quick time. In reality, things are much more complicated. It's not possible to look through a microscope and "see" whether one person's DNA is a match to another one's; rather, a great deal of the research requires scientists to operate with scientific and statistical assumptions that underlie the analyses they do.

Most people are familiar with the basics of Mendelian genetics—specific traits that individuals have are inherited from each of their parents through "genes," which are composed of a specific DNA sequence located on a specific region of a specific chromosome. The traits that are inherited are tied to hereditary factors that determine (or influence) a particular trait.

Every individual has his or her personal genetic structures and genome (all the genetic material of an organism) inherited from each parent, and they share similarities with their brothers and sisters, as well as some similarities with their cousins (the offspring of their mother's and father's siblings). The level of interrelatedness gets smaller and smaller the further away the relationships between the people get, but there are still discoverable familial relationships. Taken together, these groups form a "population" whose genetic makeup may be similar to or different from other groups of people (other "populations").

Population genetics uses large sets of genetic information to allow scientists to form hypotheses about human groups. It is based on a field of biology that studies the genetic composition of biological populations and the changes in genetic composition that result from the operation of various factors, including natural selection. Population geneticists pursue their goals by developing abstract mathematical models of gene frequency dynamics, trying to extract conclusions from those models about the likely patterns of genetic variation in actual populations. They then test their conclusions against empirical data (Okasha 2022). Basically, population geneticists are concerned with "genetic differences within and across populations, and the dynamics of how populations evolve as a result of the propagation of genetic mutations occurring within the germlines of individuals" (Burden 2019, 759).

When scientists start looking at the genetics of human populations rather than individuals, they get involved in the realm of anthropological genetics. University of Kansas anthropologist Michael Crawford (2006, 1) writes: "What distinguishes anthropological genetics from human genetics is its [anthropological genetics'] emphasis on smaller, reproductively isolated, non-Western populations, plus a broader, biocultural perspective on evolution and on complex disease etiology and transmission." This means that anthropological geneticists are interested in the ways that human culture might influence the genetic information that they encounter and/or try to model.

In looking at genetics and human culture, one familiar example of the connection between genetic variability, culture, and the environment is lactose intolerance. Lactase is an enzyme that humans need to process lactose in dairy products such as milk, cheese, and ice cream; adults who are lactase deficient are unable to process lactose, often experiencing diarrhea, stomach cramps, and other gastric discomfort after ingesting dairy products. The geographical distribution of the genetic materials responsible for giving adults the ability to process lactose after the weaning stage (lactase persistence, or LP) seems to be correlated in locations where past and present pastoral peoples who relied heavily on milk products have lived (Durham 1991). Biomedical researchers Augusto Anguita-Ruiz, Concepción Aguilera, and Ángel Gil (2020, 7) published a review of medical information on the genetics of lactose intolerance, noting:

> The frequency of LP varies greatly among populations, ranging from 0% to almost 100%, with the highest rates found in people of northern European descent and some populations from West Africa, East Africa, and the Middle East. . . . There is a very low level of LP in the Asiatic countries (15% in China, and 0% in South Korea, Vietnam, and Cambodia).

By looking at genetic changes in human genomes over time in relation to human culture, scientists can, as anthropologists Jason A. Hodgson and Todd R. Disotell (2010, 387) note, "infer the evolutionary history of humans." This is one of the things that drives anthropological geneticists to examine the DNA of past populations—to find an evolutionary history of humans and to gather information to establish relationships between human populations and the time of their divergence. Geneticist Sarabjit Mastana (2007, 373) of Loughborough University in the United Kingdom argues that research on the molecular level of specific human genetic material—at genetic polymorphisms—creates the possibility to estimate "the contribution of different gene pools to the make-up of present-day populations and test hypotheses about origin of linguistic and historical population movements." Polymorphisms, as it refers to genetics, refers to the presence of two or more variant forms of a specific DNA sequence that can occur among different individuals or populations.

Using these types of study methodologies, it is possible to get a general idea of the length of time from divergence based on the number of differences in DNA between two or more populations (see Hodgson and Distell 2010, 388–94, for a more detailed discussion of this process). Scientists can get a better understanding of population histories by using DNA "fingerprints"—a combination of genetic markers that relate to "discrete, segregating genetic traits which can be used to characterize populations by virtue of their presence, absence, or high frequency in some populations and low frequencies in others" (Crawford and Beaty 2013).

While science is often seen as neutral and value free, it is important to understand that, as anthropologist Jonathan Marks (2012, 170) notes, "human genetics is not value neutral and is not disconnected from contemporary social and cultural politics." He goes on to write that the value of anthropology for contemporary genetics probably lies in "helping to explore the cultural assumptions that inhabit the production and interpretation of its data" (170). This means that the science of genetics, coupled with the humanistic insights derived from anthropological studies, can provide information to help better understand the long-term histories of human populations across the globe.

In the past, people have misused human genetics for social and political purposes to enforce such outmoded beliefs that drove American eugenics, Nazi race hygiene, and corporate genomics. In 1911, Charles Davenport published *Heredity in Relation to Eugenics*, in which he argued that many human traits were genetically inherited and that it would therefore be possible to selectively breed people for desirable traits to improve humanity. In 1916, naturalist Madison Grant published *The Passing of the Great Race*, which explained human history in terms of the racial superiority of the Nordics and called for the immediate sterilization of the American unfit, "extending gradually . . . and perhaps ultimately to worthless race types" (47). This same ideology was taken to extremes by Nazi Germany.

Human genetics and genomic research are just two tools for those who study human populations, and it can be applied in both positive and negative ways. As noted in the previous chapter, some American Indian / Native American tribal groups use DNA studies to confirm or reject claims by tribal members of relationships to other tribal members (TallBear 2013); in Southeast Alaska, human genetics research demonstrates genetic connections between a young woman from circa 2,950 years ago and contemporary tribal groups in the area, noting that she "is most closely related to present-day individuals from the Tlingit, Haida, Nisga'a, and Tsimshian territories along the northern Pacific Northwest Coast" (Aqil et al. 2023, 12). Such research could be used to support tribal land claims; alternatively, such research *might* be used against tribal claimants if the results were thought to be negative or ambiguous.

A Genetics-Informed Population History of the Japanese Archipelago

It is within the broad systemic search for the origins of the human populations within the Japanese archipelago that the origin of the Ainu has been the subject of research. The questions of Ainu origins have been subject to investigation for nearly 150 years, beginning with American zoologist Edward S. Morse's 1879 hypothesis based on his archaeological excavations in Japan that the Neolithic populations known as the Jomon were replaced by (that is, a newer population came into the area and became the dominant population) the Ainu, who were then replaced in regions other than Hokkaido by populations ancestral to the modern Japanese who had migrated from somewhere on the Asian mainland (the pre-Ainu theory). Austrian physician Phillip Frans von Siebold (1897) proposed that the Ainu were actually the descendants of the Japanese Neolithic population. Anatomist Yoshiko Koganei, using osteological studies of one hundred Ainu skeletons in 1888–89 (Hanihara 1991, 2), believed the Jomonese were the ancestral form of Ainu, who were then replaced by the population that gave rise to the modern Japanese. A more recent discussion of the early development of anthropology and archaeology in Japan and its involvement in trying to determine the ancestors (the "missing link") of Japanese culture can be found in Hyung Pai's *Heritage Management in Korea and Japan: The Politics of Antiquity and Identity* (2013), especially chapter 4.

Scientific studies during the 1930s and 1940s proposed two theories for the development of the Japanese populations, each one offering different conclusions regarding the Ainu. Pathologist Kenji Kiyono's "hybridization theory" (1943, 1949) proposed that the Jomonese were the direct ancestral population of the modern Japanese but were morphologically altered through social and physical intermixture with the surrounding populations. He proposed admixture (admixture occurs when previously isolated populations interbreed, resulting in a population that is descended from multiple sources) between Jomon and south Asian populations giving rise to the Japanese, and between Jomon and north Asians giving rise to the Ainu. In contrast, Kotondo Hasebe's (1940) "continuity theory" proposed the idea that there were merely minor physiological changes between the Jomonese and the modern Japanese populations and did not offer conclusions concerning the Ainu.

In 1966, physical anthropologist William W. Howells used statistical analyses of cranial data from Ainu, non-Ainu, Japanese, and Jomonese skulls and concluded that the populations were different lineages but that Jomon and Ainu resembled each other. He suggested that racial replacement by Asian populations had taken place as a result of the decline of Jomon populations. This "replacement theory," however, as Kazuro Hanihara notes (1991, 3), assumed stableness of physical traits from the Jomon to present day and failed to consider such external influences on the Japanese population as the role of migration, evidence of geographic variation, and secular and cultural changes in the Japanese.

Hanihara proposes a dual structure model for the history of the Japanese. In his model,

> the first occupants of the Japanese Archipelago came from somewhere in Southeast Asia in the Upper Paleolithic age and they gave rise to the people in the Neolithic Jomon age. . . . The second wave of migration from north-

east Asia took place in and after the Aeneolithic Yayoi age; and the populations of both lineages gradually mixed with each other. (Hanihara 1991, 1)

Hanihara's "dual structure model" hypothesizes that population intermixture is still going on and that the dual structure of the Japanese population is maintained even today. He proposes that physical and cultural
regional differences between east and west Japan could be explained by
the varying rates of intermixture from region to region.

These early studies were conducted based primarily on morphological features of human skeletons. In 2000, a group of researchers led by
Makoto Bannai published the results of genetic studies that suggested
that the Ainu, based on the genetic information contained in human
leukocyte antigen (HLA) molecules, were descendants of an Upper Paleolithic population different from the mainland Japanese populations.
They argued that the Ainu were part of a population that had genetically
diverged from the majority of the present-day East Asians before the
beginning of the Neolithic period and that the mainland Japanese are
primarily descended from "post-neolithic migrants who traveled from
the East Asian continent in the Yayoi (300 B.C.–300 A.D.) and Kofun
(300–600 A.D.) eras" (Bannai et al. 2000, 137).

Work done by a group of researchers led by Atushi Tajima (Tajima
et al. 2004) further refined the genetic history of the Ainu. Using both
matrilineal (mitochondrial DNA inherited from the mother's side) and
patrilineal (Y chromosome information inherited from the father's side)
genetic materials, their study compared Ainu materials with other populations from North, East, and Southeast Asia. Their analysis showed
that eleven of twenty-five mtDNA sequence types were unique to the
Ainu and that, of the fourteen shared types, the most frequently shared
type was found to be common among the Ainu, the Nivkhi of northern
Sakhalin Island (located north of Hokkaido), and the Koryaks of Kamchatka Peninsula to the northeast of Hokkaido. They concluded that the
Ainu retain a degree of their own genetic uniqueness but also have higher
genetic affinity with Japanese populations and the Nivkhi people, a group
that occupies the Amur River Basin of East Russia and Sakhalin Island,
than they do with other populations. These findings imply some level of
admixture between the Ainu and mainland Japanese populations rather

than replacement of the genetic Ainu forebears by the genetic forebears of the mainland Japanese population.

More recently, studies conducted by research teams led by geneticist Choongwon Jeong (Jeong, Nakagome, and De Rienzo 2016) and by Noboru Adachi (Adachi, Kakuda, et al. 2018) independently analyzed genetic data to gain more information on the population histories of the Ainu. Jeong's group conducted genome-wide analyses of Ainu genetic material to study the relationship between the Ainu and other East Asian and Siberian populations outside the Japanese archipelago and proposed that "the deep history of the Ainu is consistent with the archaeological record for the Jomon culture in Japan" and "the ancestors of the Ainu are likely to have reached the Japanese archipelago in an early migration event distinct from the spread of farmer populations across East Asia" (Jeong et al. 2016, 268).

Adachi's research group (Adachi, Kakuda, et al. 2018) used ancient mitochondrial DNA ("aDNA") from Ainu skeletons dated to between 1603 and 1868 that had been excavated from areas all over Hokkaido to test the hypothesis that Ainu populations still retain the lineage of Hokkaido Jomon populations but that they also have experienced admixing with local populations, including from Siberia and mainland Japan. They note that Ainu ethnic identity is generally agreed to have been established in the thirteenth century (2018, 139), influenced by contact with Siberian cultures via the Okhotsk culture of northern and northwestern Hokkaido. Their study indicates that the greatest amount of influence from the mainland Japanese is in southwestern Hokkaido, the area closest to Honshu. Their data indicated that the genetic contributions of the Okhotsk were higher than that of the Jomon (35.1 percent to 30.9 percent) and that the genetic influence of the mainland Japanese was also strong at 28.1 percent.

Yuichi Nakazawa (2017, 541) proposed six pathways for human migration into the Japanese archipelago (see figure 3). Nakazawa's first route was a migration from the Korean peninsula to northern Kyushu via the Tsushima Strait (route 1). The second Nakazawa proposed was from the Russian Far East in the north to Hokkaido via Sakhalin Island (route 2). The third possible track was also a southward migratory route, from the Kamchatka Peninsula in western Beringia to eastern Hokkaido via the Ku-

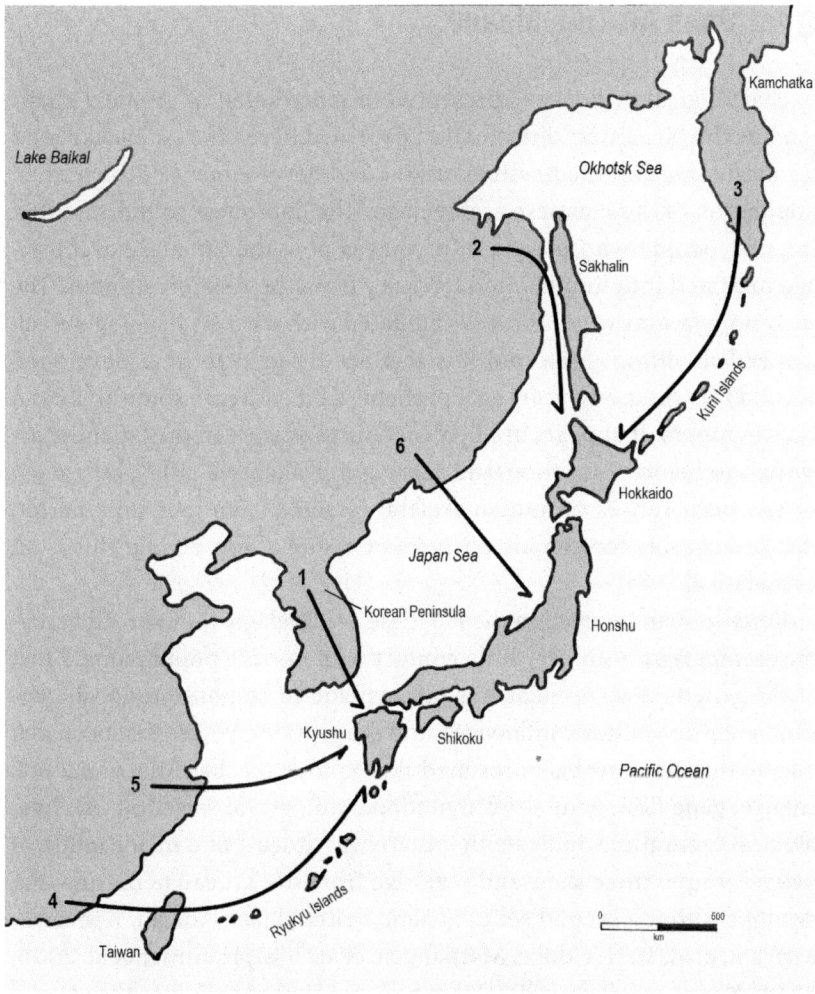

FIGURE 3 Peopling of the Japanese archipelago (adapted by Carol J. Ellick from Nakazawa 2017, 541, figure 1).

rile Islands (route 3). The fourth was a northward route that originated in southern China, extended to Taiwan Island and to the Ryukyu Islands, and crossed over the southern Pacific Ocean, eventually reaching southern Kyushu (route 4). The fifth route went east from eastern China to Kyushu and crossed the East China Sea (route 5). The sixth route was from the coastal Russian Far East to Honshu and crossed the Sea of Japan (route 6).

What Does All This Mean?

Archaeological evidence is presented in more detail in the next chapter, but the "scientific" information provided here offers a background for discussions on the possible origins and development of the human population of the Japanese archipelago. The data seem to indicate that the first people who moved into what is now the Japanese archipelago migrated into uninhabited territory from the Asian continent. The early populations were culturally affiliated with what archaeologists call Upper Paleolithic stone tool kits that are thought to have developed around fifty thousand years ago, probably a bit earlier in some areas and later in others. It appears unlikely that humans were in the Japanese archipelago before forty thousand years ago (Nakazawa 2017), but, given so few occurrences of human skeletal remains from that time period that are useable for genetic analyses or radiocarbon dating, this is all speculative.

Once humans arrived in the Japanese archipelago, they spread across the archipelago, with very little contact with outside populations. Most of the genetic development was internal and in response to local environmental and cultural influences, and the genetic changes that occurred during that time probably resulted due to four mechanisms of genetic change: gene flow, gene drift, mutation, and natural selection. Archaeological excavations indicate that there was at least one major influx of people around three thousand years ago from the Korean peninsula that brought with it a second set of genetic material (see Adachi, Kanzawa-Kiriyam, et al. 2021; Cooke, Mattiangeli, et al. 2021; Hammer et al. 2006; Jinam, Kawai, and Saitou 2021) that has contributed greatly to the genetic makeup of contemporary mainland Japanese populations. The irrigation-based rice agriculture and the ceremonies associated with it brought in by these immigrants had a major impact on those who already lived on the three main islands of Kyushu, Shikoku, and Honshu but less so on the northern (Hokkaido) and southern (Okinawa) islands.

Geneticists and other scientists recognize the influence of this migratory population on the genetics and social structures of the local populations. Scientists propose that this admixture between the two populations led to the current genetic makeup of contemporary mainland Japanese populations. They also recognize that some of the genetic traits in contemporary Japanese populations are absent in contemporary Ainu and Ryukyuan populations.

The cultural and economic innovations on the Japanese mainland (such as the wet-rice agriculture, increased use of metal and metal tool types, increased trade and social interaction with the Asian mainland, and more widespread economic interaction among the various settlements) allowed the population there to flourish and thus contributed to the foundation of the stereotypical mainland Japanese culture. The oldest recorded name for Japan—Wa—occurs in several ancient Chinese texts. From this, the Japanese word *Wajin*, meaning "the people of Wa," has been applied to the mainland Japanese people. In the northern and southern islands, however, the lack of meaningful admixture with the new population from the Asian continent left the local populations genetically "different" (generally speaking) from the initial population at this time, although it was impacted genetically by northeast Asian populations through Sakhalin and the Amur River basin people. It is these different genetic signatures that scientists talk about in their interpretations of the deep history of the Ainu and Ryukyuan populations.

Concluding Remarks

This very generalized interpretation of the genetic history of the Ainu is just that—a simple way of explaining how the peopling of the Japanese archipelago likely occurred. The local histories of the archipelago are complex, as they are everywhere, but this broad foundation offers a base onto which to layer the archaeological and historical information presented in the following chapters.

This is then the story that physical anthropologists, biological anthropologists, geneticists, and other scientists tell about the early people of the Japanese archipelago and the contributions derived from various other geographic areas of the Asian continent. The genetics of the human populations of Japan provide information that has been interpreted to offer insights into mechanisms whereby the mainland Japanese and the Ainu and Ryukyuan populations originated and developed more than forty thousand or so years ago. The next chapter will discuss the archaeological material that provides additional evidence for the development of

Japanese culture as well as the Ainu relationship with the archaeological record of the Jomon and later archaeological cultures.

Further Reading

Kazuro Hanihara's 1991 essay "Dual Structure Model for the Population History of the Japanese" has been the foundational work to examine the possible mechanisms that have been used to differentiate Ainu and mainland Japanese populations. Additionally, Hyung Il Pai's *Heritage Management in Korea and Japan: The Politics of Antiquity and Identity* (2013) has a good discussion of early studies in the development of anthropology and archaeology in Japan. More recently, Mark J. Hudson, Shigeki Nakagome, and John B. Whitman reexamine Hanihara's hypothesis in their 2020 publication "The Evolving Japanese: The Dual Structure Hypothesis at 30." Other geneticists have published works on DNA studies of human remains that have been found in archaeological excavations, and it is suggested that readers consult Noboru Adachi, Hideaki Kanzawa-Kiriyama, and colleagues' "Ancient Genomes from the Initial Jomon Period: New Insights into the Genetic History of the Japanese Archipelago" (2021); Niall P. Cooke and colleagues' "Ancient Genomics Reveals Tripartite Origins of Japanese Populations" (2021); and Timothy Jinam, Yosuke Kawai, and Naruya Saitou's "Modern Human DNA Analyses with Special Reference to the Inner Dual-Structure Model of Yaponesian" (2021).

Many of these articles are within specialized publications, but some discussions are available with basic archaeological publications on Japan, such as Junko Habu's 2004 volume *Ancient Jomon of Japan*; the 2018 volume *Handbook of East and Southeast Asian Archaeology*, edited by Junko Habu, Peter V. Lape, and John W. Olsen; and the 2022 volume *Maritime Prehistory of Northeast Asia*, edited by Jim Cassidy, Irina Ponkratova, and Ben Fitzhugh.

CHAPTER 3

• • • • • • • • •

Archaeology of the Japanese "Mainland" (Honshu-Shikoku-Kyushu)

Currently, there are no widely accepted archaeological sites within the Japanese archipelago older than 40,000–37,000 years ago, during the Upper Paleolithic. Yuichi Nakazawa and Christopher J. Bae (2018, 148) propose that the earliest occupation occurred sometime around 50,000 to 70,000 B.P., at a time during the Last Glacial Maximum when portions of the Japanese archipelago were connected via so-called land bridges with the Asian continent, creating much larger land masses and connections to the modern-day regions of southern China, Korea, and/or eastern Siberia (Nakazawa and Bae 2018, 147, figure 1). During glacial periods, when the sea level was hundreds of meters lower because of the amount of water locked up in the massive ice sheets, Hokkaido and Sakhalin were connected to the mouth of the Amur River to form the Paleo-Sakhalin-Hokkaido-Kurile Peninsula (Paleo-SHK Peninsula), a large mass of land made of what are now separate islands (Sakhalin, Hokkaido, and the Kurils). At the same time, the main islands of Honshu, Shikoku, and the Kyushu Islands were joined together to form Paleo-Honshu Island (Iizuka and Izuho 2017, 103; Nakazawa and Bae 2018, 145–46), a large expanse of land rather than three separate islands as they are today (see figure 4).

While the opportunities for human movement into the Japanese archipelago might have occurred as early as 50,000 years ago, Nakazawa

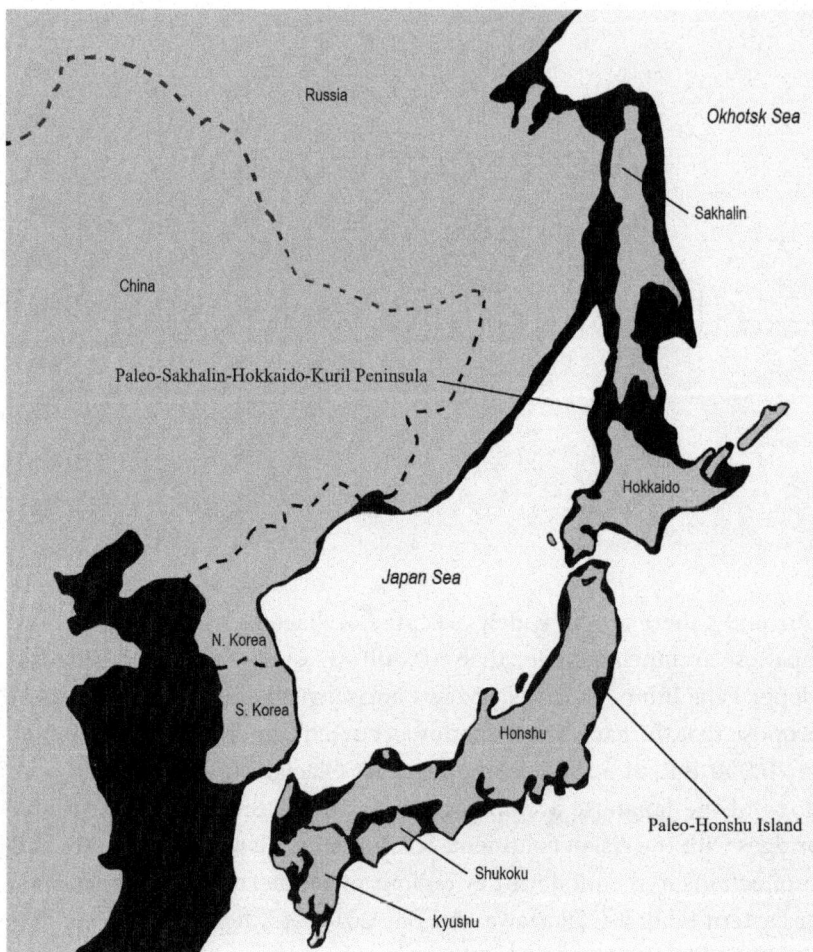

FIGURE 4 Landmasses during the Late Pleistocene showing Paleo-Honshu Island and Paleo-Sakhalin-Hokkaido-Kuril Peninsula (adapted by Carol J. Ellick from Nakazawa and Bae 2018, 146).

and Bae (2018, 152) suggest that human groups might not have taken advantage of the land bridges, arguing that "it is not until . . . late MIS [Marine Isotope Stage] 3 (40,000–30,000 years ago), [that] human arrival on the islands became more pronounced."

Archaeologist Christopher Bae (2017) suggests that researchers interested in early Japanese archaeology should not use the older tripartite division of Lower-Middle-Upper Paleolithic (sometimes called the Old, Middle, and New Stone Age) more often used to describe the development of the technology of the human species over the past two million years in Africa and Eurasia. Instead, he proposes to use Early and Late Paleolithic, as suggested by Xing Gao and Christopher J. Norton (2002), since the stone tool technology generally associated with the Middle Paleolithic of Europe (such as the Levallois technique, a specialized flaking technology) doesn't appear in northern China until later, at about the same time that stone blade technology generally associated with the Upper Paleolithic of Europe appears.

Bae's (2017, 517) "Late Paleolithic" in eastern Asia is normally associated with the appearance of blade technology (a special stone tool production technique that produced long, thin flakes of stone from a core) about 40,000 B.P., even though blade technology did not simply replace all the traditional core and flake-tool industries in the region at one time. Additionally, he draws attention to the presence of ground stone tools (tools made by grinding materials against another object until the appropriate edge and shape are reached) in Japan at about 38,000 B.P. (albeit in small numbers). Ground stone, once considered a defining part of the beginning of the Neolithic, disappeared for a while and then reappeared about 11,700 B.P.

Nakazawa's (2017) analysis of information from Paleolithic archaeology, human paleontology, and human genetics discussed in the previous chapter offers evidence for a better understanding of the complex picture of Late Pleistocene demographic history, at least in the central and southern archipelago. Nakazawa notes that the chronology of archaeological sites in Paleo-Honshu started about 40,000–37,000 B.P., while the Paleolithic record in Hokkaido is not earlier than 30,000 B.P. This appearance of older archaeological sites in the south, as well as the fact that Paleolithic sites are more numerous in southern Japan than in the north, implies, to Nakazawa, that the majority of migration into Japan came from the southwest.

Nakazawa (2017, 545) notes that there is clear evidence of Paleolithic habitation beginning about 40,000–37,000 years ago and ending about 11,500 B.P. The earlier archaeological assemblages incorporated blade technology into the flake-based assemblages, with a gradual but consistent increase in the number of tools produced on blades—end scrapers, burins, and perforators—with the blades being produced using various technological techniques, including prismatic blades.

There are, however, stone tool forms that occur here that are rare in other parts of Japan—trapezoids (defined as abruptly and/or minimally retouched small flakes), backed blades characterized by abrupt retouches and truncations on elongated flakes, blades traditionally described as knife-shaped tools, and edge-ground axes (Nakazawa 2017, 545).

Yuichiro Kudo and Fujio Kumon, working in the Lake Nojiri area of central Honshu Island, have developed some generalized chronologies on the Late Paleolithic that can serve as proxy for broader Japanese Late Paleolithic prehistory. To Kudo and Kumon (2012, 29), the Late Upper Paleolithic in the Japanese archipelago is roughly identified by backed blade industries, point-tools industries, and microblade industries and dates back to around 29,000–25,000 calendar years ago, according to a lithic typological and morphological comparison and radiocarbon dates of other areas such as the Yoda-Ogichi site and the Sakurabatakeue site.

The middle portion of the Late Paleolithic around Lake Nojiri is characterized by Sugikubo-type backed blade industry and point industry (Tani 2007) at about 25,000–20,000 years ago on the basis of radiocarbon dates. This is followed by a microblade industry, which also includes subconical microblade cores of the Nodake-Yasumiba type and wedge-shaped microblade cores made by the Yubetsu technique. These microblade industries can be placed at around 20,000–16,000 B.P. on the basis of radiocarbon dates of the Yoshioka B site and Araya sites (Kudo and Kumon 2012, 29).

Sadakatsu Kunitake's (2016, 172) research on the Kanto Plain of Honshu indicates that the hunter-gatherers of the region moved into the area before the Last Glacial Maximum, the time when the Ice Age glaciers were at their maximum. Subsequently, the region's hunter-gatherers developed efficient procurement and consumption strategies for lithic materials as a form of regional adaption that played out through the Japanese archipelago as human populations increased in number.

After the Paleolithic, most of the archaeological assemblages of the Japanese archipelago are identified by microblade production coupled with more common usage of ground stone tools and the appearance of pottery. This Neolithic ("new stone age") lifestyle, more commonly associated with plant and animal domestication elsewhere, continues to be associated with hunters and gatherers in Japan and is known as the "Jomon."

Jomon

The very long (approximately 14,000 years) Jomon period is conventionally divided into a number of phases, with broadly general beginning and ending dates: Incipient (16,500–10,000 years ago [B.P.]), Initial (10,000–7,000 B.P.), Early (7,000–5,550 B.P.), Middle (5,500–4,500 B.P.), Late (4,500–3,000 B.P.), and Final (3,000–2,300 B.P.), with the phases getting progressively shorter. Even though this period is lumped under a single name by archaeologists, considerable regional and temporal diversity occurs across the Japanese archipelago; therefore, the beginning and ending dates for each phase vary by region.

Junko Habu (2008, 572) has suggested that, because of the wide variability, "the Jomon should not be seen as a single entity characterized by a fixed set of cultural traits" the way that most/many archaeologists continue to do. It might be better to stop thinking of the Jomon as a singular archaeological culture and to consider it to be a series of archaeological traditions. An archaeological culture is a recurring assemblage of types of artifacts, buildings, and monuments from a specific period and region that may constitute the material culture remains of a particular past human society. Archaeological traditions, on the other hand, refer to the continuities in artifact design and customs passed down through generations, reflecting cultural values, identities, and practices.

The spread of broadleaf forests in the earliest Jomon provided an increased food supply in terms of plentiful nuts (and the animals attracted to them) and other forest products as well as the increase of marine resources created by the formation of continental shelves through coastal transgression. The ecological wealth and the increase in food resources led to population increase and a more sedentary subsistence strategy, as indicated by larger, more permanent settlements.

The hunter-gatherer groups in Japan during this time relied heavily on plants and animals but were not practitioners of horticulture—at least, there is little evidence that can be determined archaeologically. American archaeologist Joseph R. Caldwell proposed that, in such situations where there was abundant plant and animal species, horticulture or agriculture were unnecessary for survival. His "Primary Forest Efficiency" (Caldwell 1958) was "a subsistence strategy based on detailed knowledge of seasonal cycles and of diverse forest foods: floral and faunal, terrestrial and aquatic" (Dye and Watson 2010, 164). Jomon culture, and especially later cultures in Hokkaido, seem to fit this model, even though some archaeologists (G. Crawford 2011; Nishida 1983) would argue that cultivation of chestnut and millet occurred in the Middle and Late Jomon, coming in before rice. Terrestrial food sources used by Jomon populations meriting special mention include Sika deer, wild boar (with possible wild-pig management), wild plants such as yam-like tubers, and freshwater fish. In northeastern Honshu, marine life was another major food source, with shell middens indicating intensive exploitation of marine resources (Habu et al. 2011, 25). Generalized characteristics of the six Jomon phases are described in the following sections.

Incipient Jomon (ca. 16,500–10,000 B.P.)

The Incipient Jomon period marks the transition between Paleolithic and Neolithic ways of life (Habu 2004; Imamura 1996; Kudo 2012) (see table 2). Archaeological findings indicate that people lived in simple surface dwellings and practiced a hunting-and-gathering economy. They produced deep pottery cooking containers with pointed bottoms and rudimentary cord markings—among the oldest examples of pottery known in the world (e.g., Amemiya 1994; Murakami 2008). The earliest pottery was plain. It was followed by ridge-patterned pottery, nail-impressed pottery, and pottery with many cord impressions. This pottery was made by people living in the Kanto region on the eastern side of Honshu, the plain on which today's Tokyo is located.

   Incipient Jomon pots present a major challenge to understanding the Jomon cultures because pottery making has more often been associated with agriculture and seen as a characteristic of a more sedentary culture. In Japan, however, Incipient Jomon people were hunter-gatherers who lived in nomadic small groups, and yet they developed the craft of pottery long before agriculture was introduced into Japan. Archaeologist Peter Jordan and a diverse group of researchers (Jordan et al. 2022, 317) note that the need to store quantities of salmon after harvesting, along with the exploitation of marine resources (shellfish and other coastal resources, ocean fishing, and sea mammal hunting), might have served as an incentive for people to experiment with new types of container technologies for more efficient processing of these catches into food. The Incipient Jomon archaeological record demonstrates that pottery making is a technology independent and distinct from agriculture.

Simon Kaner and Yasuhiro Taniguchi (2017, 335–36) draw attention to the importance of the Incipient Jomon, writing that "it was from this time on that the behaviors and practices that underpinned the following eight millennia were established" (335), which they summarize as follows:

> (1) the spread in the construction of pit-dwellings and an increase in the number of settlements; (2) the development of shell middens and the establishment of fishing technologies; (3) the regular use of plant processing equipment, especially grinding stones and querns; (4) increasing amounts of pottery being made and used; (5) the possible incipient cultivation of certain plants, notably the intensive use of nuts such as chestnuts; (6) the development of distinctive pottery style zones; (7) an increase in the use of stone resources, notably obsidian, brought in from distant sources; and (8) an increase in numbers and sophistication of ceramic figurines (*dogū*). (Kaner and Taniguchi 2017, 335)

Initial Jomon (ca. 10,000–7,000 B.P.)

By the Initial Jomon period, the gradual climatic warming that had begun around 8,000 B.P. sufficiently raised sea levels so that the southern islands of Shikoku and Kyushu were separated from the main island of Honshu. The rise in temperature also resulted in an increase in the food availability, which was derived from the sea as well as by hunting animals and gathering plants, fruits, and seeds. Evidence of this diet is found in shell mounds (Habu et al. 2011), or ancient refuse heaps. Food and other necessities of life were acquired and processed with the use of stone tools such as grinding stones, knives, and axes. Like Incipient Jomon pottery, the pottery is intricately decorated in the "cord-like" structure that characterizes Jomon (Imamura 1996). Regional differences in the shape and

TABLE 2 Jomon chronology, with climate, economy, settlement, and population information

Period	Dates	Climate	Economy	Settlement	Population
Incipient	16,500–10,000 B.P.	Cool, dry	Hunting and gathering economy; plain pottery with rudimentary cord marks; bow and arrow	Simple surface dwellings	Small nomadic groups
Initial	10,000–7,000 B.P.	Slight warming	Hunting and gathering and marine resources; pottery more complex with regional differences; ground stone tools and axes	Settlement number and size increase	Population increases; larger groups
Early	7,000–5,500 B.P.	Warming continues	Hunting and gathering, with marine and coastal resources; pottery complexity and regional diversity; clay figurines (*dogu*) appear	More and larger settlements; pit dwellings common in west, less in east; economic interaction with Korea	Population continues to increase; larger and more numerous groups

Middle	5,500–4,500 B.P.	Warming trend peaks	Hunting and gathering with simple agriculture or proto-agriculture; increased production of female figurines and phallic images of stone; burials in shell mounds; rise in ritual practices	Larger settlements and larger villages; people more sedentary	Group size reaches high point; people begin living in mountains as well
Late	4,500–3,000 B.P.	Climate cooling	Innovations in fishing technology with toggle harpoons; lacquerware production; circular ceremonial sites of stones; larger numbers of figurines; increase in the importance and enactment of rituals; long-distance exchange networks of exotic goods; increasing social inequality	Communities more similar to each other, indicating closer contact	People leave mountains to enter coastal regions
Final	3,000–2,300 B.P.	Climate cooling	Resources scarcer; diminishing food supply	Settlements farther apart	Population decline

Source: Adapted from Habu 2004; Kaner and Taniguchi 2017.

pattern of pottery became apparent. In the Tohoku region and the southern Hokkaido region, the pattern changed from the impressed type, to the shell impression, and finally the cord-mark type. Most pottery had a pointed bottom.

Archaeologists Naoko Matsumoto, Junko Habu, and Akira Matsui (2017) provide a review of Jomon archaeology from the Initial to Final Jomon subperiods, with an additional comparison of geographical expressions in eastern versus western Japan. They also acknowledge that there might be different ending dates associated with the various Jomon phases because of the geographical distances and proximity to resource areas, noting that "Jomon culture shows marked temporal and spatial variability" (2017, 437). Citing Sugao Yamanouchi (1964) and Takura Izumi (1985), they suggest that the regional biodiversity of the forests in eastern and western Japan may have led to the development of "two distinct subsistence strategies, settlement patterns and social complexity throughout the Jomon Period" (Matsumoto, Habu, and Matsui 2017, 442).

Early Jomon (ca. 7,000–5,500 B.P.)

The Early Jomon corresponds to one of the most interesting intervals in human history. Between 7,000 and 5,500 B.P., the world reached its warmest in the millennia following the Ice Age—during this period, the average summer temperature was about four to six degrees Fahrenheit (ca. two to four degrees Celsius) higher than it is today. In western Japan during the Early Jomon, the presence of large settlements with large numbers of pit dwellings (a shallow pit with an earthen floor covered by a thatched roof) became common, along with an increase in the total number of sites. In eastern Japan, however, the number of pit dwellings remained low. Of importance is the appearance of the earliest examples of clay figurines (*dogū*) of humans and animals that have been hypothesized to have served as ritual objects (Matsumoto, Habu, and Matsui 2017, 442) (see figure 5).

Regional differences in the shape and pattern of pottery became more visible during the Early Jomon. In the northern Tohoku region and the southern Hokkaido region, cylindrical pottery with flat bottoms had cord-mark patterns made by rolling twisted plant fibers on the surface of the pottery vessel (Kaner and Taniguchi 2017, 334). The Jomon also developed their pottery work even further: they began to fashion figu-

FIGURE 5 *Dogū* from Hakodate Jomon Culture Center.

rines. In addition to the cord-marked earthenware cooking and storage vessels, other handicrafts produced for daily use included woven baskets, bone needles, and stone tools. It's likely that lacquerware (see figure 6) also developed in this period.

The contents of huge shell mounds adjacent to settlements show that a high percentage of people's daily diet continued to come from the oceans, including shellfish and fish. Similarities between pottery produced in Kyushu and contemporary Korea suggest that regular commerce existed between the Japanese islands and the Korean peninsula.

FIGURE 6 Lacquered bowl from the Korekawa Site, Aomori Prefect, Honshu.

Middle Jomon (ca. 5,500–4,500 B.P.)

The Middle Jomon period marked the high point of the Jomon culture in terms of increased population and production of handicrafts. The warming climate peaked in temperature during this era. Refuse heaps indicate that the people were sedentary for longer periods and lived in larger communities. They fished; hunted animals such as deer, bear, rabbit, and duck; and gathered nuts, berries, and other wild plants. This is probably the time period when they began attempting plant cultivation rather than just helping native plant environments. The Jomon began to live in very large villages and developed very simple agriculture or proto-agriculture. Matsumoto, Habu, and Matsui (2017, 444) suggest that the increase in sedentism and specialization in types of plant resources might have been able to support a larger population for a while but that a resultant decrease in subsistence and food diversity could be used to explain the population decline in eastern Japan during the Middle Jomon.

Although still largely hunters and gatherers, they also began to develop increasingly sophisticated artwork with magnificent decorations more indicative of farming societies. Pottery decorated with appliqued strips of clay was made in various areas. In the northern Tohoku region and the southern Hokkaido region, "fire-flame pottery" (cylindrical pottery with a rim shaped like four waves and clay applique on the surface) was common (see figure 7). Their figurines depicted animals and humans, and the increased production of female figurines and phallic images of stone as well as the practice of burying the deceased in shell mounds suggest a rise in ritual activities.

Late Jomon (ca. 4,500–3,000 B.P.)

Late Jomon populations migrated out of the mountains and settled closer to the coast, especially along Honshu's eastern shores, as the climate began to cool once more. Greater reliance on seafood inspired innovations in fishing technology, such as the development of the toggle harpoon and deep-sea-fishing techniques. Communities appear to have come into closer social contact, as indicated by greater similarity among artifacts. Circular ceremonial sites composed of stones, in some cases numbering in the thousands, and larger numbers of figurines in the Jomon settlements show a continued increase in the importance and enactment of rituals. This cultural period is characterized by the continued sophistication of its material culture, including lacquerware production, an increase in the number of ritual artifacts and ceremonial features, and the development of long-distance exchange networks of exotic goods (see Habu 2004, 137–39). These signs, along with an increasing diversity in burial types during the Late Jomon period, have commonly been interpreted as a reflection of increasing social inequality (see Habu 2004, 254–58).

FIGURE 7 Fire-flame pottery jar, Tokyo National Museum.

Final Jomon (ca. 3,000–2,300 B.P.)

The people of the Final Jomon period had to work more for their food because of the changing climate. The population decline that had begun during the transition between the Middle and Late Jomon continued (Crema et al. 2016). People moved further apart in order to maintain their living arrangements and to continue to survive based on a diminishing food supply. Matsumoto, Habu, and Matsui (2017, 445–46) suggest as well that the decline in population seen in eastern Japan indicates a movement of people out of eastern Japan to the west. They note the differential occurrences of the characteristics of the subperiods to be later in time as one moves from the east to the west.

Because of this movement of populations further away from each other as well as the decrease in population density, regional differences in the settlements and cultural materials became more pronounced. As part of the transition to the Yayoi culture, domesticated rice was introduced into Japan at this time, probably in the Kyushu region first and then subsequently eastward.

Jomon Economy and Daily Life

Looking at the Jomon as a whole (all six phases), the Jomon used bows, arrows, and stone spears for hunting. For these tools, slate and obsidian, both very common in Japan and suited for creating sharp blades, were used. The animals hunted included deer, boar, and hare, some of which were captured using pits as well as shot with bows and arrows. Dogs were also used for hunting.

Mountain vegetables and nuts, such as chestnuts, walnuts, and Japanese horse chestnuts, were an important source of food for the people at the time. Hard nuts were used after being crushed and milled with stone pestles, grinding stones, and stone plates. Chestnuts are edible, do not require special processing, are suitable for storage, and are preserved with minimal processing. Japanese horse chestnuts, however, must be soaked in water to remove the bitter taste, and the remains of watering places for processing them have been found.

In addition to gathering shellfish at the sea and the river, people used dugout canoes for fishing. Excavated fishhooks and harpoon heads suggest that they caught relatively large fish by line fishing and spear fishing. Stone weights are thought to have been used as fishing-net sinkers for catching small fish.

The transition from a mobile life to a sedentary life led to the emergence of semipermanent settlements. Within these, pit dwellings were built, and graves became more localized in the habitations. Over time, larger regional population hubs such as Sannai Maruyama in Aomori

City formed. Large buildings with thick pillars, mounds used as a ritual/ space, and stone circles as large monuments were also constructed in these larger regional hubs (see figure 8).

People at that time were buried in pit graves. After a sedentary life-style was established in the Early to Middle Jomon period, graves for adults, arranged in rows, were placed in the vicinity of the settlement areas. During the Late Jomon period, there are examples of graves that were placed in a single location in the settlement center but also some circumstances where graves were located away from residential areas, while the remains of children who had died were buried in pottery jars in the vicinity of other graves.

Dugout canoes were in use and contributed to the ability of people to trade with other people living longer distances away, with jade, asphalt, and obsidian being exchanged. Lacquering, which had been established around the Early Jomon period, is an integrated technique that shows the advanced skills of people at that time and requires a bit of sedentism because of the intricate and complex process. It is uncertain whether lacquerware was developed independently in Japan or whether the lac-quered pieces originated on the Asian mainland (Hudson 1996, 48).

Many clay figurines used for rituals and accessories were also made. This suggests that the Jomon people had a rich spiritual world. Many remains of religious and ritualistic items whose purpose has not been identified have been found, including chipped stone and bone artifacts in the shapes of people, animals, and swordlike stones. These are thought to have been used in rites for fertility and safety at hunting, memorial services for ancestors, and as prestige goods.

Yayoi

About 2,600 years ago, there was an influx of intensive agriculture prac-tices, including wet-rice production and the cultivation of barley, wheat, millet, and other dry crops (Crawford 2011, 337). "Yayoi" (2,600 to about 1,950 B.P.) is the name that has been given to the era that is associated with this change in crops and social structures that were part of the large-scale changes over the Honshu-Shikoku-Kyushu islands of main-land Japan.

FIGURE 8 Reconstructed long house at Sannai Maruyama, Aomori City, Honshu.

The name "Yayoi" derives from the name of the district in Tokyo where the distinct pottery of this time period was first found in 1884 and drew the attention of scholars because the pottery was thinner and more symmetrical than Jomon pottery. Yayoi pottery was turned on wheels and fired at higher temperatures than Jomon pottery. It is distinguished partly by this marked advance in technique and partly by an absence of the decorative features that characterized Jomon pottery. Along with this distinctive pottery style, Yayoi settlements have more metal objects and are associated with irrigated cultivation of rice and its associated ceremonies.

Although the Yayoi period was initially viewed as a replacement of the Jomon, Seiji Kobayashi (2001) proposes that there were indications it was a fusion of two cultures—a new culture brought by the newcomers from the Korean peninsula in the west and the existing Jomon cultures of the archipelago. Fumihiro Sakahira and Takao Terano (2016, 281) have examined physical differences between the Jomon and Yayoi populations and note that there were significant genetic influences from Chinese and Korean populations in the Yayoi that were absent in the previous Jomon (see chapter 2 for details on the genetics of Japanese populations).

The people who migrated into the Japanese archipelago during this time brought with them economic systems that differed from those of the Jomon. The dependence on rice and long-distance trade created cultural differences that centered primarily in Kyushu, Shikoku, and western Honshu. The development of this economic system brought with it associated administrative and culture systems that created internal political unification. Ultimately, the groups on the Honshu-Shikoku-Kyushu islands reached sizes and complexity and further political unification that allowed them to establish links with foreign countries as a country of their own.

The following discussion draws heavily on Koji Mizoguchi's (2017) work and his synthesis of Yayoi archaeology. He notes that the Yayoi are considered in two different ways. First, some archaeologists divide the Yayoi into five phases—the Yayoi I–Yayoi V phases, occasionally with the "Initial" phase added to the beginning of the Yayoi I phase—while others use a three-phase system of Early, Middle, and Late Yayoi. However, the distinction of the Initial Yayoi phase is less useful in a broad sense because, as Mizoguchi (2017, 561) notes, "it is only applicable to the northern Kyushu region where the earliest rice-farming villages emerged in limited spots prior to the spread of the paddy field rice agriculture-based socio-cultural complex across western Japan."

In the three-phase system, Yayoi I is treated as the Early Yayoi; the Yayoi II, III, and IV phases are consolidated into the Middle Yayoi; and Yayoi V is considered the Late Yayoi. In this tripartite scheme, dates for the Yayoi vary, but the beginning of the Early Yayoi is generally placed at about 2,600 B.P.; the beginning of the Middle Yayoi between 2,400 and 2,200 B.P.; the beginning of the Late Yayoi from around 2,000 B.P.; and the beginning of the Yayoi VI/Yayoi–Kofun transitional phase around 1,750 B.P. (Mizoguchi 2017, 562).

Initial Yayoi and Yayoi I (ca. 2,800/2,600–2,400/2,200 B.P.)

This period is generally equated with the beginning of indications of rice paddy field agriculture in Kyushu (see figure 9; table 3). A new type of house, consisting of round and rectangular subtypes, was introduced to the archipelago from the Korean peninsula (Nakama 1987). V-sectioned ditches, which often enclosed the settlements, were introduced from the Korean peninsula as well. Additionally, burial grounds became separated from the dwelling area rather than placed at the center of the settlement as they were in Jomon settlements.

The archaeological material culture of local populations adopted some artifact types and shapes from the immigrants while adapting others. Mizoguchi (2017, 563) suggests that new artifacts were adopted if there were no functional equivalents in the existing material culture, while artifacts for which there were existing counterparts in the local cultural groups were adapted to fit the needs of the new economies. He also notes that the eastward spread of people during the second half of the Yayoi I period probably resulted from a combination of small-scale migrations and the adoption of the migrants' customs by local communities, result-ing in new villages and assemblages exhibiting local characteristics.

Along with this influx of people and technology, new methods for burying the dead appear. The adoption of dolmens—burial structures composed of large capstones generally supported by small stones placed on the ground over a cobble-walled chamber, or a pit—to encapsulate burials usually contained either a cist or a composite wooden coffin. The use of such structures originated in the Korean peninsula and occurred in Japan first along the coastal communities of northern and northwest-ern Kyushu. However, as their use spread eastward, some characteristics dropped out until, eventually, more eastern populations stopped using the capstone and the burials ended up as flat graves with a cist or cist-like stone arrangement set around a coffin or pit burial (Mizoguchi 2017, 565, fig. 34.4; 566–67).

TABLE 3 Yayoi chronology, with subsistence and settlement pattern information

Period	Dates	Economy	Settlement	Population
Early Yayoi (Yayoi I)	2,800–2,200 B.P.	Rice paddy agriculture; some artifact types adopted while others adapted; plain, thinner, wheel-thrown pottery; stone daggers and willow-shaped polished stone arrowheads	Round and rectangular houses; V-sectioned ditches enclose settlements; burial grounds separate from settlement; adoption of dolmens to encapsulate burials; arrangement of graves and inclusion of specific associated grave goods evidence of social stratification?	Major influx from Korean peninsula; small-scale migrations from west to east; admixing of Yayoi and Jomon people
Middle Yayoi (Yayoi II–IV)	2,200–2,000 B.P.	Maturation of rice-farming communities	New settlement system with new sites "budding off" when carrying capacity in area reached; burial compounds often square, mounded, and with large cemeteries and buildings associated with them	Population increases due to migration and general population growth
Kyushu Horizon		Closest to the Korean peninsula; direct influences from the west in technologies (bronze weapon production; iron forging) and imported materials from the Early Han empire of China	Regional centers, indicative of a settlement hierarchy, also began developing during this time	Continued population growth

Western Horizon	Intermediary between Kyushu and Eastern Horizons; *dotaku* bronze bells and weapon-shaped implements; iron tools later	Settlement hierarchy similar to that in Kyushu; huge cemeteries; large, rectangular buildings repeatedly rebuilt at the same spot over time	Continued population growth
Eastern Horizon	Furthest from Korean peninsula and closest to continuing Jomon economies; pottery cord marked; bronze and iron scarce	No apparent settlement hierarchy	Continued population growth
Late Yayoi (Yayoi V) 2,000–1,750 B.P.	Increasing amount of Chinese influence	Abandonment of settlements across Kyushu and western region; elite-precinct-type compounds in settlements in Kyushu and west; fewer formal burials; dead buried in square, clearly defined compounds; burial of infants and children in the same manner as adults in compounds seem to indicate *ascribed* status as opposed to *achieved* status	Continued population growth

Source: Derived from Mizoguchi 2017.

FIGURE 9 Archaeological remnants of Early Yayoi rice paddies, Sunazawa Site, Hirosaki City, Aomori Prefect, Honshu.

Other characteristics, such as stone daggers and willow leaf–shaped polished stone arrowheads, the arrangement of graves, and the inclusion of specific associated grave goods, are seen by Yasuo Yanagida (1986, 141) as early indications of social stratification. However, Mizoguchi disagrees, arguing that such evidence is not strong enough at this time to make that association.

Middle Yayoi (Yayoi II–IV) (circa 2,400/2,000 B.P.)

Mizoguchi characterizes this period as a time of the maturation of rice-farming communities. He writes as well that three broad regional units developed, archaeologically recognized as "large pottery style zones" with "distinct ways of organizing settlements, burying the dead, and praying for the well-being of their communities" (Mizoguchi 2017, 570). He also notes the differences between the eastern horizon and other two horizons—the Kyushu horizon and the Western horizon (from present-day Chugoku and Shikoku regions to the Tokai and Hokuriku regions).

The Kyushu Horizon
This horizon is the closest to the Korean peninsula both geographically and in many cultural characteristics. Mizoguchi (2017, 570–75) presents some of what he recognizes to be direct influences from the east, including technologies (bronze weapon production; iron forging) and evidence of imported materials from the Early Han empire of China. Regional centers, indicative of a settlement hierarchy, also began developing during this time, interpreted by Mizoguchi to be indicative of some sort of more formalized control over interactions between differing regions and/or communities.

The Western Horizon
Mizoguchi (2017, 575–77) describes the Western Horizon as an intermediary between the Kyushu and the Eastern Horizons. There was a unique bronze assemblage composed of dotaku bronze bells and weapon-shaped implements, and iron tools show up later in the period. Settlement hierarchy similar to that in Kyushu exists here as well, along with huge cemeteries and large, rectangular buildings repeatedly rebuilt at the same spot over time.

The Eastern Horizon
This area is the furthest removed from the Korean peninsula and the closest to the continuing Jomon economies and cultures of the northern Tohoku Region of eastern Honshu and Hokkaido. As such, it was influenced by the two separate culture expressions: (1) the pottery continues to be cord marked, and bronze and iron are scarce (although not absent);

and (2) there doesn't appear to be any settlement hierarchy (Mizoguchi 2017, 577). Of particular note is that there was an extensive practice of re-burial in the Eastern Horizon that, according to Hideshi Ishikawa (2000, cited in Mizoguchi 2017, 577), prolonged the relationships between the living and the dead.

In general, the Middle Yayoi is marked by the development of new settlement systems with new habitation sites "budding off" when carrying capacity in one area was reached. It appears that the new locations were composed of kin-based groupings with shared storage areas. The larger settlements acquired "central-place-like" attributes situated at economically advantageous locations. Burial compounds were often square, mounded, and with large cemeteries and buildings associated with them. In the east, however, intercommunal ties were probably strengthened or developed through the use of secondary burial/reburial of the deceased. This changed, however, with the continued expansion of ideas from the west.

The Late Yayoi and the Yayoi–Kofun Transitional Phase (2,000–1,750 B.P.)

Mizoguchi (2017, 582) begins his description of this phase with the subtitle "Turmoil" and draws attention to the increasing amount of influence China had in the region at this time. Turmoil certainly seems to be apparent, with the abandonment of settlements across the Kyushu and Western Horizons at this time. Mizoguchi (2017, 582) associates this turmoil with the Xin Dynasty of Wang Mang from A.D. 9 to A.D. 23. In his opinion, the disruption of access to materials from China (finished objects as well as raw materials necessary for the production of bronze) likely created the internal strife experienced by the Kyushu and Western Horizons at this time and onward through about A.D. 30.

He notes that an important part of the Yayoi V phase is the development of hierarchy in the form of elite-precinct-type compounds in settlements across Kyushu and western Japan (Mizoguchi 2017, 583). At the same time, the number of formal burials dropped sharply, but the dead were buried in square, clearly defined compounds. The burial of infants and children in the same manner as adults in these compounds seems to indicate the occurrence of *ascribed* status (social status an individual has by virtue of birth) as opposed to *achieved* status (social status earned by an individual through work, valor, or other actions). To Mizoguchi (2017, 584), this suggests that some segments of society (probably lineages) were in some way in control of things.

The first historical mention of what is perceived to be the descendants of the Yayoi dates from A.D. 57 and explains that the "Wa" people (Chinese name given to the Japanese) regularly sent tributary delegations to China to meet with representatives of the Chinese empire. Additionally, the kingdom of Yamatai (later known as Yamato), ruled by the priestess Himiko, is mentioned in the Chinese historical text *Wei Zhi* (Cartwright 2017b).

Kofun

On the Japanese mainland, the Kofun period followed the Yayoi period and is characterized by large burial mounds, elaborate funerary pottery sculptures (called *haniwa*), ironworking (replacing bronze), and the establishment of the Shinto religion. This period is also known for the rise of the Yamato clan as a military power.

Mizoguchi (2017, 562) notes that the Kofun period is commonly divided into ten phases: Early Kofun (Kofun phases I–IV), beginning at about A.D. 250/275; the Middle Kofun (phases V–VIII), beginning about A.D. 400; the Late Kofun (phases IX and X), beginning at about A.D. 500; and the Final Kofun, between A.D. 600 and 700.

In describing the period of transition between the Yayoi and the Kofun, Mizoguchi (2017, 588) draws attention to the increasing "generation of the elite interaction network/sphere, covering the Kyushu and Western Horizons and the western portion of the Eastern Horizon." This network was embodied by a package of material items, which he names the "Initial Kofun Package (IKP)" (2017, 588), composed of a range of portable items (such as bronze mirrors, bronze and iron weapons, iron woodworking implements, iron fishing implements), nonportable ones (such as slate stone–built cists and mound-covering large cobbles), and monumental items (keyhole-shaped mounds), many of which originated in various regions of the Kyushu and Western Horizons. These items were assembled in the Kinki-core Region/Horizon (KCR) of the Osaka and Nara Prefectures, the contemporary Kansai area. This suite of items was not imposed on others by force but adopted and shared by other emerging elites seemingly voluntarily.

Throughout the remainder of the Kofun, the KCR continued to grow its dominance over the other regional polities; burial tumuli (mounds of earth and stones raised over a grave or graves) increased in size. During the Middle Kofun, items and ideas imported from the Korean peninsula continued, along with the appearance of actual communities of migrants (Mizoguchi 2017, 592). The *Book of Song* and other works compiled as official historical documents by mainland Chinese authorities recorded that five of the paramount chiefs of the KCR (Wa-no-go-oh) had dispatched their emissaries to the Jin and the Liu Sung Dynasties of China in succession (A. Yoshida 1998).

The Late Kofun saw a slight decrease in the size of the tumuli as well as a shift in the seeming location of power from the Furuichi and Mozu areas to the northern portion of the Osaka Plain. Mizoguchi (2017, 593) interprets these shifts to be related to the disruptions in the line of the paramount chiefs (or at least instability in the succession of the paramount chiefs). The emergence of clusters of small, round tumuli indicates what Mizoguchi interprets as representative of extended family-scale groups whose burials represented their accomplishments in life rather than things to which they were born. This was the time when Buddhism was introduced into the area and, Mizoguchi notes, is the border of the transition to the ancient state.

Prior to the introduction of Buddhism from China, the primary religious tradition was Shintoism. Simply put, Shinto means "way of the gods" and is the oldest religion in Japan. It has no known founder or major text that outlines its principal tenets or beliefs (Cartwright 2017c). In Shinto, gods, spirits, supernatural forces, and essences are known as *kami*; evil spirits or demons are *oni*; and ghosts are known as *obake* and require certain rituals to send them away before they cause harm. The belief that some spirits of dead animals can even possess humans (the worst being the fox) and that these individuals must be exorcised by a priest is an interesting institutionalization of widely shared animistic beliefs tracing back to pre-agricultural communities.

Buddhism came into Japanese culture from China during the sixth century A.D. (Mizoguchi 2017, 596) and was readily accepted by both the elite and the ordinary populace because it confirmed the political and economic status quo, offered a welcoming reassurance to the mystery of the afterlife, and complemented existing Shinto beliefs (Cartwright 2017a). Buddhist monasteries were established across the country and became powerful politically in their own right. Buddhism reinforced the idea of a layered society with different levels of social status, with the emperor very much at the top. The aristocracy could also claim that they enjoyed their privileged position in society because they had accumulated merit in a previous life. In addition to the reinforcement that Buddhism gave to the status quo, it was hoped that the adoption of Buddhism by the early Japanese would enhance Japan's reputation as a rising civilized nation in East Asia. Once officially adopted, monks, scholars, and students were regularly sent to China to learn the tenets of Buddhism in more depth and bring back that knowledge, along with art and even sometimes relics, for the benefit of the Japanese people (Cartwright 2017a).

Concluding Remarks

The Jomon is the basic archaeological culture that forms the foundation for modern Japanese culture prior to the introduction of wet rice agri culture from the continent. The archaeological cultures in the Japanese mainland (Honshu-Shikoku-Kyushu islands) share similarities with the Jomon of Hokkaido to the north and the Ryukyu Islands to the south. During the very long time period of the Jomon, technological development and cultural advances occurred earlier in the west and then spread eastward. Over time, in spite of local and regional variation, the Jomon is a time of cultural and technological similarities over the Japanese archipelago.

Further Reading

Information on the early archaeology of the Japanese archipelago is a little scarce in English publications except for more technical academic journals. However, general works for public readership are more common about the Jomon archaeological culture. Junko Habu's 2004 volume

Ancient Jomon of Japan provides a great deal of information about the Jomon period in Japanese archaeology. Simon Kaner and Yasuhiro Taniguchi's 2017 essay "The Development of Pottery and Associated Technological Developments in Japan, Korea, and the Russian Far East" as well as Mizoguchi's 2017 essay "The Yayoi and Kofun Periods of Japan"—both in the *Handbook of East and Southeast Asian Archaeology*, edited by Junko Habu, Peter V. Lape, and John W. Olsen—give useful information on these specific periods of time on the Japanese mainland.

CHAPTER 4

• • • • • • • • • •

The Archaeology of
Hokkaido and the Ainu

The culture histories of Hokkaido and the Japanese mainland are similar until the introduction of wet-rice agriculture in the Japanese archipelago about 2,300 years ago. Then, the increasingly complex cultural developments associated with rice production on the Japanese mainland after the introduction of cultural elements in the Yayoi shifted the trajectory of the mainland populations, but the inhabitants of Hokkaido and the Tohoku region of northern Honshu continued to maintain a Jomon lifestyle of hunting and gathering supplemented by horticulture.

At about 2,300 B.P., Hokkaido people transitioned into what is known as the Epi-Jomon culture/period in Hokkaido.[1] It is this divergence of cultural trajectories following the Jomon that has contributed to the social separation that has developed within mainland Japanese and Hokkaido cultures over the centuries. See figure 10 for a chronology of Hokkaido archaeological cultures.

As a means of trying to establish the spatiotemporal patterns of site distribution from the Paleolithic to the historic Ainu period to better understand settlement patterns in relation to the environment, a research

---

1. "Zuko-Jomon" is sometimes used instead of "Epi-Jomon" in Japanese texts, but Epi-Jomon is used here.

Period (Age ×10³ cal. yr BP)	Description
Historic Ainu 700–100	Formal cemeteries, marine and terrestrial mammal hunting, fishing, gathering, rare pigs, ritualised bear husbandry, localised rice (SW Hokkaido only) and spreading of millet and wheat farming, permanent villages, fortified stockades and the emergence of local Ainu political authorities, intensive trade, substantial social differentiation.
Satsumon 1300–700	Large formal cemeteries partly with tumulus graves, localised rice and more wide-spread millet and wheat farming, large permanent villages, more iron tools, intensive trade, substantial social differentiation.
Okhotsk 1500–800	Okhotsk Culture immigrated from northern regions, formal cemeteries, intensive marine mammal hunting, hunting-fishing-gathering, domestic pigs, ritualised bear husbandry, villages, more iron tools, substantial social differentiation.
Epi Jomon 2300–1300	SW Hokkaido - formal cemeteries, hunting-fishing-gathering, localised rice farming, first iron tools; NW Hokkaido - rare and small cemeteries, small villages, shell middens, dog breeding for food, moderate social differentiation, seasonally mobile groups; reduced trade with Honshu populations (Yayoi), use of amber increased, use of asphalt and jade decreased.
Final Jomon 3300–2300 / Late Jomon 4000–3300	Large circular cemeteries (stone circles and mound burials), elaborate burials (Late Jomon), hunting-fishing-gathering, trade of asphalt and jade across the Tsugaru Strait, adoption of lacquer ware production, settlements move to lowlands, graves remain upland, declining villages (Final Jomon), substantial social differentiation.
Middle Jomon 5000–4000	Formal cemeteries, marine and terrestrial mammal hunting, nut and intensive shellfish gathering, river and coast fishing, large villages during early period, settlement size decrease from late period (after ca. 4.2 cal. yr BP), storage, large shell middens, growing social differentiation (SW Hokkaido), seasonally mobile groups and limited social differentiation (NE Hokkaido).
Early Jomon 6000–5000	Few formal cemeteries, marine and terrestrial mammal hunting, gathering (initial chestnut exploitation), river and coast fishing, large villages with circular houses, storage, shell middens, seasonally mobile groups, disappearance of regional differences in pottery styles
Initial Jomon 10,000–6000	Few formal cemeteries (1st half - next to settlements, 2nd half - distant from settlements), marine and terrestrial mammal hunting, gathering, river and coast fishing, shell middens, small hamlets with pit-houses, storage, seasonally mobile groups, round-bottom and flat-bottom pottery in SW + NE Hokkaido, respectively, lacquered yarn production (SW Hokkaido), migration of the Blade Arrowhead Culture people into eastern Hokkaido by ca. 8000-7000 cal. yr BP.
Incipient Jomon 14,000–10,000	Initial use of pottery and microblade technology, terrestrial mammal hunting, gathering, river and coast fishing, highly mobile groups (no pit-houses).
Palaeolithic period 35,000–14,000	Artefacts mostly lithics, burned cobbles and charcoal, probably terrestrial mammal hunting as main subsistence, high residential mobility, settlements on fluvial terraces, probably tent-like dwellings, living in groups of many (1st half of Late Palaeolithic) and single (2nd half of Late Palaeolithic) families.

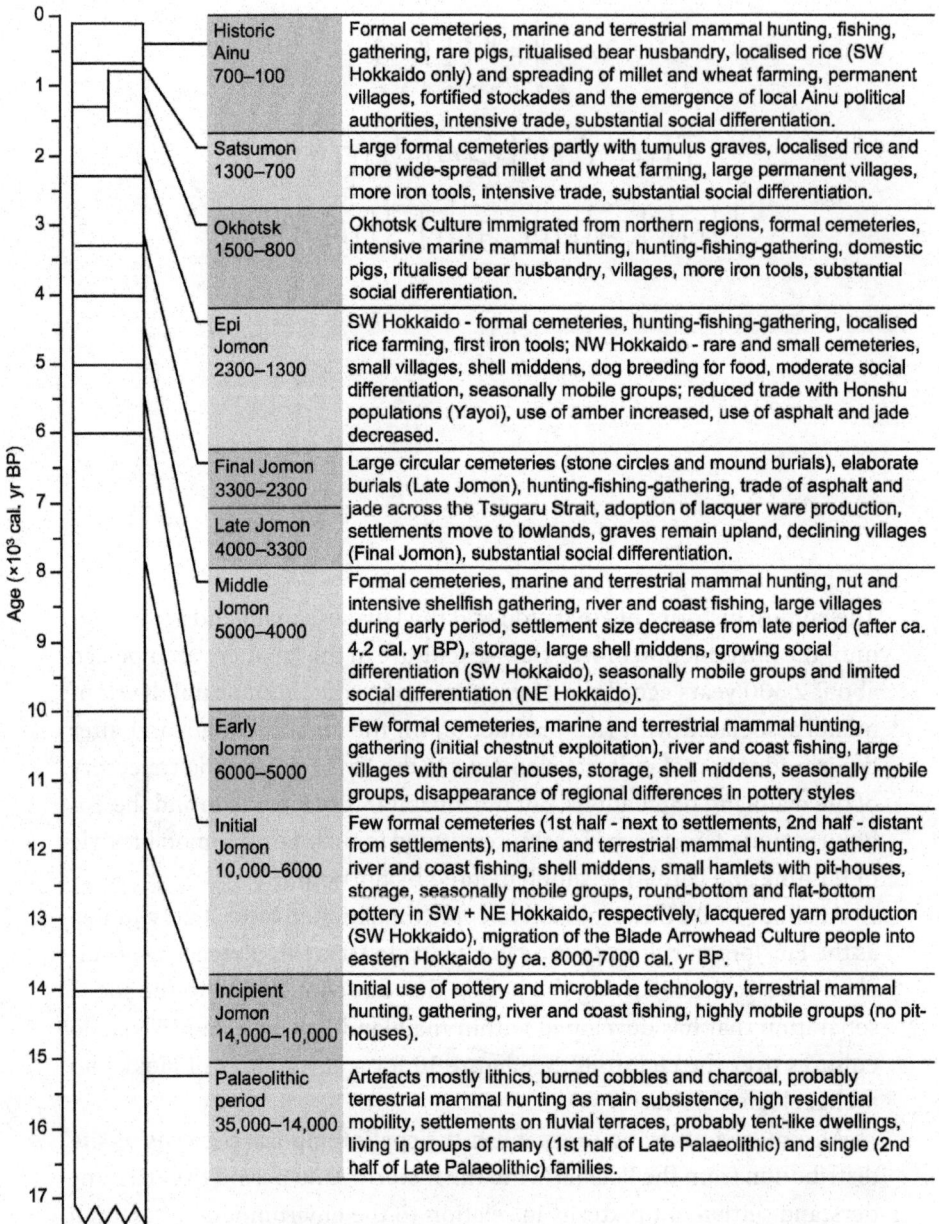

FIGURE 10 Chronology of Hokkaido archaeological cultures (adapted by Carol J. Ellick from C. Abe et al. 2016, 1631).

project conducted by Chiharu Abe and colleagues (C. Abe et al. 2016) analyzed data on location and chronological classification of archaeological sites based on information on a Hokkaido Prefectural Board of Education database. They acknowledged two types of limitations with the data they analyzed. First, the absence of sites in areas may be related to the failure of adequate archaeological surveys in the area or the failure of the early people to use those areas. Second, some early habitations may have been destroyed by rising sea levels or other natural processes. The limitations of the data aside, the information provided by their analyses is illuminating.

The Paleolithic of Hokkaido

For a period of about six thousand years, from about 34,300 to 28,000 B.P., the occupants of what is now known as Hokkaido used a stone tool industry composed primarily of tools such as scrapers, trapezoids, and beak-shaped tools made on flakes of detached stone from discoidal and multifaceted cores (Buvit et al. 2014, 223).

With the onset of the Last Glacial Maximum (LGM) at about 26,000 years ago, two generalized stone tool industries developed. The first, dating between about 26,400 and 23,900 years ago, was primarily flake based and included end scrapers and perforators alongside many less formal tools. The second industry emerged about 25,000 B.P. and produced scrapers, burins, and other tools on large blades rather than on flakes as well as a fully developed microblade industry in southern Hokkaido.

Chiharu Abe and colleagues analyzed 671 sites associated with the Paleolithic. While the site numbers attributed to the Paleolithic are low, their spatial distribution implies that human presence was mainly confined to inland areas. About 90 percent of all sites are located a distance of more than six miles (10 kilometers) from the modern coastline. Their findings corroborate their hypothesis that the "subsistence of Paleolithic populations was mainly based on terrestrial foods with a likely focus on (large) terrestrial mammals and suggest that marine food resources did not play an important role" (C. Abe et al. 2016, 1631).

Paleolithic/Incipient–Initial Jomon Transition (35,000 to 10,000 B.P.)

After the Paleolithic, the transition between the Incipient and Initial Jomon phases is marked by a slight increase in total site numbers, with an indication that people chose to locate closer to the sea. This suggested shift in subsistence strategy includes marine adaptation along with the emergence of the Jomon pottery period, proposed by Chiharu Abe et al. (2018, 1634) to be associated with a period of climate amelioration associated with a deglacial period between two colder glacial periods. The disappearance of large terrestrial mammals at that time probably forced Hokkaido communities to diversify their food sources and shift to hunting smaller terrestrial mammals such as hare for meat sources.

There is also a clear shift in site concentration from the northern to the southern part of Hokkaido, perhaps because of the availability of more favorable living conditions in the south during the late glacial and early Holocene, due to milder climate or the availability of abundant marine fauna providing rich hunting and fishing grounds. More favorable growing conditions in southern Hokkaido are indicated by a greater abundance of perennial shrubs, nuts, and annual herbaceous plants that have been found in the remains of plants in Initial Jomon sites on the Kameda peninsula (G. Crawford 1983, 2011).

Early and Middle Jomon (ca. 6,000–4,000 B.P.)

The number of Early Jomon sites located within one kilometer of the sea continued to increase through time until the Middle Jomon, when in all parts of Hokkaido, including the north, the frequency of coastal sites decreased in favor of more inland sites. Chiharu Abe and his colleagues (2016) see these changes in site number and distribution reflecting the process of increasing settlement ("sedentarization"), as postulated by Habu (2004) for insular East Asia.

The diversification of food resources during the early stage of the Jomon was followed by subsistence specialization, where a few food sources were intensively exploited and stored. The broad abundance of sites along the coastlines as well as in the interior of Hokkaido during the Middle Jomon clearly illustrates a subsistence specialization (e.g., marine/inland fishing and hunting and exploitation of plants) dependent on localized environments (see also Takase 2020). There was a notable increase in the presence and density of acorn, chestnut, horse chestnut, walnut, and hazelnut along with other temperate plants producing edible fruits, roots, and berries (G. Crawford 2011; Habu 2004; Yamada and Shibauchi 1997) as well as evidence of the possible usage of buckwheat and foxtail millet during Early and Middle Jomon (G. Crawford 2008). Chiharu Abe et al. (2016, 1640) believe that "the climate deterioration seen in the environmental proxies" can be used to explain the combination of diversification and intensification in the use of natural plant resources during the Middle Jomon phase.

Late to Epi-Jomon (ca. 4,000 to 1,300 B.P.)

The subsequent Late, Final, and Epi-Jomon stages are characterized by a continuous decline in the total amount of sites across Hokkaido. Chiharu Abe and colleagues (2016) also note that for several regions in Central Japan, settlement sizes shift from relatively large sites with high numbers of pit dwellings during the Middle Jomon to smaller sites during the Late and Final Jomon (see also Imamura 1996). The site distributions seem indicative of more occupation in southern Hokkaido during the Late and Final Jomon, with few sites in the northern regions. Abe and colleagues (2016, 1641) propose that local populations could "no longer [balance] the decline in food resources caused by climate deterioration" with more food sources required of growing population numbers.

Archaeologists Keiji Imamura (1996) and Daisei Kodama (2003) have suggested that the appearance of stone circles (burial and/or ceremonial sites) on hilltops in southwestern Hokkaido and the Tohoku region of northern Honshu during the Late Jomon stage is evidence for shifts in social organization as a result of climate deterioration (see figures 11 and 12). In addition, Douglas Bailey (2009) associates the increase in ceramic and stone figures and Oki Nakamura (1999) correlates an increase in grave goods with these same shifts in social organization.

FIGURE 11 The Kiusu Earthworks Burial Circles Site, Chitose City, Hokkaido.

FIGURE 12 Jichinyama stone circle, Otaru, Hokkaido.

Hokkaido Post-Jomon Sequences

On the island of Hokkaido, the post-Jomon archaeological sequence is divided into five main cultures: the Epi-Jomon, the Okhotsk of northern Hokkaido, the Satsumon of southern Hokkaido, the Tobinitai of eastern Hokkaido, and the Ainu (Hudson 2017, 698; Kato 2018, 3–5). In the following sections, I will discuss each one briefly.

Epi-Jomon (2,300 to 1,300 B.P.)

The people of the Epi-Jomon period, largely restricted to Hokkaido, are believed to represent a continuation of Jomon culture sustaining a hunter-gatherer lifestyle (Aikens and Higuchi 1982). Compared with the Final Jomon, the frequency of sites located within one kilometer of the sea is significantly higher during the Epi-Jomon, with a clear shift in sites to northern Hokkaido, especially on the Sea of Okhotsk coast (C. Abe et al. 2016, 1641). However, Epi-Jomon communities are characterized by a higher mobility and a lower degree of plant exploitation. Plant food is mainly represented by nuts as well as shrub and vine fruits, with no clear evidence for plant cultivation (G. Crawford 1987, 2011; D'Andrea 1995). The primary subsistence strategy was based on river fishing, with salmon as the major prey, as well as the use of maritime foods (Okada 1998). The large number of sites (approximately 40 percent) situated in direct proximity to the sea and probably to river estuaries supports these interpretations.

Looking at the Epi-Jomon on Hokkaido, it is apparent that it was solidly based on the previous Jomon, even as it absorbed some cultural influences from the Yayoi and later Kofun of Honshu, especially in portions of southern Hokkaido. The Epi-Jomon also reveals a direct connection to the subsequent cultures of Hokkaido—the Satsumon and the Ainu (Zgusta 2015, 53–54).

At first glance, the Hokkaido Epi-Jomon cultures followed characteristics of the Jomon, especially in the versions found in Hokkaido and northern Honshu, including the Kanto, Hokuriku, and Tohoku regions (see figure 13). However, the Hokkaido Epi-Jomon economies were based on salmon fishing, land and sea animal hunting, and gathering of walnuts, lily bulbs, and other forest products as well as the use of shellfish on the coast (Takase 2020).

84   CHAPTER 4

Honshu Island   **Hokkaido Island**

Chronological Framework based on State Formation Processes

Modernizing State	Meiji	Present Day
Feudal State	Edo Period (Shogunate)	AD 1900
	Sengoku	AD 1600
	Muromachi	AD 1500 / AD 1400
	Kamakura	AD 1300 / AD 1200
Classic State	Heian Period	
	Nara Period	AD 900
	Asuka Period	AD 800 / AD 700
Early State	Kofun Period	
	Yayoi Period	AD 300
	Rice Cultivation / Metal Introduction	---AD/BC--- / 300 BC
	Jomon Culture Complex Hunter-Gatherer	c. 3000-10000 BC
		c.14000 BC / c.15000 BC
	Paleolithic Culture Pleistocene Hunter-Gatherer	

Hokkaido side: Meiji; Historical Ainu; Satsumon Culture; Okhotsk Culture; Epi-Jomon Culture; Jomon Culture Complex Hunter-Gatherer; Paleolithic Culture Pleistocene Hunter-Gatherer

Stages: Modernizing Stage; Contact Stage; Sustainable Hunter-Gatherer Stage

Chronological Framework based on non-State Formation Processes

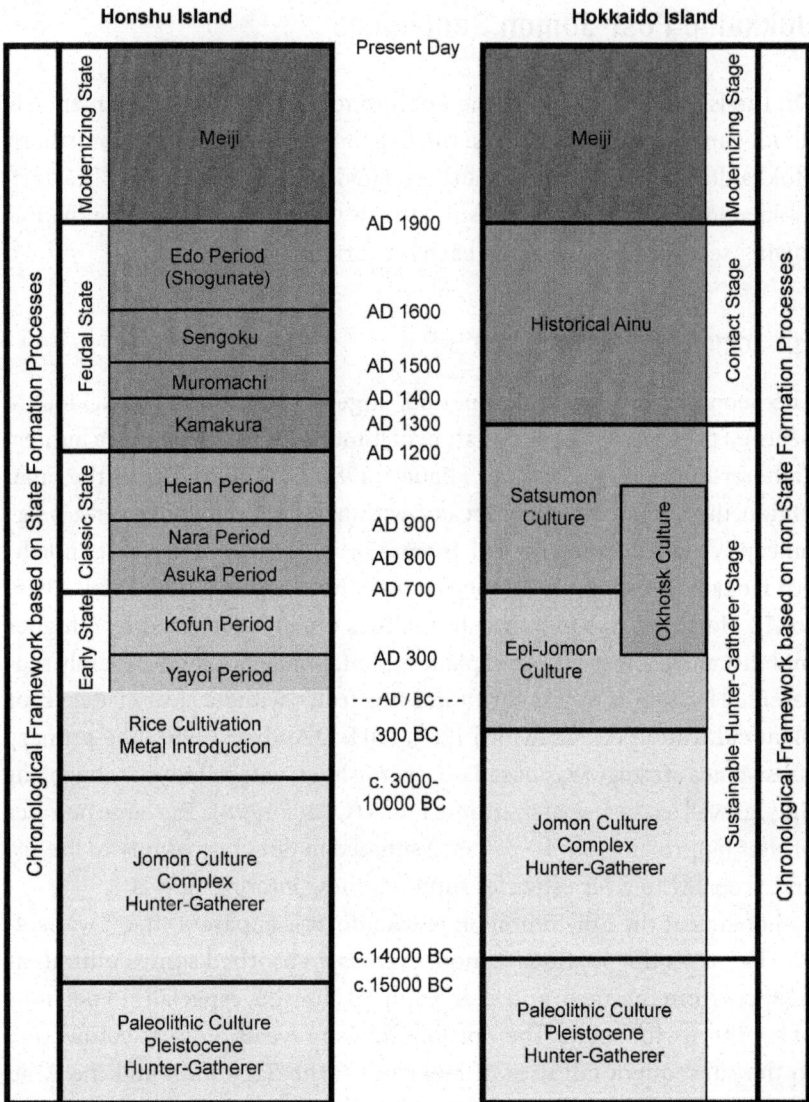

FIGURE 13 Chronology comparison between Honshu and Hokkaido (adapted by Carol J. Ellick from Kato 2018, 4, figure 1).

The material culture of these Hokkaido groups indicates an awareness of the changing cultures on the Japanese mainland (Zgusta 2015, 54), but the Hokkaido cultures continued to use their own methods of survival. Earthenware decoration patterns, though still essentially Jomon, show an increase in Yayoi influences. The appearance of iron in archaeological sites is indicative of trade relations with Yayoi groups of Honshu and possibly the Asian continent. Stone, bone, antler, and ivory continued to be used for tools; iron, however, eventually replaced other materials for tool construction, ultimately supplanting flaked and ground stone blades in harpoon toggles, knives, and other tool types. Because Hokkaido was not suitable for rice production, people traded northern marine products for rice and other agricultural foodstuffs from Honshu (Zgusta 2015, 54–55).

This Epi-Jomon culture dominated Hokkaido until about the seventh century, when new cultural elements entered southwestern Hokkaido from Honshu (Zgusta 2015, 58; Kato 2018, 5). Hokkaido pottery, in many ways indistinguishable from that of northern Honshu, continued to use Jomon-like decoration motifs. Localized ceramic cultures and subsistence economies developed in Hokkaido, associated with certain ecological zones and localized niches (Hudson 2017, 698). Jomon round pit dwellings were gradually replaced by rectangular ones with rounded edges and had both central open hearths and earthen ovens. Southern Hokkaido people continued to rely on salmon fishing and land animal hunting, but the barley, millet, buckwheat, and other crops were added to their economies. Crop production spread from southern Hokkaido, but it was less important in the north and northeast portions of the island.

Okhotsk Culture (1,500–800 B.P.)

About 1,500 years ago, the people of the archaeological Okhotsk culture started to move southward from Sakhalin Island through Rebun and Rishiri Islands along the northeastern Hokkaido coastline toward the Nemuro Peninsula and the southern Kuril Islands. Mark J. Hudson (2017, 698, citing Segawa 2005) suggests that this migration might be the result of people following "Epi-Jomon populations in search of iron." Artifacts like pottery, iron, and bone tools, as well as phylogenetic studies (Takehiro Sato et al. 2007), suggest that this culture has its origins in the lower Amur River region of the Russian Far East. Domesticated pigs, dogs, crops, and different wild plants were used as food sources (Amano 2003; G. Crawford 2011), and their major subsistence activities (marine fishing and especially sea mammal hunting) are well reflected in the coastal distribution of sites. Figure 14 shows a habitation structure used by Okhotsk peoples.

FIGURE 14 Reconstructed Okhotsk pit structure, Hokuto Site near Kushiro, Hokkaido (photograph by Carol J. Ellick).

The Okhotsk culture had extensive trade relations with cultures to the north and south. Goods like iron, bronze, coins, and jasper were obtained from outside the Okhotsk domain (Amano et al. 2013; Kikuchi 1986) in exchange for sea mammal furs and walrus ivory (Yamaura 1998). However, it is not widely accepted that trade played a major role in the Okhotsk culture beyond the acquisition of prestige items (see discussion in Hudson 2004).

A particularly high affinity to sea environments is suggested for the northern Hokkaido-affiliated Okhotsk culture, with about 84 percent of sites located less than one mile (1–2 kilometers) from the modern coastline.

Satsumon Culture (1,300–700 B.P.)

While the Okhotsk culture was thriving in the north, in southwest Hokkaido the Satsumon culture, which was strongly influenced by the Kofun and Nara cultures of the Japanese mainland, formed around the seventh century A.D. (Kato 2018, 5). Satsumon culture developed out of the Epi-

Jomon through immigration and contact with northern Honshu farmers. Major influences from Honshu include pottery-making traditions, mortuary systems, and iron weapons and tools.

Especially notable is the rise in the number of archaeological sites during this period. Many of the newly established sites were located along the northern and northeastern coastlines of Hokkaido, while more sites were abandoned than newly established on the Oshima Peninsula. Considering the increase in settlement size (Weber, Jordan, and Kato 2013) in comparison to the Epi-Jomon subperiod, the rise in site frequency may be satisfactorily interpreted as a rise in population.

A possible explanation for the rise in population at this time might be immigration from northern Honshu. Cultural traits such as pit dwellings and pottery types in the Hokkaido archaeological record have been suggested (Zgusta 2015, 58) as the result of a strong influence on the Satsumon culture by the "final Kofun" of the Tohoku region. Gary W. Crawford (2011) suggests that people of the Kofun culture were forced to migrate toward the north by territorial claims of the first state in southwestern Japan. The abundant remains of a variety of crops—including barley, wheat, foxtail millet, broomcorn millet, buckwheat, melon, flax, and soybean—suggest the possibility of exchange of agricultural goods for products gained by hunter-gatherers in the north. Tohoku immigrants pushed the local Epi-Jomon population to northern and northeastern Hokkaido and settled the southwestern regions of the island, which were more favorable for farming.

Tobinitai Culture (1,000–800 B.P.)

After the tenth century, the Satsumon population expanded into northeast Hokkaido and integrated with the Okhotsk culture. This hybrid Satsumon–Okhotsk culture is found in large areas along the northeastern coast of Hokkaido, where it is known archaeologically as the Tobinitai culture; similar versions are also present in northern Hokkaido and the southernmost Kuril Islands.

Tobinitai culture pottery is generally of typical Satsumon forms but decorated with the "noodle" design of Okhotsk earthenware. The Tobinitai continued the Satsumon preference of freshwater fishing over Okhotsk marine hunting, northern cultural traits that later became essential parts of Ainu culture.

One major example of these northern cultural traits that continued within Ainu culture involved the Ainu relationship with the bear. The bear was venerated by the Satsumon, as it had been by their Jomon ancestors, but there is no indication that the Satsumon groups practiced what later became known as Iyomante—raising captured bear cubs as family members to ritually send their spirits back to the divine world by killing them during winter ceremonies. However, it was associated with the prehistoric Okhotsk and ethnographic Nivkh and Amur cultures of the Amur-Sakhalin region of East Asia.

The Iyomante is the most important ritual of the modern Ainu (Zgusta 2015, 61), and it serves as a symbol of their cultural and ethnic identity, a "kernel of Ainu culture" (Hudson 1999, 209). It probably entered the Ainu culture via the Tobinitai culture of Okhotsk–Satsumon convergence. Thus, the modern Ainu culture as described in ethnographic reports and as can still partly be seen today most likely came into being during the thirteenth century as a result of an Okhotsk contribution to the ethnic Ainu Satsumon culture, itself a continuation in a modified form of the Jomon culture (Zgusta 2015, 60–61).

However, zooarchaeologist Takao Sato (2019, 391) of Keio University notes that "up until the beginning of the last century, the Hokkaido Ainu also performed sending ceremonies for adult and sub-adult bears killed by hunting . . . either in their settlement or at the location of the bear's capture, depending on the circumstances." He also discusses the archaeological evidence of such ceremonies based on bear skulls found in archaeological excavations at Otafuku-iwa Cave and five other archaeological sites that "date the practice to around the 12th or 13th centuries, which corresponds to the closing period of the Satsumon culture" (394). I will return to this point in chapter 8.

The Protohistoric Ainu

The last stage of Hokkaido's hunter-gatherer sequence is represented by the protohistoric Ainu. Today, it is widely accepted by archaeologists that the modern Ainu emerged from an amalgamation of the Okhotsk and Satsumon cultures (Kato 2018; Utagawa 2002; Zgusta 2015). The transition to the Ainu culture period is marked by a substantial reduction in sites, with the abandonment of a large number of sites in both northern and southwestern Hokkaido as well as in the Kuril Islands. The main concentration centers of archaeological sites are in the eastern part of Hokkaido, the Ishikari Lowlands, and along the coast southwest of the Hidaka Mountains. The onset of the Ainu culture coincides with the onset of the "Little Ice Age" (Lamb 1965), a cool climate period that is believed to have been of global scale (Broeker 2001), with lowest temperatures between about 550 and 250 years ago (Mann et al. 2009). This climate deterioration reflected by a weaker summer monsoon is also evident from northeastern China (Chen et al. 2015). However, its impact on Hokkaido's hunter-gatherer populations is still an open question.

Concluding Remarks

The cultural and economic influences from the Korean peninsula about 2,300 years ago brought about a major change in the Japanese mainland but had much less of an effect on the people of Hokkaido. On the Japanese mainland, the Yayoi and the Kofun form the foundation of the Japanese state, while the post-Jomon archaeological cultures of Hokkaido continue a relatively uninterrupted trajectory established during the Jomon, perhaps with influences from the north. Through the cultural integration of the Satsumon and Okhotsk cultures, the historical Ainu culture can be rather firmly established in the thirteenth century. The tradition of animal rituals by the Ainu, such as whale worship and bear worship, was passed on from the Okhotsk culture to the Ainu. On the other hand, cultural traditions such as the use of iron items, certain woodcrafts, and millet farming were passed on from the Satsumon culture to the Ainu culture. In the thirteenth century, which was the transition period from the Satsumon culture to the Ainu culture, the pottery-making tradition disappeared and the housing style continued changing from pit dwelling to flatland dwelling in Hokkaido Island as it had begun two centuries prior.

Further Reading

For the archaeology of Hokkaido, the reader should consult chapter 2, "Hokkaido Island: Ainu," of Richard Zgusta's 2015 volume *The Peoples of Northeast Asia Through Time: Precolonial Ethnic and Cultural Processes Along the Coast Between Hokkaido and the Bering Strait.* Hirofumi Kato's 2017 essay "The Ainu and Japanese Archaeology: A Change of Perspective" and his 2018 essay "Hokkaido Sequence and the Archaeology of the Ainu People" offer a different perspective on the relationship between Hokkaido archaeology and the connections to contemporary Ainu people.

Additionally, a good general volume about the development of Japanese and Ainu cultures is Mark J. Hudson's 1999 volume, *Ruins of Identity: Ethnogenesis in the Japanese Islands,* as well as his 2014 essay, "The Ethnohistory and Anthropology of 'Modern' Hunter-Gatherers: North Japan (Ainu)," in the *Oxford Handbook of Archaeology and Anthropology of Hunter-Gatherers,* edited by Vicki Cummings, Peter Jordan, and Marek Zvelebil.

CHAPTER 5

· · · · · · · · ·

History of Japanese Colonization and Assimilation of the Ainu

Research about the archaeological past of Hokkaido highlights some of the issues with the separation between "archaeological" and "historical" approaches to discussing and interpreting "the past." The mainland cultures of the Honshu-Shikoku-Kyushu (HSK) islands used their associations with and proximity to the Chinese mainland to develop written "history" that tied into existing chronicles on the continent. Hokkaido, however, continued to maintain archaeological cultures peripheral to, and yet a part of, the main islands' chronicles. Archaeologists generally call this period "protohistory" and define it as "the moment when the past appears to come within the reach of written texts" (Foxhall 2018)—not quite "prehistory" and not quite "history." The term is problematic as it may prioritize one culture (the recording group) over another (see Foxhall 2018 for an in-depth discussion). In spite of its problems, however, the term continues to be used as a more convenient generalized marker for discussion purposes, which is how I use it here.

In this case, the Okhotsk, Satsumon, and Tobinitai archaeological cultures of Hokkaido came into existence coevally with the development of early Japanese chronicles. Hudson (2017, 698) writes that, around the third century A.D., Epi-Jomon groups moved southward into the northern Tohoku area, where they interacted with Yayoi- and then Kofun-period societies. He also notes that one of the earliest Japanese histories, the *Nihon Shoki*, describes that, in the third month of A.D. 660, during the reign of empress Saimei (who reigned from 655 to 661), military expeditions led by Abe no Omi were sent to the north against a group referred to as the "Sushen," who were attacking the Emishi people. Hudson suggests that the Sushen (citing Segawa 2011 and Matsumura et al. 2006) might have been Okhotsk culture bearers pushing southward along the Japan Sea coast.

Thus, there is an overlap between "history" of the mainland Japanese and that of those populations of Hokkaido that were the foundations for historical Ainu populations. In addition, there is a likelihood that regional groups existed in the past that were likely separate people who later became subsumed under the more generic term *Ainu*. Most researchers talk about the "Ainu" as if it was a single population, whereas the group known as Ainu today was composed of many different groups oriented around local social and economic practices across northern Honshu and Hokkaido Islands, Sakhalin Island, and the Kuril Islands. For example, in the Tohoku region of Japan, there were notable differences between groups on the Japan Sea coastal side of the area and those on the Pacific Ocean side in terms of their economies and their relationships with cultures in the western and eastern areas of Hokkaido, respectively. Therefore, the idea of a "single Ainu history" is unsound.

David L. Howell (2014, 103) notes that "narratives of Ainu history [in Japanese historians' work] tend toward extremes, portraying a timeless and often idyllic [lifestyle] before Japanese conquest and a nearly invisible [one] after modernity in which the Ainu are reduced to bit players." He expands on this by stating: "Historians thus find themselves torn between the twin desires to give the Ainu agency as the subjects of their own history and to insert the Ainu's experience into mainstream narratives of Japanese history" (104).

Hudson (2014a, 121) also notes the limited nature in which the Ainu are presented in broader works: "The current position of Ainu in Japanese archaeology is thus characterized by the paradox that, although most physical anthropologists and some archaeologists argue that Ainu are descended from Jomon ancestors, the Jomon is usually viewed as a part of *Japanese* rather than Ainu history."

The question of the relationship between the historic Emishi of the Tsugaru region of northern Honshu and the Ainu of Hokkaido shows some of the issues involved in looking at the ethnogenesis of the Ainu. Historical records indicate the ultimate alliances and amalgamation of the later Ainu, apparently melded groups that at one time exhibited animosity to the other.

Kazuro Hanihara (1990, 46) writes that, because the Ainu and non-Ainu Japanese were in a transitional stage of separation during medieval times (A.D. 1185 to 1603), the differences between them were not as large as they are today. He goes on to say that "the question whether the group called Emishi belonged to Ainu or to non-Ainu Japanese is not applicable." Sakurako Tanaka (2000, 16–18), on the other hand, considers the Indigenous residents of Tsugaru as Ainu:

> The separate fates of the remaining Ainu (or members of other indigenous peoples) in Tsugaru and Hokkaido have thus been shaped by the sociohistorical changes these regions went through during the Edo [Tokugawa] period; and this process had been governed primarily by the official attitudes of the regional governments towards them, and the public cultural differences enforced by them. (2000, 101)

Thus, Tanaka argues that the Emishi were separate people who became subsumed under the broader term *Ainu* through governmental policy and actions. She also presents a more detailed history of the Tsugaru region in relation to the Japanese state separate from that of the Hokkaido Indigenous people. The interested reader should consult Tanaka's work for more information and a comparative history.

In some ways, the situation of "the Ainu" might be likened to that regarding American Indian groups and colonists of North America. While contemporary groups are lumped into the broader "American Indian / Native American" terminology, historically the individual groups had broad and varying interactions with others across the continent. Additionally, the relationships between the different European colonists with the groups with which they came into contact varied as well: to put it simplistically, the Spanish attempted to conquer the groups they encountered; the English entered into treaties with them; the French entered into treaties, but individual French explorers often created familial relationships; Russians traded with those they encountered and also created familial relationships but rarely used treaties with Native groups.

However, it is important to open this discussion with information on the Emishi. These people, as noted, were considered to be non-Japanese because they operated outside Japanese state culture and control. They were more likely derived/descended from archaeological culture bearers of local Epi-Jomon populations who interacted with, yet remained separate from, the Yayoi agriculturalists who moved into their territories.

The Emishi

Richard Siddle (1996, 27) indicates that one of the earliest mentions of the group of people who lived in the regions beyond the borders of the early Yamato Kingdom is found within the *Nihon Shoki* (compiled around A.D. 720). The Chinese ideograph for "eastern barbarians" (different ideographs were used for the barbarians of the other three directions) was used in describing the Emishi (or Ebisu). However, Siddle also notes that other Emishi were known from "Watarishima" (the island now known as Hokkaido) who were different from the Tohoku Emishi: the Tohoku Emishi paid "tribute" with horses while the Watarishima Emishi used furs and skins—it seems more likely that the "tribute" was seen as trade by the Emishi.

Thus, it seems that the groups of Epi-Jomon people who operated outside the Yamato kingdom were generally subsumed under a broad categorization of "the Other." This distinguished them, not necessarily by language or other expressions but primarily by the recognition that they were not "civilized" according to a moral order derived from Confucianism (Siddle 1996, 28), that is, "barbarians." The Emishi were considered uncivilized because they did not participate in "the consumption of the 'five kinds of grain'" as well as by the easily discernable differences between "customs that differed from the 'civilized' groups, such as ways of dress, hairstyles, or the eating of meat (which came to be regarded as taboo after the introduction of Buddhism in the sixth century)" (Siddle 1996, 28).

In addition, even though there were obvious differences between the Emishi of the Tohoku region and the Sushen (as noted by the military expeditions), both were generically subsumed under the single identifier. Thus, it seems unlikely that the Emishi and the other groups that contributed to the formation of the Ainu were not all derived from a single group or culture but rather from a variety of groups that contributed in varying degrees to the group ultimately known as "Ainu." This lumping of various groups into "Ainu" seems to be derived only in the sense that they were in opposition to the colonizing forces of the Japanese state.

Generally, the Ainu "homeland" is considered to be northern Honshu and Hokkaido. However, historically, the Ainu were known to have expanded into Sakhalin Island and the Kurils as well as other areas of the continent. Archaeologist Mark Hudson (2014b, 1054) notes that "Ainu people also traded and lived in the Amur Basin and Kamchatka" even if they might not have lived there permanently. Hudson (2017, 696) also explains: "Ainu people traded . . . from the Amur River to Kamchatka to Akita in north Japan, an area equivalent in size to a triangle linking London, Tunis, and Warsaw." Historian Richard Siddle (1996, 26) estimates that "a population of perhaps forty thousand Ainu lived throughout Hokkaido, the Kurils, and Sakhalin." He notes, however, that the region's inhabitants were not homogenous, and that "while the Ainu shared broad cultural and linguistic similarities, regional variations in dialect and culture were evident, especially in Sakhalin and the Kurils, where the Ainu were in close contact with other northern peoples" (27).

Hudson (2017, 697) notes that Ainu expansion into Sakhalin involved "military operations against other groups in Sakhalin, fighting successfully against the Mongol empire in the thirteenth century." In discussing the Ainu war with the Mongol empire, Hudson (2017, 703) notes: "Historical records from the Mongol Yuan dynasty explain how the Jilimi people on Sakhalin, who had already submitted to the Mongols, were attacked every year by the Guwei." Yuan and later Chinese texts associate the "Jilimi" with the Nivkh and the "Guwei" with the Ainu (Hudson 2017, 703). Hudson also writes that "the Mongols sent soldiers to Sakhalin in 1264, 1284, 1285, and 1286 in an attempt to subdue the Ainu" (703).

Archaeologist Ben Fitzhugh and colleagues (B. Fitzhugh et al. 2002, 72) note that "very little has been written about the development or expansion of the Ainu culture into the Kurils." Their research as part of an International Kuril Island Project documented eleven archaeological sites, with the oldest deposits dating to at least 2,500 years ago. In the conclusion, they write, "It is reasonable to see the Kurils as having contributed directly to Ainu ethnogenesis, given hints of continuity between Okhotsk and Ainu spirit-sending ceremonies . . . and the persistence of pit house dwellings among the Kuril and Sakhalin Ainu" (B. Fitzhugh et al. 2002, 87).

In spite of this broad expanse of territory occupied by the Ainu historically, by the nineteenth century, their territory was greatly limited. Sakhalin became Russian territory under the 1875 Treaty of St. Petersburg between Japan and Russia, and the Kurils became Russian territory after Russia's annexation of the northernmost four islands at the end of World War II. For this reason, unless specifically indicated otherwise, when I refer to "the Ainu," I refer primarily to the Ainu population of Hokkaido Island. In some specific circumstances, however, I discuss non-Hokkaido Ainu populations from northern Honshu, Sakhalin, and the Kuril Islands.

The following historical narrative deals mainly with the relationships between the Wajin and the Ainu of Hokkaido but includes some history of the Ainu of the island of Honshu, especially as the discussion approaches more contemporary issues. In some situations, Japanese historians use the term *Ezo* or *Ezochi* to describe the island now known as Hokkaido. *Ezo* replaced the term *Emishi* as a descriptor of the Native people under the Kamakura bakufu (A.D. 1185–1333), the first administration to bring all of Honshu under its nominal control (Siddle 1996, 29). Thereafter, the ambiguity inherent in the use of *Emishi* also faded as *Ezo* came clearly to refer to the "foreign" inhabitants of the islands across the Tsugaru Strait. While both the "Ezo" and the "Emishi" were culturally different groups of people, the connotations of "barbarism" inherent in the term continued intact. The island was renamed "Hokkaido" (meaning "Northern Sea Circuit") by the Japanese government of Honshu during the Meiji Restoration in 1869.

Wajin–Ainu Economic Interaction

Economic interaction with populations of Hokkaido is known archaeologically, as discussed in the previous chapter, from at least the thirteenth century onward. Satsumon culture bearers of the thirteenth century were in the process of subsuming the Okhotsk culture and were involved in trading with the Mongol empire in Sakhalin and the Amur River basin of what was then Manchuria (Howell 1994, 76). The Ainu then adopted an intermediary role in the trade between the Japanese state and northeast Asia (B. Walker 2001, 129).

Evidence for economic interaction in the form of trade between the Ainu and the Wajin shows up in the form of metal and lacquerware in the Satsumon archaeological cultural complexes along the southern portion of Hokkaido. In the fourteenth century, trade between the people of Honshu and those of Hokkaido increased, with items from Honshu, China, and northeastern Asia becoming more evident in Hokkaido archaeological contexts (Loy 2010, 43). By the fifteenth century, there were trading posts established for regularizing trade between Ezo and Honshu.

There was conflict between Wajin and Ainu warriors, however, and in 1457 friction erupted into open warfare. Koshamain's Rebellion (or War) was ostensibly sparked by an argument over a short sword sold by a Japanese blacksmith to an Ainu youth (Howell 1994, 76). Throughout the next two hundred years, conflict between the Japanese and the Ainu was commonplace, primarily based on economic issues regarding the unfair trade advantages taken by the Japanese traders.

In 1551, the Kakizaki clan (later known as the Matsumae clan) came to an agreement with the Ainu chieftains Hashitain and Chikomotain over profit sharing between the Ainu suppliers and Honshu merchants. In return, the clan was granted exclusive control over the territory along the southern one-third of the Oshima Peninsula.

During the Tokugawa era (also known as the "Edo" Period), from 1603 to 1867, Wajin culture was somewhat codified by various regulations issued by the military government in Tokyo (Loy 2010, 46–50). The Ainu were further excluded from what was expected of the "Japanese" people since they were depicted as "so different in physical appearance, custom and language that the idea of assimilation with the rest of Japan was initially unthinkable" (Loy 2010, 53). Moreover, the Ainu increasingly became exemplars of what was patently *not* Japanese in the emerging national imaginary of Tokugawa Japan. Howell (1994, 87) writes that it wasn't the forceful segregation of Ainu in actuality but rather that the Matsumae authorities were "more concerned to regulate visible emblems of ethnicity, such as clothing and hairstyles," as a means of emphasizing their role as "middlemen" between the barbarian Ainu and the civilized Edo government. He sees this as an attempt to "preserve the Ainu's alien ethnicity while simultaneously (and paradoxically) incorporating that alien ethnicity into the Japanese social-status hierarchy" (88).

At this time, the Ainu were considered useful primarily for trade or labor. The Matsumae clan had extensive contacts under the basho system (territories set aside for the exclusive use by specific traders) with the Ainu of Hokkaido. The Matsumae held exclusive rights to trade with the Ainu communities of the island and to guarantee the security of Japanese interests there. The Matsumae essentially subcontracted their territory to mainland traders for "contracting fees" (Siddle 1996, 36). In this way, the traders were the first line of authority in relation to the Ainu, with the Matsumae exerting control over them. In a manner similar to frontier governments around the world, the Edo government exercised very little direct influence over the Ainu, instead relying on the reports and results of the Matsumae trade enterprises.

With the expansion of Matsumae trade enterprises between the Ainu and the Wajin, the exploitation of Ainu resources and Ainu labor increased as well. With the increase in trade goods, local resources became more scarce; as local resources decreased (or were harvested to beyond sustainable levels), Ainu men became more reliant on working for the Japanese traders in a wage economy than on hunting and gathering within their home locations. The Shakushain revolt of 1669–72 grew out of Ainu discontent with Matsumae trading and hunting practices as part of the impact they had on local subsistence resources and practices. While there were other conflicts between Ainu groups and the Wajin, this rebellion is generally considered by historians to be the last significant armed resistance by Ainu in Ezo (Siddle 1996, 34–36).

A hundred years later, in 1782, Kyubei Hidaya began commercial fishing operations in the area. Hidaya's men maintained a high degree of brutality against the Ainu: labor was coerced and Ainu who resisted were threatened, beaten, and, if they repeatedly disobeyed, poisoned. Ainu women were routinely raped by Hidaya guards and managers. In May 1789, an Ainu chief was purportedly given poisoned liquor. In retaliation, forty-one Ainu attacked a guard outpost in Tonari, killing twenty-two Wajin. The violence spread, and in total seventy-one Wajin were killed. The uprising, known as the Menashi-Kunashir rebellion, was eventually quelled by Ainu elders who convinced the leaders of the revolt to stop, but the subjugation force from Matsumae executed thirty-seven alleged members of the revolt. Howell (1994, 84) attributes the actions of the Ainu elders to such self-serving desires as the continued reliance on Japanese commodities and goods. Another option is that the elders were hoping to reduce the brutality of the inevitable Wajin response.

In 1799, the Matsumae clan lost control of the trade in Hokkaido to the military government in Edo. Under the Hakodate Edict of 1802, the Ainu were "encouraged" by the Tokugawa government to adopt Japanese language and customs as a means of assimilating in Japanese culture (Loy 2010, 64). This policy appears to have been intended to develop allies for the Tokugawa government against the influence of Russia from the Kurils and Sakhalin Island. Many Ainu men rebelled against the more distasteful policies, such as those related to shaving beards and cutting hair (Siddle 1996, 41).

The Matsumae regained control of the trade in Hokkaido in 1822 and reinstated the prohibitions against the Ainu use of Japanese language and customs (Matsu'ura 2002, 34–36). However, the increasing cost of resources led once again to increased exploitation of the Ainu work-force. The use of fixed shore nets in the ocean near river mouths led to a dramatic plunge in salmon populations and further impoverishment of Ainu communities that relied on the yearly runs of salmon for food and winter stores.

The military government in Edo retook control of Ezo and the Ainu in 1855 following the opening of trade between Japan and Western countries America, Britain, and the Netherlands. As a result of this, the Edo government redoubled its efforts to force Ainu assimilation by copying American techniques of forced assimilation of American Indian groups as well as by trying to persuade Ainu men to stop wearing earrings and discourage Ainu women from tattooing their faces and hands (Howell 1994, 90). Japanese government officials also encouraged the Ainu to undertake agriculture as the American government had encouraged American Indians to do as a means of making the colonization of Ainu lands a reality.

The Ainu During the Meiji Period

In 1868, the Tokugawa shogunate lost power, and the emperor was re-stored to the supreme position. The land was administratively divided into prefectures that functioned through bureaucratic structures orig-inally developed by the daimyo. Ezo was renamed "Hokkaido" in 1869, and the Hokkaido Development Commission (Kaitakushi) was created to guide the process of surveying, clearing, and establishing areas for Wajin colonists and industrial interests.

In looking at Japanese history of this time, Siddle (2003, 451) notes that the relationship between the Japanese and the Ainu had been based on trade of some sort since the seventh century with interactions with the Satsumon and other Emishi. He writes, however, that "it was with the inauguration of the Colonization Office (*Kaitakushi*) in 1869 that the Ainu fell under the complete control of the Japanese state" (451).

Ken S. Coates (2004) offers a good summary of Japanese policies toward the Ainu during this period, noting that during the Meiji era, the Japanese made a concerted attempt to join with the Western industrial nations. To Coates (2004, 182), "the desire to perform like the West resulted in a virtual replication of British and colonial European indigenous policies." The assimilation of the Ainu was an integral aspect of that policy. During its first decade in power, the new regime not only banned visible markers of Ainu ethnicity, such as earrings and tattoos, but also forbade the Ainu to practice their religion or to hunt on ancestral hunting grounds.

Hokkaido officials began entering Ainu into the system of household registers (*koseki*), the basic administrative apparatus through which the emerging modern state established surveillance and control over its subjects. The 1871 Family Registry Law "inducted" the Ainu in the Japanese nation, where they were listed with other Japanese as commoners but also marked as "former natives." In November 1878, as Howell (1994, 91) notes, the state stripped the Ainu of their ethnicity in legal terms by renaming them "former aborigines" (*kyudojin*). During the next several years, the Ainu became subject to taxation, Japanese civil and criminal law, and conscription under the same conditions as other Japanese subjects.

The Ainu were given Japanese names, often with their Ainu names transcribed in katakana next to the kanji. Christopher D. Loy (2010, 80–81) notes that sometimes entire villages were given the same surname, regardless of kinship relationships. They thus became Japanese citizens, and the Japanese family system, the basis of the modern state, "was imposed upon them through the family register system" (Kojima 2014, 103). Along with this move toward inclusion in Japanese society, traditional customs such as tattooing the mouth and hands of Ainu women, ear piercings on men, and the funerary ritual involving burning the house of the deceased were banned.

Ainu lands were nationalized in 1872, as the Meiji government completed the formal dispossession of Ainu resources. Officials believed the failure of the Ainu to become "good Japanese" was attributed not to specific colonial policies but to the innate propensities of the Ainu themselves (Siddle 2003, 451). The social Darwinism that enjoyed the status of "scientific truth" in Meiji Japan supported the idea that the Ainu were destined to disappear (much as the American Indians in the United States were supposed to be "disappearing") because their savage race was less developed than the modern Japanese and, therefore, ill adapted to survive.

In 1875, Japan signed the Treaty of St. Petersburg with Russia, giving up Sakhalin Island and forcing any Ainu living there to relocate to Hokkaido Island. This later created issues when, as a result of the stringent land policies aimed at turning the Ainu into farmers, many Sakhalin Ainu left Hokkaido and returned to Sakhalin, then under Russian rule.

SOCIAL DARWINISM

Social Darwinism was the theory that human groups and races are subject to the same laws of natural selection as Charles Darwin perceived in plants and animals in nature. According to the theory, strong cultures grew in power and cultural influence over the weak, who were in turn diminished in power while their cultures declined. Social Darwinists held that the life of humans in society was a struggle for existence ruled by "survival of the fittest."

Assimilation measures, aimed at turning the Ainu into productive and localizable Japanese citizens, were enacted piecemeal in the first thirty years of the Meiji era. Japanese policies were remarkably similar to those in other settler countries like the United States, Canada, Australia, and New Zealand, and for good reason: the Japanese government used "strategic idioms" derived from U.S. domestic policies. As Katsuya Hirano (2019, 606) notes: "Ainu dispossession . . . was shaped predominantly by American frontier politics."

The United States used homesteading policies as a part of westward expansion to fulfill its "Manifest Destiny"—a nationalist moral imperative. The Meiji government implemented a similar version of Manifest Destiny or civilizing mission as a means of bringing Hokkaido and its Ainu under the Japanese system. To do this, the Meiji government brought in "advisors from the United States, including Horace Capron as a chief advisor, to share their experiences with tribal removals and resettlement in the U.S. context" (Lightfoot 2019, 619). Hirano (2019, 606) draws attention to the explicit similarities in the dispossession of land by the Ainu and other Indigenous peoples at the hand of their colonial governments: "By 1900, both Native Americans and Ainu had been stripped of lands on which they had lived for millennia, and forests, rivers, and land had been utilized for the capitalist development of their respective governments."

Horace Capron, a commissioner in the U.S. Department of Agriculture, journeyed to Japan in 1871 to serve as a special adviser to the Japanese government. Capron urged the Japanese government to adopt liberal homesteading laws similar to those enacted in the United States in 1862, resulting in the enactment of the "Regulations for Sale and Lease of Hokkaido Lands" in 1872. This law, Hirano (2019, 603) notes, "declared Ainu Mosir to be *terra nullius* ['unoccupied land'] and state property. This law set the price of 3,300 square meters of fertile land at 1.5 yen, and for poorer land, at just one yen or even half a yen."[1]

This led to an explosion of Japanese settlers into Hokkaido for the "free land" and resulted in the decimation of Ainu land ownership, previously held in common for members of each Ainu *kotan* or town. Japanese leaders encouraged the systematic migration of former soldiers and ordinary citizens—in particular, displaced farmers and peasants—to Hokkaido by supplying them with land and financial support. At the same time, they counted on American experts, who offered various technologies of colonization, to reshape Ainu Mosir into a land suitable for Japan's capitalist modernization.

Throughout the late nineteenth century, other American scientists involved in helping the Japanese colonial effort in Hokkaido included William Smith Clark, William Wheeler, and David Penhallow (Hennessey 2020). These three professors aided the Hokkaido Development Commission in its work to find resources for extraction as well as mechanisms for turning Hokkaido into a profitable enterprise. Clark was the first president of Sapporo Agricultural College (now Hokkaido University); Wheeler was responsible for surveying routes for roads and railways and

---

1. Ainu Mosir is an Ainu term meaning "land of the Ainu" or "land of the humans."

providing the Kaitakushi with expert advice on their construction; Penhallow was charged with researching a wide range of potential cash crops and other natural products from Hokkaido. The Americans "played an essential role in physically transforming Hokkaido into a Japanese territory" (Hennessey 2020, 58), so much so that their actions in abetting the Japanese government's colonization of Hokkaido brought about great hardship for the Ainu, particularly in their ecological effects. Later, the professors were seen to be "actively spreading the view of the Ainu as a primitive race with no history that would soon disappear in the wake of Japanese settlement" (Hennessey 2020, 58).

These actions toward assimilation culminated in the 1899 Former Aborigines Act, which "aggressively sought to alleviate the suffering of Ainu communities in Hokkaido through a mixture of assimilation and welfare policies" (Loy 2010, 78). The act granted up to five hectares of land (12.35 acres) per Ainu household, with covenants against alienation except to an heir. If the land was not cultivated within fifteen years, the state would regain the land. And, while schools and hospitals were supposed to be built in Ainu communities, this segregation policy continued to enforce the Ainu separation.

As mentioned in chapter 1, Ainu were featured at the 1903 Osaka Industrial Exposition and again at the 1904 St. Louis Exposition as part of the "human zoo" exhibits along with other so-called primitive cultures. In keeping with ideas of unilinear social evolution promoted by Great Britain anthropologist Edward Tylor and American anthropologist Lewis Henry Morgan (Graber 2010), the "primitive" Ainu acted as a backdrop for the "civilized" Japanese exhibit in much the same way the United States positioned itself among its Native American and Filipino exhibits. Images of the Ainu wearing traditional clothing were placed in contrast to Japanese houses and gardens. This cemented the Japanese government's idea that the Ainu people were a "vanishing race," much the same as American Indians, Canadian First Nations, and the Australian Aborigines.

Political scientist Sheryl Lightfoot (2019, 618) discusses how Japanese colonial policies were derived from a basic idea that "the Japanese are racially and ethnically homogenous but also inherently superior to the Ainu." She goes on to note how "a major objective of Japan in Hokkaidō was to 'civilize' Ainu people" (619) by bringing them up from their primitive hunting and fishing economies to a level equal to those of "civilized" countries such as the United States. Thus, to the Japanese government, cultural assimilation was regarded as necessary in the interest of the Ainu's own survival. A key aspect of this mission in Hokkaido was the introduction of settled farming and private property, much as the view of the United States regarding American Indian progress was framed.

Concluding Remarks

Non-Japanese historians and researchers have tended to look at the history of the Ainu as a broadly generalized population outside of (or on the peripheries of) Japanese history in one form (or for one reason) or another, with differential focus: Brett Walker's work (2001) focuses largely on conditions in eastern and northeastern Hokkaido, while Howell (2005) deals almost exclusively with southern and western Hokkaido. Wage labor is central to Howell's portrayal of Ainu society in the Tokugawa period, while Walker's writing focuses much more on trade. As noted previously, Tanaka's discussion of the Emishi offers insights into that population of people who existed in northern Honshu during the early Japanese state formation.

Relationships between the Japanese state and the non-Japanese "barbarians" on the northern borders were often driven by trade. The people of prehistoric Hokkaido (precursors to the groups who ultimately became the Ainu) seem to have had minimal contact with the people of Honshu until about 700 B.P., when evidence of trade with Honshu, China, and northeastern Asia becomes more prominent (see table 4).

By the fifteenth century, trade was established with the Ainu of southern Hokkaido. The trade and the impact that the native products needed as part of that trade appear to have put pressure on local groups. Conflict developed between the Wajin and Ainu warriors, and it took nearly a hundred years for the two groups to reach an agreement for the hostilities to subside sufficiently for the groups to resume relatively peaceful trade relations. Conflict arose again during the Tokugawa period, when competition for both resources and the items those resources fetched in trade led to tension among the Ainu villages and again to conflict. It wasn't until 1807 that the Japanese government sought to "civilize" the

TABLE 4 Important dates of Ainu and Japanese government interaction

Year	Event
2020	Upopoy ("Singing together" in Ainu) National Symbolic Space and Museum opens
2019	Passage of Act Promoting Measures to Achieve a Society in which the Pride of Ainu People is Respected (The Ainu Measures Promotion Act, or AMPA)
2018	Foundation for Research and Promotion of Ainu Culture (FRPAC) merges with Ainu Museum of Shiraoi to become the Foundation for Ainu Culture (FAC)
2009	Hokkaido Utari Kyokai reverts to Hokkaido Ainu Association
2008	Diet passes "Resolution calling for the Recognition of the Ainu People as an Indigenous People of Japan"
	Creation of the Advisory Council for Future Ainu Policy
2007	Japan ratifies United Nations Declaration on the Rights of Indigenous Peoples
2006	Amendments to "Act on the Promotion of Ainu Culture, and Dissemination and Enlightenment of Knowledge about Ainu Tradition, etc." become "Law for the Promotion of Ainu Culture and for the Dissemination and Advocacy for the Traditions of the Ainu and the Ainu Culture"
1997	Nibutani Dam case finds Ainu are "indigenous people"; Nibutani Dam illegal
	Japanese Diet passes "Act on the Promotion of Ainu Culture, and Dissemination and Enlightenment of Knowledge about Ainu Tradition, etc.," which fully revokes the 1899 Former Aborigines Protection Act and creates the Foundation for Research and Promotion of Ainu Culture (FRPAC)
1961	Hokkaido Ainu Association becomes Hokkaido Utari Kyokai
1937	Former Aborigines Protection Act is revised and Ainu-only schools are abolished
1930	Hokkaido Ainu Association forms
1904	Ainu exhibit at Louisiana Purchase Exposition (also St. Louis Exposition), United States
1899	Former Aborigines Protection Act passes
1875	Treaty of St. Petersburg forces Sakhalin Ainu to move to Hokkaido as Sakhalin becomes Russian property
1872	"Regulations for Sale and Lease of Hokkaido Lands" nationalizes Ainu land
1871	Family Registry Law passes and inducts Ainu into Japanese nation
1869	Ezo is renamed "Hokkaido"
	Hokkaido Development Commission (Kaitakushi) is created

(continued)

TABLE 4 (*continued*)

Year	Event
1868	Meiji Restoration
1856	Edo government retakes control of Ezo from Matsumae Clan
1822	Matsumae Clan regains Ezo; reinstates prohibitions against Ainu
1802	Hakodate Edict allows Ainu to take on Japanese customs
1799	Matsumae Clan loses control of trade of Ezo
1782	Menashi-Kunashir rebellion against Wajin merchant Hidaya
1669	Shakushain's revolt begins; ends in 1672 with Shakushain's poisoning
1514	Kakizaki Clan (later Matsumae Clan) gains economic control of Ezo; prohibits Ainu from taking on Japanese customs
1456	Koshamain's War
720	*Nihon Shoki* first mentions Emishi or Ebisu as "eastern barbarians"
660	Military expedition by Abe no Omi against Sushen, who were people from the north
57	First mention of the "people of Wa" (Wajin) in Chinese histories

Ainu and assimilate them rather than trying to keep them socially and economically separate.

Assimilation policies of the Japanese government toward the Ainu beginning with the Meiji government's annexation of Hokkaido were informed by, and generally followed, assimilation policies of the United States. American "advisors" in Japan suggested American policies of assimilation such as language disruption, land seizure and allotment, and converting the Ainu into farmers.

Further Reading

The primary sources relating to Ainu history as part of their relationships with mainland Japan are David Howell's 2005 volume *Geographies of Identity in Nineteenth-Century Japan*, Richard Siddle's 1996 volume *Race, Resistance and the Ainu of Japan*, Brett Walker's 2001 volume *The Conquest of Ainu Lands: Ecology and Culture in Japanese Expansion, 1590–1800*, and Christopher Loy's 2010 dissertation, "The Ainu of Northern Japan: Indigeneity, Post-national Politics, Territoriality." Additionally, Mark Hudson's 1999 *Ruins of Identity: Ethnogenesis in the Japa-*

nese Islands and ann-elise lewallen's 2016 *The Fabric of Indigeneity: Ainu Identity, Gender, and Settler Colonialism in Japan* offer good insights into the Japanese and Ainu situations.

Moreover, a workshop held in British Columbia, Canada, in 2018 led to the publication of articles focusing on the 150th anniversary of Japanese settler colonization of Hokkaido. The 2019 special issue by Tristan R. Grunow and colleagues, "Hokkaidō 150: Settler Colonialism and Indigeneity in Modern Japan and Beyond" (in the journal *Critical Asian Studies*), offers pointed insights into specific aspects of Ainu–Japanese relationships.

CHAPTER 6
• • • • • • • • •

Assimilating the Indigenous
Other Colonial Policies of Assimilation

This chapter offers very brief discussions of policies of the United States, Canada, Australia, and New Zealand in relation to the Indigenous peoples of these countries. Its purpose is to provide readers with brief historical material for comparison of Japanese policies related to the Ainu. Ken S. Coates (2004, 180–81), in *A Global History of Indigenous Peoples*, generalizes about the initial relationships between colonizing nations and the people they encountered:

> [C]olonial expansion rested uneasily with the indigenous population. The rapid expansion of migrant populations threatened the stability of local ecosystems and drained available resources. The ideology of the new order, based on personal or government land ownership was imposed on indigenous territories. Indigenous peoples were quickly displaced by farms, ranches, plantations, town sites, commercial fishing developments, mines, or other intrusions of the new economic order.

More importantly, he writes, the Indigenous people "had to be controled [*sic*] and managed so as to ensure that they did not interfere with the activities of the incoming colonial settlers" (Coates 2004, 181) who intended to take over everything of importance.

The United States and American Indians

Ann Irish (2009, 23) quotes David Penhallow, an American scientist who lived in Hokkaido from 1876 to 1880, as saying

> the relations of the Aino [*sic*] to the Japanese were and are precisely those of the American Indian to the European. . . . It is the same story of pacific intentions, bold demands, aggressive acts, and continual wars, resulting in the final subjugation and extermination of a weaker race.

Penhallow was wrong, of course—the American Indian was *not* exterminated. In January 2024, there were 574 federally recognized tribal entities in the United States, each one with its separate and distinctive name. "American Indian" and/or "Native American" are the two primary terms used to identify the Indigenous population of the United States, although occasionally one might encounter "Native American Indian," but that term is a bit of overkill. The terms are not necessarily used interchangeably, but usage of one or the other is often a matter of personal or professional preference. For example, the National Congress of *American Indians* (emphasis added) is the most widely representative organization relating to tribal issues in the United States, whereas the *Native American* Rights Fund (emphasis added) is perhaps the most widely recognized representative legal organization. In this chapter (as elsewhere), I use the two terms interchangeably even though I recognize the political implications of each.

The relationships between the U.S. government and tribal nations changed after the American Revolution of 1776. Even though Indian tribes were not included in the Constitution under which the new United States of America was formed, they were mentioned specifically in two places in terms of taxation and commerce. Table 5 at the end of this section provides important dates of American Indian and U.S. government interactions.

The early U.S. federal government was intent on exerting federal authority over American Indian affairs above that of the individual states. The Supreme Court ruling in the case of *Johnson v. McIntosh* (1823) set the judicial precedent that, through the Doctrine of Discovery, European countries and, ultimately, the United States had secured a superior legal

TABLE 5 Important dates of American Indian and American government interaction

Year	Event
2010	U.S. government "supports" the United Nations Declaration on the Rights of Indigenous Peoples
1975	Indian Self-Determination and Education Assistance Act (ISDEA) allows tribes to take over government programs
1972	AIM Trail of Broken Treaties
1971	Alaska Native Claims Settlement Act (ANCSA) provides land to Alaska Natives
1969	Alcatraz takeover by AIM activists and tribal members
1968	Indian Civil Rights Act ends "termination"
	American Indian Movement (AIM) founded in Minneapolis, Minnesota
1956	Indian Relocation Act moves tribal members to cities
1953	House Concurrent Resolution passes for "termination" of federal supervision of tribes
1934	Wheeler-Howard Act / Indian Reorganization Act passes as part of "Indian New Deal"
1890	Wounded Knee Massacre
1879	Establishment of Carlisle Indian Industrial School as Residential School
1877	General Allotment Act (Dawes Severalty Act) passes
1876	Custer's Last Stand
1871	End of treaty making
1868	Treaty of Fort Laramie with Sioux and Arapaho is last treaty ratified by Congress
1864	Long Walk of the Navajo
1837	Chickasaw Nation is removed to lands west of the Choctaw in Indian Territory
1836	Muscogee Creek Nation is forcibly removed to Indian Territory
1832	*Worcester v. Georgia* establishes tribal sovereignty over tribal lands
	Treaty of New Echota gives Cherokee two years to move to Indian Territory
1831	*Cherokee Nation v. Georgia* establishes federal government, not states, has rights over tribes
	Choctaw Tribal Nation is removed on "Trail of Tears" to Indian Territory to the west
1830	Treaty of Dancing Rabbit Creek requires relocation of Choctaws to lands to the west
1823	*Johnson v. McIntosh* establishes U.S. superior legal right to tribal lands
1778	Treaty with the Delaware Tribe is first U.S.–Indian Nation treaty
1776	United States of America is formed
1607	England begins colonizing what is now the United States

title to Indian lands. "Indian land rights were not entirely disregarded," David Wilkins (2011, 122) writes, "but were necessarily reduced even though native peoples were not direct parties in this lawsuit and were in fact separate nations."

Until the end of treaty making in 1871, the federal government enacted policies to move Indian tribes from their lands in the east to make those lands available for American farmers. Some tribes agreed to "relocate" to these lands, while others were forced to move to the west where "reservations" (lands reserved for the exclusive use of the tribal members) were established. In 1871, the federal government began a policy of "Allotment, Assimilation, and Acculturation" (Wilkins 2011, 127–28). Much of the vast Indian lands of the west were allotted to individuals under the General Allotment Act of 1887 (also known as the Dawes Act) as a mechanism for creating "citizen farmers" to speed up assimilation. Allotment resulted in the loss of nearly ninety million acres of land (Wilkins 2011, 128).

In addition to allotment, Indian boarding schools and the education system were used as a mechanism for assimilation. Indian youth from reservations were sent to boarding schools, divested of their Indian clothes, forced to speak English, and punished for speaking their own languages. Colonel Richard Henry Pratt ([1892] 1973, 261), the founder of the Carlisle Indian Industrial School in 1879, encouraged the government to "kill the Indian in him and save the man." Other boarding schools across the United States followed similar practices of forced assimilation and denigration of tribal customs, languages, and dress.

Federal policy changes during the 1920s–1940s allowed tribes a minimal amount of self-rule. The policies of the period, highlighted by three pieces of legislation known collectively as "The Indian New Deal," were an attempt to provide limited tribal self-governance. Of these, the Indian Reorganization Act had the most impact as it brought an end to the allotment policy and authorized the establishment of tribal governing and economic institutions. It specifically authorized tribes to organize and adopt constitutions, bylaws, and incorporation charters subject to ratification by vote of tribal members. It continues to cause issues, however, as it has effectively created tribal copies of the federal system of governance and has somewhat limited the influence of traditional tribal leaders.

After World War II, Congress felt the Indians had become sufficiently acculturated and no longer needed the federal government to act as their trustee. House Concurrent Resolution 108 of 1953 set about processes to "terminate" the federal supervision of tribes and their members; the passage of Public Law 280 a few weeks later conferred full criminal and some civil jurisdiction over Indian reservations (with certain reservations being exempted) upon five states (California, Minnesota, Nebraska, Oregon, and Wisconsin).

In addition, the federal government initiated a second policy of relocation: the Indian Relocation Act of 1956. Tribal adults were encouraged to leave the reservation and relocate to urban areas such as Chicago, Dallas, Denver, Minneapolis-St. Paul, San Francisco, and others. As Benjamin Strout (1982, 29–30) points out, the program mostly failed. There were no special programs to help the transplanted individuals adjust to city life, and, without familiar family and social structures, many of those who participated moved from rural poverty to urban poverty.

From 1968 through the 1970s, many of the tribal victories were tied to the broader civil rights struggles of the time (Wilkins 2011, 131–32). The 1968 passage of the Indian Civil Rights Act formally ended the policy of termination and created new goals aimed at raising the standard of living of the Indian, providing individuals with the option of remaining on a reservation or moving to a city, and increasing the Indian's opportunity to share in the benefits of modern America (McKee and Murray 1986, 125). In June 1970, Congress repealed the termination act; in July 1970, President Richard Nixon proposed "self-determination without termination." In conjunction with the Alaska Native Claims Settlement Act of 1971 and the Indian Self-Determination and Education Assistance Act of 1975, tribal governance received support from the government rather than a push for dissolution. This act allowed tribes to take over control of monies spent on federal programs for the benefit of each tribe, thus allowing tribes to maintain effective control over their own destiny through managing the "purse strings" previously held by federal agencies. Many tribes in contemporary America are deeply involved in providing benefits to their tribal members, and the federal government continues to provide funding for programs that benefit the tribes and their members.

Much of American Indian policy change was driven by American Indian activism led by the American Indian Movement (AIM). AIM, originally founded by Dennis Banks and Clyde Bellacourt in Minneapolis, Minnesota, provided an opportunity for mostly urban Indians to react to local issues. With the takeover of Alcatraz Island in San Franscisco Bay in 1969, AIM's influence grew. It drew national attention to American Indian issues and governmental inequities through its 1972 Trail of Broken Treaties, when hundreds of Native Americans drove in caravans, beginning on the West Coast, to Washington, D.C., where they occupied the offices of the Department of the Interior. While many American Indians might have disagreed with the methods AIM used, AIM did serve to drive change.[1]

In addition to legislative actions that impacted American Indian policy, the Executive Branch of the federal government also provided guidance to federal agencies concerning their relationships with American Indians. Actions by Presidents William J. Clinton, George W. Bush, and Barack Obama crafted U.S. initiatives to promote government-to-government relationships with tribal governments aimed at improving the lives of Indigenous peoples in the United States and its territories, but actions of the Donald Trump administration (2017–21) were in many ways in opposition to those of previous presidents. Reporter Anna V. Smith (2020) draws attention to this disparity, writing: "Many of the decisions over the last four years will have a lasting impact on Indian Country no matter how quickly the new Biden/Harris administration works to reverse them."

Canada and First Nations

Relationships between the Canadian government and its Aboriginal populations (First Nations, Métis, and Inuit) are complicated by the fact that colonization of the area now known as Canada involved both the French and the British. As John Leonard Taylor (2006) notes, during most of the political interaction between the colonists and the Indigenous people of the area up until the early nineteenth century, "Aboriginal policy was diplomatic and military in orientation because Aboriginal peoples constituted sovereign and independent nations."

---

1. See "American Indian Movement (AIM)," History.com, October 31, 2022, updated September 28, 2023, https://www.history.com/topics/native-american-history/american-indian-movement-aim.

Mark Aquash (2013, 121) notes that the term *Aboriginal* "refers to three unique groups of Indigenous people: First Nations, Métis, and Inuit." Like Aquash, I use the term *First Nations* as it is specific to Indigenous nations previously referred to as *Indians* in Canada. Most of the federal policy interactions related to the Indians effectively ignored the Inuit until the 1940s, and the Métis (individuals of mixed Native and European ancestry) and non-status Indians until the late twentieth century. Following a brief discussion of Inuit and Métis relations with the Canadian government, I will focus primarily on Canadian relationships with the First Nations.

The Inuit are the predominant Indigenous people of the Far North, stretching from the Bering Sea to Baffin Bay. Barry Zellen (2010, 58–59), past director of the United States' Naval Postgraduate School's Arctic Security Program, describes Inuit development in northern Canada as "a two-step process. The first step addressed the question of land. . . . With land claims settled across the region, the next step in the process of northern development was the pursuit of new systems of aboriginal self-governance."

Anthropologist/ecologist Milton M. R. Freeman (2011) writes about the Inuit Land Use and Occupancy Project as the mechanism that initiated and formed the evidence for Inuit land claims that led to the establishment of Nunavut in 1999. After Nunavut, the evolution toward more distinctly Indigenous self-governing structures continued, as reflected in the 2005 Labrador Inuit Land Claim, the first truly Inuit self-governing structure. Carole Brice-Bennet edited a 1997 volume on Innu (a subgroup of Inuit) land use and occupancy in Labrador as initial support for a land claim there.[2]

The Truth and Reconciliation Commission of Canada (TRCC) uses the term "Métis to describe people of mixed descent who were not able, or chose not, to be registered as Indians under the Indian Act" (TRCC 2015, 3). It notes that this term was applied to

---

2. More details on the Labrador land claim can be found on the Government of Canada website, "Land Claims Agreement Between the Inuit of Labrador and Her Majesty the Queen in Right of Newfoundland and Labrador and Her Majesty the Queen in Right of Canada," December 29, 2010, https://www.rcaanc-cirnac.gc.ca/eng/1293647179208/1542904949105.

the large number of Aboriginal people who, for a variety of reasons, chose not to terminate their Treaty rights, or for those women, and their children, who lost their Indian Act status by marrying a person who did not have such status. These individuals were classed or identified alternately as "non-status Indians," "half-breeds," or "Métis." (TRCC 2015, 3)

In 2019, Rhiannon Johnson, a reporter for the Canadian Broadcasting Company (CBC), provided an article as part of a series on exploring Identity. In "Who Are the Métis and What Are Their Rights?," Johnson notes that "Métis have a distinct collective identity, customs and way of life, unique from Indigenous or European roots" and that "what distinguishes Métis people from everyone else is that they associate themselves with a culture that is distinctly Métis."

Johnson describes how two Canadian Supreme Court cases established rights of the Métis and of non-status Indians. The 2003 Supreme Court of Canada decision *Regina v. Powley* established rights of the Métis. The *Daniels v. Canada (Indian Affairs and Northern Development)* Supreme Court of Canada decision in 2016 established that Métis and non-status Indians are considered Indians under Section 91(24) of the 1982 Constitution and that the federal government must accept responsibility for negotiating programs and services for Métis communities.

Julieta Uribe (2006, 3) places Canadian policy within a background of a complex system of laws derived from First Nations customs and conventions as well as French, British, and U.S. common law. Conflicting alliances between the French and the English with the Aboriginal inhabitants of the areas were often based on economic interests; the French fur-trading interests did not require the cession of land, while the British colonial expansion to the west led to treaty negotiations and land cessions. The British took over the majority of relationships with Aboriginal peoples following the collapse of French imperial power after the Seven Years' War (1756–63) under the Royal Proclamation of 1763, which established a basis of government administration in the North American territories and the constitutional framework for the negotiation of treaties with the Aboriginal inhabitants of large sections of Canada. These treaties were used to extinguish Aboriginal rights as more and more land was needed by the colonists for farming, grazing, development, mineral extraction, and other "necessities." Table 6 at the end of this section pro-

vides important dates of First Nations and Canadian government interactions.

Aquash (2013, 126) discusses the assimilation policies developed as a
result of the Bagot Commission of 1844 (see Leslie 1982), including cen-
tralized control of all First Nations matters and individual ownership of
parcels of land. This "sense of greed and materialism" would theoretically
lead First Nations individuals to "civilization." Anthropologist Michael
Asch has also written extensively on these topics, including his 2014 volume *On Being Here to Stay: Treaties and Aboriginal Rights in Canada*.

With the passage of the Gradual Civilization Act of 1857, Indian people were encouraged to abandon Indian status for enfranchisement as
Canadian citizens. The passage of the Indian Lands Act of 1860 provided
for the transfer of federal authority over Indians and Indian lands to the
Superintendent of Indian Affairs (Aquash 2013, 126–27). Section 92 of
the Constitution Act of 1867 delegated legislative authority over Indians
and their lands to the federal government, while Section 93 gave jurisdiction of education to provinces across Canada. The Gradual Enfranchisement Act of 1869 eliminated status of First Nations women who
married non-status men to dispossess Indian lands and impose Canadian
citizenship through enfranchisement, essentially promoting assimilation.

In 1876, the government consolidated the Gradual Civilization Act
and the Gradual Enfranchisement Act into the Indian Act of 1876 (Henderson 2006). The Indian Act gave the government sweeping powers
with regard to First Nations and was an attempt to homogenize a vast and
varied population of people and assimilate them into non-Indigenous
society. Subsequent amendments made it illegal for First Nations peoples
to practice religious ceremonies such as the potlatch in 1884, and others
in 1894 and 1920 required First Nations children to attend industrial or
residential school.

The Indian Act was revised in 1951, and in 1968 the Hawthorn Report
proposed rejection of the idea of assimilation and recognition of the special status of First Nations individuals. In opposition, Pierre Trudeau's
White Paper (its Statement of Indian Policy) of 1969 attempted to abandon its trust responsibility toward First Nations and delegate programs
and social services to provincial governments. The White Paper was met
with outrage from First Nations peoples and was immediately countered
by the "Red Paper" (Henderson 2006). Due to the fierce and continued

TABLE 6 Important dates of First Nations and Canadian government interactions

Year	Event
2021	Canadian government ratifies the United Nations Declaration on the Rights of Indigenous Peoples
2019	Supreme Court of Canada decision *Daniels v. Canada (Indian Affairs and Northern Development)* establishes that Métis and non-status Indians are considered Indians under Section 91(24) of the 1982 Constitution
2014	*Tsilhqot'in Nation v. British Columbia* holds that Tsilhqot'in Nation has Aboriginal title to land and the right to decide land use; right to enjoy, occupy, and possess the land; and right to proactively use and manage the land and its natural resources
2008	Government of Canada offers formal apology for the assimilative practices of the government, forced removal of children from their families, the abuse suffered by many of those children, and the resulting effects of these policies Truth and Reconciliation Commission is established to document the history and lasting impacts of the Canadian Indian residential school system on Indigenous people
2003	Supreme Court of Canada decision *Regina v. Powley* establishes rights of the Métis
1999	Territory of Nunavut is established under Inuit governance
1997	*Delgamuukw v. British Columbia* holds that Aboriginal title still exists in British Columbia
1982	Constitution Act: Section 32 defines Aboriginal peoples of Canada as Indians (or First Nations people) and includes Inuit and Métis for the first time
1951	Indian Act revision allows return of tribal ceremonies; land claims are allowed; First Nations women are given voting rights and allowed to participate in tribal governance
1894	Amendment to Indian Act of 1876 requires First Nations children to attend industrial or residential school; further amended in 1920
1884	Amendment to Indian Act of 1876 makes it illegal for First Nations peoples to practice religious ceremonies such as the potlatch
1876	Indian Act of 1876 combines Gradual Civilization Act and the Gradual Enfranchisement Act
1871	British Columbia joins Canadian Confederation
1869	Gradual Enfranchisement Act eliminates status of First Nations women who married non-status men to dispossess Indian lands and impose Canadian citizenship through enfranchisement
1867	Constitution Act: Section 92 gives legislative authority over Indians and Indian lands to federal government; Section 93 gives jurisdiction over education to provinces
1860	Indian Lands Act transfers federal authority to Superintendent of Indian Affairs

(continued)

TABLE 6 (*continued*)

Year	Event
1857	Gradual Civilization Act encourages First Nations to abandon Indian status
1844	Bagot Commission centralizes control over First Nations
1763	Royal Proclamation establishes government and constitutional framework for treaties
	Great Britain wins Seven Years' War with France to gain what is known as Canada
1583	England begins colonizing what is now Canada
1543	France begins colonizing what is now Canada

opposition by Indigenous groups and their supporters, the Canadian government quickly withdrew the White Paper.

As a result of political activism, Section 35 of the Constitution Act of 1982 affirms existing Aboriginal and treaty rights and defines "Aboriginal peoples of Canada" as Indians (or First Nations peoples), Inuit, and Métis. Self-government agreements, based on the inherent right of First Nations to self-governance as declared in the Constitution Act of 1982, involve Canadian federal, provincial, and territorial governments and individual First Nations, Inuit communities, and Métis settlements (Taylor 2006). Since then, First Nations have continued to expand their internal control of administration in a move toward self-determination and self-governance, while federal and territorial governance has lessened its involvement on First Nations' affairs. More recently, the Department of Justice has issued "Principles: Respecting the Government of Canada's Relationship with Indigenous Peoples," which "reflect a commitment to good faith, the rule of law, democracy, equality, non-discrimination, and respect for human rights" (Canadian Department of Justice 2018, 3) as a means "to engage in partnership, and a significant move away from the status quo to a fundamental change in the relationship with Indigenous peoples" (4). It also references the United Nations Declaration on the Rights of Indigenous Peoples (UNDRIP) as necessary for the survival, dignity, and well-being of Indigenous peoples around the world.

The situation is different in British Columbia, primarily because British Columbia was settled under the doctrine of terra nullius, meaning that the land was legally deemed to be unoccupied or uninhabited. Once British Columbia joined the Canadian Confederation in 1871, the federal government assumed responsibility for Indians and lands reserved for Indians, while the province had responsibility for non-Aboriginal civil matters and resources. With few exceptions (the Douglas Treaties of Fort Rupert and southern Vancouver Island), no treaties were signed between the Indigenous peoples and the British Columbia government until 1998. Many Native people wished to negotiate treaties, but the province refused until 1990.

A major development in British Columbia–First Nations relations resulted from the 1997 decision of the Supreme Court of Canada in the *Delgamuukw v. British Columbia* case, which held that Aboriginal title still exists in British Columbia. In 2014, the Canadian Supreme Court, in its decision in the *Tsilhqot'in Nation v. British Columbia* case, held that the Tsilhqot'in Nation had Aboriginal title to land being clear-cut under license of the British Columbia government without adequate consultation and communication with the Nation (MacCharles 2014). The court held that "Aboriginal title" constitutes a beneficial interest in the land, the underlying control of which is retained by the Crown, but that rights conferred by Aboriginal title include the right to decide how the land will be used; rights to enjoy, occupy, and possess the land; and rights to proactively use and manage the land, including its natural resources. But the court set out a mechanism by which the Crown can override Aboriginal title in the public interest if the Crown has carried out consultation and accommodation, if the Crown's actions have been supported by a compelling and substantial objective, and if the Crown's actions have been consistent with its fiduciary obligation to the Aboriginal body in question.

Australia and Its Aboriginal Peoples

When the British colonizers arrived in Australia in 1788, they regarded the continent as terra nullius (similar to the situation as noted for British Columbia), thereby bypassing any encumbrances required by treaty making. Because of this, Australia's Indigenous people do not enjoy any constitutional or treaty recognition, unlike in New Zealand, Canada, and the United States, where treaties have been signed.

The first apparent consequence of British settlement occurred in April 1789 when a disease—probably smallpox—struck Aboriginal people in the Port Jackson area. As in other countries, European diseases decimated Native populations who had not developed immunities. Other European diseases such as chicken pox, influenza, and measles spread in advance of the frontier of settlement. Communities with greater population densities were impacted the most. Although massacres of Indigenous populations by colonists occurred, disease was the principal cause of population decline.

The second consequence of British settlement was competition for, and appropriation of, land and water resources. While Aboriginal Australians were considered to be nomads by the British settlers because of the absence of permanent built shelters, the idea that they held no concept of land ownership was false. British colonists, similar to those of the United States and Canada, felt that the land must be productive and that farming or grazing needs far outweighed Indigenous uses. Table 7 at the end of this section offers important dates of interactions between Australian peoples and Australian governments.

There were few significant changes in the manner by which Aboriginal Australians were governed after the establishment of the federation in 1901. Six separate, self-governing colonies of Britain became states of the Commonwealth (and one territory) with existing state government policy and legislation relating to the Aboriginal populations remaining in effect. The Commonwealth became involved in a secondary manner through legislation that limited access to citizenship and welfare rights. Aboriginal people were mentioned in the original Australian Constitution, but only to ensure that they were excluded from certain provisions. It was only with the passage of the referendum to change the Constitution in 1967, passed by approximately 90 percent of Australian voters, that these two negative references were removed.

In the mid-twentieth century, a theoretically more benign period of assimilation was ushered in, but laws intended to "protect" or advance people's "welfare" quickly became laws that further alienated Indigenous people. The removal of children from Indigenous parents shifted from being an ad hoc state practice to a strategy agreed on by state and federal governments that resulted in what has been called the "stolen

TABLE 7 Important dates of Australian Aboriginal and Australian government interaction

Year	Event
2023	Defeat of the Australian Indigenous Voice Referendum to revise the Australian Constitution to establish "Aboriginal and Torres Strait Islander Voice" to "make representations to the Parliament and the Executive Government of the Commonwealth on matters relating to Aboriginal and Torres Strait Islander peoples": 39.94% in favor; 60.06% opposed
2009	Australian government ratifies the United Nations Declaration on the Rights of Indigenous Peoples
2008	Australia issues formal "Apology to the Stolen Generations"
1997	*Bringing Them Home* report describes government policies that resulted in removal of Aboriginal children
1995	*Western Australia v. Commonwealth* holds Land (Titles and Traditional Usage) Act 1993 of Western Australia invalid
1993	Native Title Act sets up a land management regime to deal with the Native title rights and interests of Indigenous Australians
	Native Title Act (Queensland) sets in place mechanisms for processing Native title claims in Queensland
1992	*Mabo v. Queensland 2* case recognizes Native title as part of Australian common law
1988	*Mabo v. Queensland* case holds that legislation to extinguish Native title to the Murray Islands without payment of compensation was inconsistent with the Racial Discrimination Act 1975
1984	Aboriginal and Torres Strait Islander Heritage Protection Act passes
1976	Aboriginal Land Rights Act (Northern Territory) recognizes Aboriginal land ownership
1971	*Milirrpum v. Nabalco Pty Ltd* case (Northern Territory) holds that Aboriginal people do not own Arnhem Land reserve and that "Native title," if it ever existed, has long been extinguished
1970	Aboriginal Lands Act (Victoria) is first recognition of Aboriginal land rights
1967	Referendum to Change the Constitution removes exclusion of Aboriginal people from Constitution
1966	Aboriginal Land Trust Act (South Australia)
1915	Aborigines Protection Amending Act (New South Wales) gives the Board for the Protection of Aborigines authority to remove Aboriginal children without having to establish in court that the children were subject to neglect
1901	Australian Federation is established as Commonwealth of Australia
1883	Board for the Protection of Aborigines is established (New South Wales)
1869	Aboriginal Protection Act (Victoria) allows removal of Aboriginal people of mixed descent from stations or reserves to force them to assimilate into white society
1789	Aboriginal peoples of Port Jackson are decimated by new diseases brought by English colonists
1788	Australian colonizers arrive in Port Jackson, Australia, and establish penal colony at New South Wales

generation." In February 2008, an official apology was made to the stolen children by the governments of South Australia, Western Australia, Tasmania, the Australian Capital Territory, and New South Wales and by various local governments and churches across the country.

The first major recognition of Aboriginal land rights by an Australian government was the Aboriginal Lands Trust Act of 1966 enacted in South Australia. However, in *Milirrpum v. Nabalco Pty Ltd* (1971)— also known as "the Gove Land Rights Case"—the Northern Territory Supreme Court ruled that Aboriginal people did not own the Arnhem Land reserve. It further held that Australian common law was incapable of recognizing Indigenous land laws, that Native title does not form part of the law of any part of Australia, that even if Native title did once exist, it would have been extinguished, and, even if it did still exist, the Yolngu could not prove the elements necessary to establish Native title.

The passing of the Victorian Aboriginal Lands Act of 1970 resulted in the presentation of title deeds to residents of Lake Tyers and Framlingham as the first recognition of land rights in Victoria. The Aboriginal Land Rights (Northern Territory) Act of 1976 provided recognition of Aboriginal land ownership and established Aboriginal Land Commissioners, Aboriginal Land Trusts, and the Aboriginal Benefit Trust Account. The Aboriginal and Torres Strait Islander Heritage Protection Act of 1984 provided for the protection and preservation of objects and sites of religious, historic, and cultural significance to Indigenous peoples where state and territory laws were ineffective or not being used.

Perhaps the greatest impact in relation to Native land rights in Australia came from the *Mabo v. Queensland* cases of 1988 ("Mabo 1") and 1992 ("Mabo 2"). Eddie Mabo, Dave Passi, and James Rice brought an action against the State of Queensland and the Commonwealth claiming "native title" to the Murray Islands. In Mabo 1, the High Court judged that Queensland legislation to extinguish Native title without payment of compensation was inconsistent with the Racial Discrimination Act 1975. On June 3, 1992, the High Court handed down its decision in Mabo 2, ruling that the Meriam people of the Murray Islands of Mer, Dauar, and Waier held Native title to their islands. The High Court also found that Australia was occupied by Aboriginal and Torres Strait Islander peoples who had their own laws and customs and whose Native title to land survived the Crown's annexation. Thus, the court recognized the existence of Native title as part of Australian common law. The judgment necessitated new policies, legislation, and public administration procedures.

The passage of the Native Title Act of 1993 set up a land management regime to deal with the Native title rights and interests of Indigenous Australians as recognized by the common law in the Mabo decision. In relation to states, the Native Title (Queensland) Act of 1993 set in place mechanisms for processing Native title claims in Queensland; the Land (Titles and Traditional Usage) Act 1993 of Western Australia, which extinguished Native title across Western Australia, was found invalid by *Western Australia v. The Commonwealth* in 1995.

Starting in the 1960s, the Commonwealth began to reform the system within its own jurisdiction, removing various legal liabilities from Indigenous Australians and sponsoring a referendum that cleared the way for greater Commonwealth involvement in the policy area. Successive Commonwealth governments then led policy in this area through phases underpinned by expressions such as "self-determination," "self-management," "reconciliation," "practical reconciliation," and "closing-the-gap." These were punctuated with the setting up and dismantling of several different administrative and consultative mechanisms and woven through with issues such as how to facilitate the gaining of socioeconomic equality and the recognition of land and other rights.

In April 2009, the Australian government made a statement in support of the UN Declaration on the Rights of Indigenous Peoples, which had been adopted by the United Nations in September 2007. As a nonbinding declaration, it did not need to be signed or ratified, nor even endorsed, to be used, but the statement reversed the previous government's position.

New Zealand and the Māori

The history of British–Māori relations began with the earliest explorers of the region, Dutch navigator Abel Tasman (1642) and Captain James Cook (1769). Mark Derby (2012) presents a good, encyclopedic overview of New Zealand–Māori relations and will be somewhat summarized here. From the late eighteenth century, the country was regularly visited by explorers and sailors, missionaries, traders, and adventurers.

In 1839, Captain William Hobson took possession of New Zealand on behalf of the British Crown. Hobson and his advisers drew up the Treaty of Waitangi to obtain the voluntary transfer of sovereignty by Māori. The treaty was first signed on February 6, 1840. Its Māori-language version promised Māori some degree of control over their resources and customs, but the English-language version indicated that the Crown's sovereignty would not be shared with Indigenous people. These differing understandings eventually led to warfare and a long process of reinterpretation and compensation. Table 8 at the end of this section offers major dates of interactions between Māori and the Aotearoa New Zealand government.

Early government policies toward the Māori were aimed at "protecting" Māori from the harmful influences of colonists, advising the governor on Māori issues, and purchasing Māori land. Voting rights were tied to land ownership with the New Zealand Constitution Act 1852, but since communally held Māori land was not recognized, almost all Māori were effectively denied the vote.

Since they lacked political power through the electoral system, Māori set up their own unofficial *rūnanga* (tribal councils) where chiefs and elders could hear disputes and administer their own people. Legislation passed in 1858 set up "native districts" headed by rūnanga, but again, little effort was made to implement the new laws.

In 1858, the Māori formed a large intertribal movement headed by a Māori king. The Kīngitanga ("King movement") aimed to foster unity between tribes and give Māori greater authority in national affairs. One of its main goals was an end to sales of tribal land, in direct opposition to the goal of New Zealand governor Thomas Gore Browne. In 1860, this land sale policy led to war between Māori and the government, first in Taranaki and then in other parts of the North Island. To end the Kīngitanga conflict, a plan was proposed to give tribes significant administrative and legal authority in their own districts. The plan set up twenty Māori districts, each headed by a Pākehā ("white") civil commissioner who presided over Pākehā resident magistrates and Māori district rūnanga. Each rūnanga selected its own Native magistrates. Few district rūnanga were successfully established, however, because some districts remained suspicious of the government's intentions. As a result, in 1863, war broke out again.

TABLE 8 Important dates of Māori and Aotearoa New Zealand government interaction

Year	Event
2010	Aotearoa New Zealand "supports" the United Nations Declaration on the Rights of Indigenous Peoples
2002	Māori seats in Parliament increase from four to seven
1989	Māori Affairs Restructuring Act purports to increase Māori sovereignty but creates bureaucracy
1967	Māori Affairs Amendment Act makes Māori land owned by four people or less reclassified as "European land"
1960	Hunn Report argues for planned migration to the cities and assistance with training, employment, and accommodation
1953	Māori Affairs Act removes communal ownership of land to ease assimilation
1900	Māori Councils Act sets up Māori councils and marae committees
1867	Māori Representation Act creates four "Māori seats" in Parliament
1865	Native Land Court begins negotiating Māori land sales
1860	War between Kīngitanga and New Zealand
1858	Māori establish Kīngitanga ("King movement")
1855	Sir George Grey uses "Aotearoa" in relation to New Zealand
1852	New Zealand Constitution Act
1840	Treaty of Waitangi is signed between the British Crown and Māori
1839	William Hobson takes possession of New Zealand for the British Crown
1769	Captain James Cook explores New Zealand
1642	English explorer Abel Tasman explores New Zealand

In 1865, Andrew Russell began to dismantle the rūnanga system to assimilate the Māori into New Zealand lifestyles. His under-secretary, William Rolleston, set up a colony-wide system of schools for Māori. These taught in English and lasted well into the twentieth century. They gave some Māori an opportunity to engage effectively with non-Māori society but indirectly contributed to the loss of Māori language.

Land loss continued to be problematic for Māori. Once the Native Land Court began operating in 1865, the Native Department ceased to be the government's land-purchasing office, but its main activity remained the negotiation of sales of Māori land. By 1870, some tribes no longer owned enough land to sustain their people, and others had withdrawn to remote regions where they had little contact with Europeans.

The Māori Councils Act 1900 set up Māori councils and *marae* (a sacred and communal meeting ground central to Māori culture and identity) committees in almost every Māori district in the country, giving these councils authority comparable to those of local governments. From 1906 through 1922, the reestablished Native Department negotiated the purchase of a further million acres of Māori land by the government, and an even larger area was alienated by other means.

Governmental policies in the 1930s pushed economic development through funding to develop large blocks of tribally owned land in some of the country's poorest districts. The program also developed a large-scale Māori housing program to provide homes on the newly developed blocks. Following World War II and into the mid-1950s, the amount of state compensation offered for nineteenth-century land confiscations was increased and Māori land development and housing schemes were extended. Māori urbanization was also considered to be irreversible, and the New Zealand government policy became to ease the path of Māori into urban life.

The Māori Affairs Act 1953 aimed to help Māori achieve equality through economic development, by removing tribal (communal) ownership of land and creating situations where Māori land was to be owned by one person or by a comparatively small group of substantial owners to make it easier for the government to deal with them. Later, under the Māori Affairs Amendment Act 1967, Māori land owned by no more than four people was reclassified as "European land," making it easier to alienate remaining areas of tribal land.

Urbanization and its impact on governmental approaches to the Māori led to the 1960 Hunn Report on the Department of Māori Affairs, produced by Deputy Chairman of the Public Service Commission Jack Kent Hunn. The report identified three types of Māori: a minority who were completely detribalized, with very little or no Māoritanga; the majority of Māori, who were generally at home in either Māori or non-Māori society; and a minority of Māori who were "complacently living a backward life in primitive conditions" (quoted in Hill 2009, 94). According to Richard S. Hill (2009, 90), the Hunn report offered that the best that could be achieved was for remnants of Māori culture to be perpetuated in the process of Māori procurement of full equality before the law and socioeconomic parity with white New Zealand. The report argued for planned migration to the cities and assistance with training, employment, and accommodation, including a governmental policy of "targeted measures and a policy of short-term or medium-term positive discrimination in the interests of long-term equality" (Hill 2009, 93).

Eventually, as more Māori gained positions of power within the New Zealand government, government policy toward its responsibilities under the founding Treaty of Waitangi became more focused. During the 1984 Labour government, New Zealand extended the powers and resources of the Waitangi Tribunal and instructed all government departments to take the principles of the treaty into account in new legislation. The government also transferred some government funding spent on Māori to the control of tribally based Māori organizations.

Under the Māori Affairs Restructuring Act of 1989, a new policy advice and monitoring ministry, Manatu Māori / Ministry of Māori Affairs, came into being. According to Hill (2009, 237), the Ministry of Māori Affairs was tasked with giving "substance to the principle of partnership embodied in the Treaty of Waitangi by generating an environment which encourages Māori people to express their rangatiratanga" (roughly defined as "absolute sovereignty"). But significantly, this was qualified by the words "in ways that enhance New Zealand's economic, social, and cultural life" (Hill 2009, 237). The administrative structures that came into place on October 1, 1989, forced any *iwi* (local group of people, roughly equivalent to "tribe") wanting to opt into the new system to comply with strict operational and policy guidelines, including strict reporting, accountability, and audit procedures that had been approved by government. Critics argued that rangatiratanga was thus "reduced to an 'autonomy' that was granted in accordance with Government edicts," with further Māori subordination to the Crown.

Hekia Parata (1994) draws attention to the lack of a consistent public policy framework in Māori affairs, and how it results in a number of inefficiencies and structural exclusions. She writes in the journal *Te Urupare Rangapu* that the Ministry of Māori Development has often been seen by other government agencies as the representative of Māori, whereas the Māori community (or at least most of it) sees the Ministry as an agent of the state, which it clearly is. Parata (1994, 7) writes, "The equation was: to be Māori is to be worthless; to be Pākehā is to be worthy."

New Zealand government policy has been directed at this goal—to turn a Māori into a brown Pākehā. The policy has masqueraded in various disguises as assimilation, integration, separation, and then back to assimilation. There has been marginal success, with the inner core of Māori culture and belief fragile but still largely intact. The only short-lived attempt by a government to work with the resilient Māori cultural structures of *whānau, hapū, iwi,* and *marae* was the brief flirtation with iwi self-management and departmental responsiveness outlined in *Te Urupare Rangapu.*

Māori have continued to become involved in the "mainstream" New Zealand governance system. According to the Inter-Parliamentary Union (Riedl 2014, 7), Māori individuals in the New Zealand Parliament offer Indigenous representation that surpasses Indigenous representation in society. The number of Māori electoral districts increased from four in 1996 to seven since 2002, based on the Māori electoral population. In addition, another fifteen representatives of Māori descent have gained seats aided by the Mixed Member Proportional electoral system adopted in 1993, which allows for a number of strategies to elect Māori representatives to parliament. The Māori position is that the reserved seats are a symbol of state acknowledgment of the Māori people's right to self-government and that the political parties' willingness to place Māori members high on their party lists is an indication of the integrated nature of New Zealand's society at large.

Government Policies Toward Indigenous Populations

The treatment of Indigenous populations in these nations has common characteristics: economic exploitation, forced relocation, restriction in the use of Native languages, policies of assimilation, religious persecution, and systematic racial discrimination. These groups have found ways of recovering from those policies, and the United Nations Declaration on the Rights of Indigenous People has helped when the host countries' governing bodies have chosen to ratify and implement it.

The varieties of governmental policies relating to Indigenous nations within the governments of Japan, the United States, Canada, Australia, and New Zealand indicate a very general battery of policies aimed at assimilation. Parata's (1994) statement—that the idea, implicit and explicit in different New Zealand policy statements, that if Māori are treated as if they were white, then they would become white, or at least behave as if they were white—serves as a general model for most of the Indigenous groups discussed. In the United States and Canada, policies relating to American Indians and First Nations were initially aimed at segregation (the "reservation period"), then assimilation, then urbanization, and then (ultimately) self-governance.

As Coates (2004, 141) explains:

> Governments of the new nation-states placed a premium on the proper use of land and resources and, unilaterally, deemed aboriginal use to be "inefficient." New legal systems, involving courts, land registries, and a variety of concepts of land tenure, provided the administrative manifestation of the ideas that land was divisible, that it could be owned and used for the benefit of individuals, and that the original owners could be dispossessed with little concern for their longstanding relationship with their territories.

Economic Exploitation

In Japan, the Tokugawa basho system exploited Ainu individuals and Ainu resources. In the United States and Canada, global markets drove capitalist ideals that led to the wholesale exploitation of natural resources without regard for Native needs. In Australia and New Zealand, land was the primary resource that was exploited for farming and grazing, leading to economic hardships for those local groups who tried to maintain a traditional way of life. Ultimately, when the local Native groups became unable to exist as they traditionally had existed, they were often forced to become reliant on government programs to survive.

Forced Relocation and Land Loss

In the United States, various tribes were forcibly moved from their traditional homelands to other areas to provide new areas for settlement. In addition, the reduction of communally owned land through allotment and other land alienation schemes served to further reduce Indigenous domains. In Australia, the concept of terra nullius, as in British Columbia and essentially in Japan, allowed colonists to proceed as if the local populations were almost nonhuman competitors standing in the way of the "proper" use of the country. The New Zealand government crafted land policies to remove Māori social and political ties to the land as a means of integration and assimilation as a way of turning them into "productive" New Zealand citizens.

Forced Restriction in the Use of Native Languages

The governments' restriction of the use of Native languages created situations where Native identity was replaced with local concepts of what it meant to be a part of the national identity. In Japan, the Ainu initially were prevented from speaking Japanese until after 1802 and then were expected to "become" Japanese by giving up their Indigenous customs, including their language. In the United States and Canada, boarding schools prevented Native students from speaking tribal languages to quicken assimilation.

Religious Persecution

Missionaries and missionizing by practitioners of established religions contributed to further erosion of traditional ways of life among Indigenous groups. Religion became a way of reaching into social and cultural lives, not only through proselytizing but through associated actions. Among the Ainu, traditional religious practices were outlawed; in the United States, it became a federal crime for American Indians to practice their religions; in Australia and New Zealand, established Western religions were given inroads into Native areas through governmental actions.

Government-Wide Policies of Assimilation

Governmental policies aimed at creating "contributing members of the dominant society" generally relied on removing cultural characteristics that differentiated Indigenous people from others. In the United States and Canada, policies relating to American Indians and First Nations were aimed at turning the Indians into productive citizens as defined by the dominant government, not the Indian people themselves. Similarly, in New Zealand, the Māori were subjected to assimilation from the outset, with urbanization and limited self-governance becoming programmatic approaches in the latter decades of the twentieth century.

Systematic Racial Discrimination

The Indigenous peoples of these countries all have experienced systemic racial discrimination as a result of their cultural backgrounds. In Japan, Mai Ishihara (2019) talks about the fear of being publicly identified as Ainu in her mother's generation; in the United States, American Indians were often subjected to racist taunts and discriminatory acts until the civil rights movements of the 1960s. National and international organizations continue to examine the impacts of racial discrimination on Indigenous groups.

Concluding Remarks

As outlined in this chapter, colonial powers, including others not specifically discussed, generally used some or all of these six approaches to dispossess the people who inhabited the lands that came under colonial control. Programmatic approaches to dispossession and integration of the Indigenous into the nation have followed similar trajectories, with similarities and differences of the results depending on the country (see tables 4–8). Contemporary Indigenous groups have benefited from immediate access to information and global communication networks to take advantage of experiences of various international Indigenous groups with their home governments. It seems likely that local Indigenous developments will come to follow similar trajectories as this international communication network expands.

More recently, Indigenous groups have been able to move beyond the colonialist policies and more toward concepts of self-governance, at least in terms of their own internal practices. In the United States, American Indian groups have strengthened their self-governance and have become politically strong within their states. Even though these groups exist within (and somewhat with the permission of) their country's governments, they are continuing to expand their independence and self-governing capabilities.

Further Reading

A good but a little dated summary of colonialist policies in relation to Indigenous populations in the United States, Canada, Australia, and New Zealand in relation to Indigenous well-being can be found in Martin Cooke et al.'s 2007 article "Indigenous Well-Being in Four Countries: An Application of the UNDP'S Human Development Index to Indigenous Peoples in Australia, Canada, New Zealand, and the United States." More specific information on Australia can be found in Anita Heiss's article "Government Policy in Relation to Aboriginal People" (n.d.). A systematic review of attitudes toward Aboriginal and Torres Strait Islanders in Australia is available in a 2022 article by Thomas Falls and Joel Anderson, "Attitudes Towards Aboriginal and Torres Strait Islander Peoples in Australia: A Systematic Review." Other sources provide focused comparisons of various aspects of government affairs, including education (Wade Cole's 2011 book *Uncommon Schools: The Global Rise of Postsecondary Institutions for Indigenous Peoples*), health (Lisa Jackson Pulver et al.'s 2010 article "Indigenous Health—Australia, Canada, Aotearoa New Zealand, and the United States—Laying Claim to a Future That Embraces Health for Us All"), health care (Katrina Alford's 2005 article "Comparing Australian with Canadian and New Zealand Primary Care Health Systems in Relation to Indigenous Populations: Literature Review and Analysis" and Nang Thet Hsu Hnin and Nang Khin Mya's 2021 article "Comparison of the International Health Care Systems Through the Consideration of Population Health and Performance Indicators in Canada, Australia and New Zealand: A Systematic Literature Review"), policing (John Kiedrowski's 2013 volume *Trends in Indigenous Policing Models: An International Comparison*), and poverty (Stephen Cornell's 2005 article "Indigenous Peoples, Poverty and Self-Determination in Australia, New Zealand, Canada and the United States").

A more detailed account of Métis history and relationships with Canadian governments can be found in Gerhard J. Ens and Joe Sawchuck's 2016 volume *From New Peoples to New Nations: Aspects of Métis History and Identity from the Eighteenth to the Twenty-First Centuries.* Mark Derby's 2012 *Encyclopedia of New Zealand* article "Ngā Take Māori— Government Policy and Māori" is quite useful as well. Additionally, the general reader interested in Australia might like Henry Reynolds's 1999 book *Why Weren't We Told? A Personal Search for the Truth Behind Our History.*

CHAPTER 7
· · · · · · · · ·
Organizing and "Becoming" Indigenous

As the previous chapter has shown, Western governments enacted policies that were intended to assimilate the Indigenous groups within their borders as a means of gaining land and engulfing the people who once lived (and relied) on that land. In spite of the policies created by those governments, however, the Indigenous groups have survived. The Ainu population of Japan has also survived policies imposed by the government in its attempt to erase them.

With the annexation and colonization of Hokkaido in 1869, the Meiji government fully initiated policies to nominally integrate the Ainu into Japanese society. Their idea was that, even though the Ainu were "Former Aborigines" and former Natives, they would benefit from the civilizing forces of Japanese culture, laws, education, and economies.

The nineteenth century saw Japan surging onto the global stage as an industrial power, yet the Ainu were still considered barbarians. Mimicking U.S. policies toward its Natives seemed the quickest way for the Japanese government to convert the Ainu populations from a "problem" into contributing members of Japanese society, and the first step necessary was to remove them from standing in the way of the march of progress.

In this chapter, I discuss some of the governmental policies that not only influenced who the Ainu became during the early years within the Japanese system but also influenced who the contemporary Ainu *are* in this century. This review is selective and does not cover all aspects of Japanese impacts on the Ainu, but these are what I believe have impacted contemporary Ainu the most. In addition, during my year in Hokkaido, many of these points arose in discussions with Ainu people and in meetings with Ainu individuals in Chitose, Teshikaga, and other communities.

The Ainu and the Former Aborigines Protection Act

As described in chapter 5, the passage of the Former Aborigines Protection Act in 1899 "enshrined official policy" (Siddle 2003, 452) toward the Ainu populations of Japan. It attempted to erase the Ainu as a recognizable group by turning them into members of the Japanese peasant class through land allotment and welfare programs. As the Japanese government modeled its policy for land distribution on the United States' Dawes Severalty Act of 1887, the Ainu suffered much the same fate as the American Indians. The privatization of the previously communally held American Indian land broke up the tribal reservations, and the government was able to install its newer "tax paying" citizens onto those lands.

The Former Aborigines Protection Act granted land to Ainu households and, much like the U.S. government policies it was emulating, the Japanese government felt that turning the former hunting and gathering cultures of the Ainu into farmers would instill in them an appreciation of private property. However, as noted by Kohei Hanazaki (2001, 120), the act "only provided land to Ainu engaged in agriculture. Those involved in other pursuits such as fishing received no assistance."

The schools constructed for the Ainu were instruments of assimilation rather than of education. Surprisingly, though assimilation was the goal, the segregation of Ainu students from the Wajin children continued to enforce the fact that they were different. Ainu children learned that they would have to give up the things that made them "Ainu" if they wanted to succeed in the Japanese culture. And, as Siddle observes (1996, 126), it wasn't until 1922 that Ainu children received "more or less the same education as their Wajin counterparts," even if in separate institutions. Not surprisingly, the paucity of Ainu examples and the invisibility of Ainu even in contemporary textbooks continues to enforce this idea, even if indirectly.

After the passage of the Former Aborigines Protection Act, Hokkaido was no longer terra nullius but had been partitioned and surveyed and the majority of the lands the Ainu had hunted on and cared for disposed of. The Former Aborigines Protection Act of 1899 remained in effect in one form or another until 1997, when it was abolished with the passage of the Ainu Culture Promotion Act.

Ainu Association of Hokkaido—The Early Years

In 1930, after an ill-fated attempt by Ainu people and their supporters, including John Batchelor, to find a way to revise the Former Aborigines Protection Act, 130 leading Ainu representatives from all over Hokkaido attended a convention in Sapporo to discuss revisions of the Protection Act. One agenda item called for a vote on the establishment of an organization to represent all Ainu in Hokkaido. Amid applause, the motion was carried unanimously and the Hokkai Ainu Kyokai (soon to become the Ainu Association of Hokkaido) was born (Siddle 1996, 134).[1]

The Ainu Association of Hokkaido was established as a "government organization intended to help the Ainu successfully assimilate into Japanese society through a variety of social measures" (Loy 2010, 90). In spite of its assimilationist goals, the organization established a network through which Ainu from all over Hokkaido could meet and discuss the shared experience of being Ainu. Much like American perceptions of "Indians" in the United States, the Japanese generally considered the Ainu a single people. However, despite obvious differences in geographic location, language, and customs, it is uncertain whether the Ainu had ever considered themselves as having such an explicitly shared identity, even if there might have been some aspects of regional identity on occasion. It wasn't until the founding of the Ainu Association that Ainu people began

---

1. Historian Richard Siddle and anthropologist Christopher Loy consistently use "Hokkaido Ainu Association," whereas Teruki Tsunemoto, president of the Foundation for Ainu Culture, professor emeritus of law at Hokkaido University, and a member of the Council for Ainu Policy Promotion, prefers "Ainu Association of Hokkaido." I will primarily use the latter but will use the former when citing the work of others who prefer it.

to consider the idea of uniting for common purposes. The Ainu Association became important for laying the "groundwork for a trans-local identity that would later provide grist for the indigenous rights movement in the later half of the twentieth century" (Loy 2010, 91).

In 1937, the Ainu Association of Hokkaido met its goal of revising the Former Aborigines Protection Act. A draft revision of the Protection Act was submitted for consideration to the Diet in 1936 and accepted by the Diet in the following year. Under the 1937 revisions of the act, the Native schools were abolished and restrictions on land ownership were eased so that it was possible to sell allotments with the permission of the governor. Welfare measures such as benefits for the poor to cover the cost of medicine and tuition fees continued, but other programs were extended to those engaged in occupations outside of agriculture. Funds were made available for housing reconstruction. Richard Siddle (1996, 144) writes that "the original objective of the Protection Act, the Japanisation of the Ainu, was seen as having been largely accomplished, and the revised Act now took on the nature of a straightforward welfare act."

The Ainu Association persevered until disbanding in 1944, before reincorporating and establishing a new constitution in 1946 following a meeting of about two hundred Ainu men and women at Shizunai on February 24, 1946 (Siddle 1996, 148). Prior to this reincorporation, following the end of World War II, the Ainu were purportedly offered an opportunity for their own "republic." In 1945, Major General Josef Swing, the officer in charge of SCAP in Sapporo, purportedly asked if the Ainu desired independence from Japan, but the Ainu leaders were said to have responded that the Ainu only desired to be good Japanese citizens (Loy 2010, 117; Siddle 1996, 148).

Following its reincorporation, the association had a flurry of activity in 1946–47 on proposed changes to land tenure policies (see Siddle 1996, 148–151). Ultimately, the Land Reform Ordinance of 1948 appropriated a full one-third of the arable land held by Ainu in Hokkaido, resulting in the loss of 34 percent of total arable Ainu lands (Loy 2010, 117).

There were few records of the organization other than the publication of *Kita no Hikari* (Light of the North) in October 1948 and the construction of a sanitorium at Noboribetsu Hot Springs in 1948 (Siddle 1996, 151). With the exception of these two actions, the newly reincorporated

Ainu Association fell into disarray and limped along with a mere 180 members between 1948 and 1960 (Loy 2010, 117).

The Hokkaido Ainu Kyokai officially changed its name to the Hokkaido Utari Kyokai in 1961, based on the widespread dislike among Ainu people that the term "Ainu" was used as a pejorative term by the Wajin (Siddle 1996, 159). The importance of social gatherings during the early parts of activism that developed during the 1960s helped the Ainu develop more integrated information resources. As Christopher Loy (2010, 125) writes, "the establishment of community centers across Hokkaido in the 1960s provided places where Ainu would meet in large groups and practice traditional craft, ritual, and language in spaces outside of the dictates of a tourist economy." As more Ainu individuals gathered together, Ainu culture witnessed a rebirth. At the same time, social unrest and calls for racial equality in the United States led to a more global awareness of the issues minority groups faced, leading to increased Ainu involvement with political and cultural movements on a global scale.

The aims of the association remained the raising of living standards and the elimination of prejudice but continued to be geared toward the eventual assimilation of the Ainu into mainstream society. In 1961, it helped the government in the implementation of a welfare program that resulted in improvements in sanitation and housing as well as in the construction of sixteen communal halls (Siddle 1996, 159–60). This drew the Utari Kyokai further into a corporate relationship with the authorities. In effect, the association functioned as an arm of the government, from which it received both financial and personnel assistance.

However, as Loy (2010, 121) notes, by the 1970s assimilation was no longer a desirable outcome for the Ainu, and the leaders of the Utari Kyokai began to reframe themselves as an Indigenous group seeking a degree of legal separation from the Japanese government and the majority ethnic Japanese. This new trajectory was largely influenced by the Utari Kyokai's involvement with international organizations that promoted Indigenous rights throughout the world such as the United Nations Educational, Scientific and Cultural Organization and the United Nations Commission on Human Rights.

In 1982, the Utari Kyokai presented a new strategy concerning the articulation of Ainu history: the Ainu version of the past in the face of sanitized official histories of Hokkaido and the adjoining islands. The General Assembly of the association adopted a proposal declaring that the Ainu, as the Indigenous people of the disputed Northern Territories, possessed Indigenous rights in the region and thus should be included in any discussions on its future (Siddle 1996, 182). Among other issues and actions at this time, the Utari Kyokai began assembling the "Ainu New Law" (Ainu Shinpo) to replace the 1899 Former Aborigines Protection Law and the Ainu welfare countermeasures that were set to expire. This is discussed later in this chapter.

Loy's research on the Utari Kyokai provides insights into not only the history of the organization but also its structure. He writes: "the overriding issue, since the repeal of the 1899 Hokkaido Aborigines Protection Act and the passage of the 1997 Act for the Promotion of Ainu Culture . . . has been securing for the Ainu rights of self-determination and some form of territorial sovereignty as framed by the emerging international discourse, increasingly promoted by the United Nations, regarding the rights of indigenous peoples" (Loy 2010, 135).

In 2009, the association reverted to its former name—the Hokkaido Ainu Kyokai (Ainu Association of Hokkaido). Over time, the Utari Kyokai has changed from an organization designed primarily to provide state-controlled welfare initiatives to the Ainu population of Hokkaido into an organization active in Indigenous peoples' rights and openly opposing the state on a variety of issues. As Loy (2010, 134) notes, "the organization has, with varying degrees of precision, been able to anticipate government reaction to their initiatives."

Even though the Ainu Association of Hokkaido has played an important role in the development of the Ainu as a political entity, some of the various policies it has supported have been problematic. For example, in the 1930s, the association sought to overcome discrimination and social problems by promoting assimilation into the broader Japanese society. In the 1960s and 1970s, while known as the Hokkaido Utari Kyokai, it reversed its course and eschewed assimilation and embraced cultural and linguistic revivalism (Loy 2010, 97).

More recently, Ainu community members have indicated mixed support for the association. The 2020 Report on Japan to the International Work Group for Indigenous Affairs (Uzawa and Gayman 2020, 269–70) calls attention to criticism of the Ainu Association of Hokkaido over what was perceived to be weak negotiations with the government over the new law. In addition, the association's support for what was perceived by some Ainu to be "the immoral transfer of Ainu ancestral remains to the memorial facility in Shiraoi" (Uzawa and Gayman 2020, 270) was strong enough to cause half of the Shizunai Ainu Community to form a new Ainu association. Additional criticism of the Ainu Association of Hokkaido grew out of the association's approval of the controversial set of ethical standards proposed by Japanese scholastic societies that would allow scientific research on Ainu ancestral remains buried before 1868.

It remains to be seen how the new Shizunai Ainu Association and other Ainu groups critical of the Ainu Association of Hokkaido will be treated by local municipalities under the funding structures of the new law. This indication of criticism and loss of support for the existing Ainu Association of Hokkaido will be important in the continued development of a unified Ainu future.

Becoming Indigenous

"Becoming indigenous," Loy (2010, 130) writes, "appears to be as much about positing a specific kind of legal, political, and cultural relationship to the state as it is about uncovering or perpetuating certain cultural practices over others." Still, Ainu involvement with other global Indigenous groups and access to interaction afforded by the United Nations and other global organizations helped the Ainu gather information and garner support for their movement.

In some ways, 1997 might be construed as the genesis for the Ainu as "the Indigenous people of Japan." Two events happened that impacted the relationships between the Japanese government and the Ainu; that these occurred within two months of each other indicates that the Japanese government and the Ainu were poised to move forward into another realm regarding interaction with each other.

On March 27, 1997, the Sapporo District Court, in its ruling on the Nibutani Dam case, reached two important findings. First, it determined that the Ainu fit its definition of an Indigenous people; second, it determined that the Japanese government's decision to construct Nibutani

Dam on the Saru River "exceeded the government's administrative discretion and was illegal" (Levin 2001, 464).

The second event was the passage by the Japanese Diet of the "Act for the Promotion of Ainu Culture and Dissemination of Knowledge Regarding Ainu Traditions, etc." on May 8, 1997. The law fully revoked the 1899 Hokkaido Former Aborigines Protection Act, which had been used as a mechanism for assimilation of the Ainu. The new law stated that it aimed "to realize the society in which the ethnic pride of the Ainu people is respected and to contribute to the development of diverse cultures" in Japan by implementing measures to promote Ainu culture, referring to the "Ainu traditions and culture from which the Ainu people find their ethnic pride" (Cheung 2003, 955).

Nibutani Dam

In the early 1980s, Tadashi Kaizawa and Shigeru Kayano, two landowners and prominent leaders of the Nibutani Ainu community, refused to acquiesce to the expropriation of land they owned for the large-scale construction of a river dam in the immediate vicinity of Nibutani, their ancestral village. Their refusal triggered a legal contest in the Japanese courts, the first in Japanese history to consider the relationship of Japan as a nation-state with an Indigenous people living in its territory.

From 1982 through 1984, representatives of the Hokkaido Development Bureau negotiated with landowners to be affected by the construction of the Nibutani dam. Mark Levin (2001, 452) notes, "the government refused to acquiesce to Kayano and Kaizawa's demands for compensation and ameliorative measures addressing the losses that would be suffered by the Nibutani's Ainu community because of the dam project." Therefore, in 1986, the Hokkaido Development Bureau applied to the Minister of Construction for a "Project Authorization" that became the statutory basis for the compulsory takings of the Kayano and Kaizawa properties. It wasn't until February 1989 that the actual expropriation of the two properties occurred. The Ainu filed a lawsuit in court challenging the government's right to take their land and to construct the project.

In spite of the nearly three years' delay, construction continued, even though the two Ainu landowners filed administrative appeals to the action. Construction continued as the appeal process was ongoing. Ultimately, the Ministry of Construction denied the appeal four years later, in April 1993. By this time, Tadashi Kaizawa had died, and in 1992 his place in the court case had been taken over by his eldest son, Koichi Kaizawa. In May 1993, Koichi Kaizawa and Kayano filed their lawsuit against the Hokkaido Expropriation Committee; the government of Japan joined the lawsuit on the side of the defense at a later date.

In December 1996, the court heard final arguments. It reached its decision four months later. Even though the dam had been constructed and numerous sites of cultural and religious importance to the Ainu had been inundated and/or destroyed, the court held that the expropriation of the land and the construction of the project had been illegal. Of importance to contemporary Ainu was the court's invocation of Article 13 of the Japanese Constitution, which "guarantees to the plaintiffs the right to enjoy the distinct ethnic culture of the Ainu people, which is the minority to which the plaintiffs belong" (quoted in Levin 2001, 463). Based on this interpretation, the court held that "the Ainu people fit its definition of an indigenous people" (464). Additionally, the court held that, under international covenants ratified by the Diet (specifically, the International Covenant on Civil & Political Rights ratified in 1979) and Article 98(2) of the Constitution, treaties have legal force and, therefore, the Ainu have rights as "indigenous minorities" (Browning 2019, 220). In addition, as Kaori Tahara (1999, 3) notes, "the effect of the District Court's decision in the Nibutani Dam case was to awaken Japanese society to the indigenousness of Ainu people."

The court case had definite positive impacts in future Ainu–Japanese government relationships; Georgina Stevens (2014, 218) notes that "success in the Nibutani case and the court's judicial activism in recognizing Ainu minority and Indigenous status inspired other activists to attempt to utilize domestic courts for similar purposes." Additionally, the government offered compensation that resulted in the creation of the Historical Museum of the Saru River and other facilities in the general area showcasing regional Ainu culture.

The Act for the Promotion of Ainu Culture

The passage of the "Act for the Promotion of Ainu Culture and Dissemination of Knowledge Regarding Ainu Traditions" by the Diet in 1997 revoked the Hokkaido Former Aborigines Protection Act of 1899 and reinforced the idea that Ainu culture was worthy of protection from being lost. "Ainu Culture" in this law, as Sidney Cheung notes (2003, 955), meant the Ainu language, music, dance, crafts, and other cultural properties that have been inherited by the Ainu people, and the other cultural properties developed from these. Even though the 1997 Ainu Culture Promotion Act carefully avoided recognizing the "indigenousness" of the Ainu, it, in conjunction with the Nibutani Dam decision, gave a form of tacit recognition to the Ainu as the Indigenous minority within Japanese territory, at least those Ainu who lived in Hokkaido.

The Special Committee of the Utari Kyokai had begun to study proposals for new legislation in 1979; in 1984, it delivered a draft proposal for a law that was intended to provide rights and guarantees to enable Ainu to gain guaranteed political participation (a special "Ainu" seat in local and national representative bodies). It was intended as well to provide economic benefits in the form of a "self-reliance fund" based on the principle of compensation for historical dispossession to be administered by Ainu themselves. It was also intended to enhance Ainu rights to cultural identity, in particular the use and revitalization of the Ainu language (Loy 2010, 131–32; Siddle 1996, 184; 2003, 455).

The 1997 law that passed, however, was different from the law proposed by the Special Committee of the Utari Kyokai. The final law did not include any special accommodations for political participation of the Ainu in local or national political situations, nor did it provide any form of financial compensation directly to Ainu individuals or to any Ainu organizations. Instead, as stated in "Article 1 (purpose)" of the law, it focused on "the education of the nation, referring to the situation of Ainu traditions and culture."

Even though the law itself was seen by some Ainu people as "too little, too late," with not enough concrete change, it did lead to extended opportunities for cultural preservation of language and cultural traditions. It resulted in an increase in financial support for various kinds of cultural activities as well as more support for conference, exhibition, and cultural exchanges with other Indigenous groups in other countries, providing increased recognition of the Ainu as "Indigenous" on an international stage. However, as Simon Cotterill (2011, 3) notes, shortcomings of the act were that it failed to address issues of political participation, land rights, and the Ainu's Indigeneity.

TABLE 9 FRPAC's five basic policies and relevant major activities in promoting Ainu culture

Policies	Major Activities
1. Promotion of comprehensive and practical research on the Ainu	Provide research subsidies and publication subsidies for outstanding projects
2. Promotion of the Ainu language	Training language instructors; language classes; radio courses; speech contests
3. Promotion of Ainu culture	Training storytellers to pass down oral Ainu literature; a manual for Ainu lifestyles and culture; dispatching advisers on Ainu cultural activities; contests and exhibition for Ainu traditional craftwork; Ainu cultural festival, cultural award, and international exchange
4. Dissemination of knowledge on Ainu traditions	Distributing textbooks for elementary and junior high school students; home page; seminars and lectures; establishing Ainu Culture Society and Ainu Culture Center
5. Revival of Ainu traditional lifestyle	Utilization of spaces; development of natural materials; experience of cultural exchange; fostering transmitters of Ainu culture

Source: Adapted from Cheung 2003, 956; Foundation for Ainu Culture n.d.

At the institutional level, the Foundation for Research and Promotion of Ainu Culture (FRPAC) was established in 1997, almost at the same time as the enactment of the Ainu Culture Promotion Act. FRPAC started with an endowment of JPY 100 million (JPY 90 million from the Hokkaido government and JPY 10 million from fifty-six municipalities in Hokkaido that include Ainu residents) allocated to support diverse activities. Cheung (2003, 956) presents four basic policies that FRPAC was operating under in promoting Ainu cultural traditions in Japan and the rest of the world. In 2018, the Foundation for Research and Promotion of Ainu Culture was renamed the Foundation for Ainu Culture (FAC); its website indicates there are five basic policies under which it operates (see table 9), having added "Revival of Ainu traditional lifestyle" as an additional policy goal.

The Japanese government used the Ainu Culture Promotion Act to serve as the guiding principle for the future development of governmental policy to help contemporary Ainu preserve their culture in the belief that this would contribute to the retention of the aspects of "Ainu-ness." However, Siddle (2003, 455–56) draws attention to the differing ways that the law was interpreted: either that it is "the government's strategy is to focus on 'culture' in order to de-politicize the Ainu problem and disconnect it from the international struggle for indigenous rights" or that the "formal acquisition of cultural rights is a first step to the full practice of the political, civil and social rights guaranteed under the 1946 constitution" (456).

The Ainu as Part of Global Indigenous Movements

The Ainu became involved in the global Indigenous movement in the 1970s and developed connections with other groups that contributed to their own internal concepts and organization. Social unrest outside Japan certainly contributed to the unrest within Japan, and student mobilization against such issues as the war in Vietnam and the continuing desire for the return of Okinawa from the American military also contributed to the stirrings of change desired by young Ainu. These incidents, as Siddle (1996, 166) notes, "contributed to the increasing politicisation of the communities as the issues that underlay continued Ainu marginalisation were brought to the surface."

Global activism on the Indigenous front by groups in North America, Australia, and New Zealand also contributed to the development of a growing idea of Ainu nationhood. In the United States, the idea of "pan-Indianism" espoused by urban Indians and other advocates for Native American rights contributed a ready-made blueprint for activists to follow. Visits by Ainu representatives to China, the United States, Canada, and Australia highlighted the similarities in struggles that the Indigenous groups faced. Siddle (1996,186) notes how the "consequence of international involvement in the worldwide indigenous peoples' movement is a heightened awareness of the concepts of indigenous rights and the celebration of indigenous culture."

Kohei Hanazaki (2001, 127) also recognizes the impact that the international global Indigenous rights movements has had on the Ainu, describing events such as the 1986 Hokkaido Utari Association request for an investigation of the Ainu ethnic question to the United Nations Human Rights Committee; the attendance by the director of the association at meetings of the Working Group on Indigenous Populations of the UN Human Rights subcommittee; the 1989 visit to Hokkaido by Indigenous representatives, mainly from the Asia-Pacific region; and the 1993 International Forum for Indigenous Peoples in Nibutani.

Thus, the activity of the Ainu in relation to the Japanese government was greatly influenced by the actions of other Indigenous groups in relation to their own governments. Through such efforts, Ainu have gained knowledge and techniques of the other groups to help them create their own agendas for working within existing structures.

Biratori Dam Project

Construction of the Nibutani Dam was completed long before the 1997 court decision was reached and the court decided that the destruction of the dam was not feasible. But the decision did have a local impact in the Saru River area beyond the immediate construction of the lake itself. Nibutani wasn't the last construction project on the Saru River.

In 2003, the Biratori area received its highest recorded amount of rainfall due to a typhoon. The resultant flooding exceeded the designated high-water levels in almost all rivers, including the reservoir impounded by Nibutani Dam. The local community requested flood countermeasures that could respond to the inundation, resulting in a change of the Saru River Comprehensive Development Project and Flood Control Plan to maximize flood control with river channel excavation and a new dam at the junction of the Nukabira and Shukushubetsu Rivers upstream from Nibutani.

Because of the Nibutani court decision and the passage of the 1997 Act on the Promotion of Ainu Culture, and Dissemination and Enlightenment of Knowledge about Ainu Tradition, and other developments, the Saru River System Improvement Plan (developed July 2002, revised March 2007) acknowledged the preservation, succession, and promotion of Ainu culture as essential measures in the area and directly involved the local Biratori Ainu Community in planning from the onset. To help with this, the Ainu Cultural Environment Conservation Investigation Committee was established specifically to be certain that consideration for Ainu culture was included and that the project took into consideration conservation measures related to the animals and plants necessary for

Ainu life, methods of practicing and retaining culture, and places for ritual etiquette.

In August 2006, the Biratori Dam Area Cultural Conservation Measures Study Group was established as a forum for examining the implementation of conservation measures. The group's discussions have been directed toward three conservation methods: (1) conservation by recording, (2) conservation by acting, and (3) conservation by creating areas within which such conservation measures might occur.

This program, which has gone on for nearly twenty years, has resulted in more involvement in the process by the local Ainu community as well as the development of a programmatic approach to recognizing and conserving (in one way or another) the aspects of Ainu culture that are impacted by the new reservoir. It has allowed the Ainu community to be involved from the beginning and to have its perspectives and ideas known and implemented throughout.

The initial process in the Biratori Dam project is described by Naohiro Nakamura (2008) in an examination of the cultural impact assessment that was undertaken. More recently, Hideki Yoshihara and Noriko Inoue (2018) offer insights into ways that Biratori used the Act on Protection of Cultural Properties as a mechanism to protect Ainu cultural landscapes in the Saru River valley.

Recently, historical and contemporary information on the project was derived from presentations given by various members of the project offices as part of two symposia. The first, the "Symposium to Discuss River Improvement and Ainu Culture in the Saru River Basin," was held in Biratori, Hokkaido, on October 1–2, 2022. The second was part of the Global Station for Indigenous Studies and Cultural Diversity (GSI) international symposium "Indigenous Heritage and Research Ethics," held at Hokkaido University on January 20–22, 2023. At this point in time, the majority of the reports are in Japanese. Perhaps there will be translations offered in the future.

Diet Resolution 2008

"Indigenous at last!" are the first three words of the title of an article by ann-elise lewallen (2008, 1) that describes the "Resolution calling for the Recognition of the Ainu People as an Indigenous People of Japan" ("the 2008 Resolution," passed on June 6, 2008). Other authors brought attention to the passage of the act and the hoped-for impacts it would have on the Ainu.

The 2008 Resolution was passed unanimously by both houses of the Japanese Diet and represented the attainment of a goal long sought by Ainu people across Japan (Iewallen 2008, 1). Yet, while the government's official acknowledgment of the Ainu as Indigenous might have been interpreted by outsiders as "progress," some still saw it as not enough, arguing that, among other things, it "failed to lay the foundations for proper antidiscrimination legislation" (Cotterill 2011, 3).

The passage of the 2008 Resolution seems based on Japan's ratification of the UN Declaration on the Rights of Indigenous Peoples in September 2007. As noted, the Sapporo District Court held that such international covenants entered into by Japan have legal force and should affect interpretations of internal laws and policies. After the passage of the 2008 Resolution, the chief cabinet secretary issued a statement, a portion of which said:

> Not only will the government further enhance the Ainu policies taken so far, but it will make efforts to establish comprehensive policy measures, in reference to relevant clauses of the UN Declaration on the Rights of Indigenous Peoples, with the recognition that the Ainu are an indigenous people who have lived around the northern part of the Japanese Archipelago, especially in Hokkaido, with a unique language as well as religious and cultural distinctiveness.[2]

However, it should be noted that, in international law, the prevailing view is that United Nations Declarations are not treaties and therefore have no legal effect in and of themselves.

In July 2008, the chief cabinet secretary called for the creation of a high-level expert council, the Advisory Council for Future Ainu Policy, to consider principles and measures for future Ainu policy in Japan. The Advisory Council contained a "representative of the Ainu people" and

---

2. Statement of the chief cabinet secretary, June 6, 2008, quoted from Ainu Policy Promotion Headquarters, "Overview of Ainu Policy in Japan," accessed November 29, 2024, https://www.kantei.go.jp/jp/singi/ainusuishin/index_e.html.

provided a history of the Ainu and their Indigenousness in its final report, issued in July 2009.

Based on the Report of the Advisory Council, the Council for Ainu Policy Promotion was set up in December 2009 under the auspices of the Office of the Chief Cabinet Secretary. The council was established to find ways to promote Ainu policy, taking into consideration the recommendations made by the Council for Ainu Policy Promotion, which had been appointed by the government to identify policy priorities in Japan with reference to the UN Declaration. The council was composed of fourteen members: five Ainu representatives, five scholars and experts on Ainu culture and human rights, and the remaining four from national and local governments. Other than the specific Ainu seats allotted to the Advisory Council, all were Wajin.

The Council for Ainu Policy Promotion continued trying to find ways to fund Ainu issues and crafted policies associated with the development of a Symbolic Space for Ethnic Harmony. In February 2019, the government submitted a draft bill in the National Diet that aimed to implement a more comprehensive package of measures to promote local Ainu communities, industries, and internal and international exchanges through tourism.

The draft bill recognized the Ainu as an Indigenous people for the first time in national legislation; it states its objective as "realizing a society that will respect the pride of the Ainu as an ethnic group." Notice that the bill was not focused on respecting the Ainu as an ethnic group but rather on respecting "the pride of the Ainu as an ethnic group." It is this type of subtle wording that has drawn more attention than the actual products of the government in relation to the 2008 Resolution. The 2008 Resolution spurred internal policy to action, and increased action on policies have had impact on the Ainu, especially the Ainu Policy Promotion Act of 2019.

The Ainu Measures Promotion Act / Ainu Policy Promotion Act

In April 2019, the Act Promoting Measures to Achieve a Society in which the Pride of Ainu People is Respected was enacted, and it came into effect the following month. According to Teruki Tsunemoto (personal communication, 2024), because there is no formal English name of the law,

"Ainu Policy Promotion Act (APPA)," "Ainu Measures Promotion Act (AMPA)," and "Ainu Policy Measures Promotion Act (APMPA)" all refer to the same law. Therefore, in the following discussion, I will use "the act" except where an author uses a specific version of the name of the law.

The act recognized the Ainu people as an Indigenous people who have lived around the northern part of the Japanese archipelago, especially in Hokkaido. It aimed to advance a wide range of measures and programs in a manner to increase regional, industrial, and tourism promotion, in addition to the welfare measures and cultural promotion program established by previous laws, resolutions, and policy measures.

In addition to the broader goals, the act also created new subsidies as a means of providing support for projects implemented by municipalities that aimed to increase awareness of Ainu issues and to actively benefit Ainu populations. One of its measures also called for the establishment of mechanisms whereby Ainu culture practitioners could harvest forest products from state-owned forests and salmon in freshwater surfaces in order to protect and promote their traditional culture. It also established the Ainu Policy Promotion Headquarters under the chief cabinet secretary to promote Ainu policies comprehensively and effectively.

Ainu representatives met the passage of the new law with mixed feelings (see Morris-Suzuki 2018; Uzawa 2019; Uzawa and Gayman 2020). Some again said the law was "too little, too late," and that it didn't offer any land reforms or governmental apologies for the programs of the past that attempted to erase the Ainu. Authors of a 2020 report to the International Work Group for Indigenous Affairs (IWGIA), an international human rights organization, state that some Ainu activist groups noted "an absence of Ainu self-determination as well as an understanding of the new law as constraining and founded in government-driven tourist incentives . . . rather than to further economic and political self-determination" (Uzawa and Gayman 2020, 269). Others note that it did not offer any governmental acknowledgment of Ainu "collective rights" as a "people" (minzoku) but rather as Ainu individuals who had the right to practice their culture. The act, as Tsunemoto (2023, n.p.) writes, "is noted as the first act to enshrine in law the recognition of the Ainu as an indigenous people, but contains nothing that provides the indigenousness of the Ainu people with any legal effect: There is no definition of the Ainu people or a guarantee of their rights as an indigenous people."

Additionally, Tsunemoto (2019a, 2019b, 2023) provides background and justification for the structure and reasoning behind the final law as well as some points of contention in it. He notes rightfully that the act does not guarantee specific rights to the Ainu. Instead, it calls upon the regional governmental jurisdictions to promote Ainu culture in the hopes that such promotion will lead to the socioeconomic improvement mostly in the region where the Ainu live. He recognizes that it is a characteristic of Japan that it is not possible to guarantee rights, such as the rights to self-determination and land, because Ainu individuals, who are the subjects of rights, cannot be identified easily as a result of historical processes and governmental assimilation measures.

At this point in time, the act is too recent to know whether it will be effective in helping the Ainu gain some level of self-sufficiency. The idea to provide support in the regions where the Ainu people live is only an indirect means of providing economic support to Ainu communities. Direct funding to Ainu communities for specific projects would help the communities and would remove a layer of bureaucracy, but, at present, the process of determining the eligibility of Ainu organizations for any sort of financial support is uncharted.

Still, a major question exists as to whether the Ainu community (either as an island-wide organization such as the Ainu Association of Hokkaido or as individual local associations) has the necessary organization and knowledge to receive large amounts of public money and to plan and implement various projects. For this reason, the act is structured so that, for the time being, local governments will plan and implement various projects in cooperation with the local Ainu.

Perhaps most useful to the ongoing discussion about the further development of the Ainu as an Indigenous people is offered by Tsunemoto (2019a, 67): "the possibility of identifying [individual] Ainu people in an objective sense is not possible. People of Ainu identity, however, do exist, and it is clear that Ainu culture has contributed significantly to the diversity and enrichment of Japanese culture as a whole." However, there are concerns that Tsunemoto's analysis does not go far enough.

Chuo University law professor Yuko Osakada (2021, 1054) offers a discussion of the Act in relation to the United Nations Declaration: "as criticised by some Ainu people and Ainu rights defenders, the Ainu Policy Promotion Act does not provide for any indigenous rights set forth in the UN Declaration." She also draws attention to the fact that numerous Japanese officials, including Tsunemoto, use wording within the declaration's preamble as justification for not taking the act further, arguing that the act was taking into consideration the "significance of national and regional particularities and various historical and cultural backgrounds" (Osakada 2021, 1061). She addresses the problem of identifying Ainu individuals as discussed by Tsunemoto and argues that such problems should not be used "as an excuse to justify a lack of preferential treatment to indigenous individuals in general" (Osakada 2021, 1061), even though she does not offer any alternatives to the issues Tsunemoto identifies.

The authors of the reports to the International Work Group for Indigenous Affairs on Japan in 2023 deemed the act "ineffective" based on the results of "a nationwide survey of Ainu conducted by a citizens' group" (Gayman, Uzawa, and Nakamura 2023, 218). The survey, as explained in footnotes of the report, "was distributed to 80 Ainu individuals representing over 60 organizations, and responded to by 38 Ainu individuals representing 23 Ainu organizations, including branches of the Ainu Association of Hokkaido" (Gayman, Uzawa, and Nakamura 2023, 223n15). Of the thirty-eight Ainu who responded, thirty were dissatisfied with the law's system for soliciting Ainu community opinion in the enactment of promotional initiatives and twenty-seven felt that the creation of the Upopoy National Museum and Park did not improve their Indigenous rights (Gayman, Uzawa, and Nakamura 2023, 223n16). The authors also note that Ainu were concerned with "the law's failure to protect Ainu Indigenous rights, such as salmon harvesting, with its failure to address fundamental Ainu welfare issues, and with its failure to properly account for diversity within the Ainu community," without stating whether these concerns were mentioned in the survey (Gayman, Uzawa, and Nakamura 2023, 218).

In 2024, calling attention to the scheduled 2023 review of the act, the authors of the report (Gayman et al. 2024, 227) note the efforts of "Ainu individuals, in collaboration with civil society organizations," to collect signatures on a petition to offer input regarding the content of the act:

> the petition . . . calls for a thorough review of the law in terms, inter alia, of "Indigenous attributes" as Indigenous Peoples as stipulated by the UN Declaration on the Rights of Indigenous Peoples (UNDRIP), Ainu rights

to land, fishing and hunting, Indigenous education, freedom from discrimination, rights to repatriation of ancestral remains, and the right to participation in the administration of the law. (Gayman et al. 2024, 227)

As with most recent laws, the Ainu Policy Promotion Act included a clause that it would be reviewed after five years. The government has been holding hearings in Ainu communities in Hokkaido and Tokyo since 2024 to receive input regarding the act. According to Tsunemoto (personal communication, March 2025), two common requests have emerged from these discussions: new, effective measures against hate speech; and special support for elderly Ainu. It remains to be seen whether these goals are attainable.

Concluding Remarks

This chapter has explored some of the actions and events that have shaped contemporary Ainu organizations and culture in Japan over the past century as well as more recent laws and policies within basically the past decade. I have not discussed every action or court finding that might have impacted the formation of the Ainu as an Indigenous population but have highlighted those I consider to be major influences on the directions that Ainu formation and actions have taken.

The Ainu Policy Promotion Act has been seen by the Ainu as lacking. It does not deal with land rights or economic equality issues but rather focuses only on what may be identified as "cultural." The state decides which projects count as "culturally" worthwhile, which continues to marginalize Ainu communities where the relations between the Ainu and the local jurisdiction are problematic.

As I will discuss in more detail in chapter 9, the Raporo Ainu Nation court case might have repercussions on the future of the Ainu. While the Raporo Ainu Nation Lawsuit for Declaratory Judgement on Salmon Fishing Rights was denied by the Sapporo District Court in April 2024, an attorney for the Raporo Ainu Nation, Morihiro Ichikawa, has indicated that they intend to appeal. It is their hope that they can demonstrate that since there has never been a treaty or other international instrument between the Japanese state and any Ainu kotan, Ainu sovereignty has never been extinguished and continues to exist.

Further Reading

Much of the information presented here resides in specific journals. However, information on the passage of Japanese actions related to the Ainu can be found online with a search with keywords "Ainu," "Indigenous," and a specific topic of interest. Christopher D. Loy offers a wonderful and in-depth description of the history of the Hokkaido Ainu Association in his 2010 study "The Ainu of Northern Japan: Indigeneity, Post-national Politics, Territoriality." Readers interested in more information on the Nibutani Dam should consult Mark A. Levin's 2001 article "Essential Commodities and Racial Justice: Using Constitutional Protection of Japan's Indigenous Ainu People to Inform Understandings of the United States and Japan," in the journal *International Law and Politics*. Teruki Tsunemoto's 2019 and 2023 articles on the Ainu Measures Promotion Act / Ainu Policy Promotion Act (APPA) should be consulted by those more interested in the impacts the APPA might have on Ainu people.

CHAPTER 8
· · · · · · · · ·
Nationalizing the Past and Homogenizing the Present

The archaeological and historical past of Japan is complex because of the way contemporary Japanese societies have tended to view the Japanese "mainland" (HSK islands) as separate and distinct from the archaeology and history of Hokkaido. Chapter 2 discussed the genetic foundation of the archaeological and contemporary Japanese populations, chapters 3 and 4 provided the archaeological background of Japan and described the reasons for the different trajectory of archaeological cultures on Hokkaido, and chapter 5 reinforced the idea that the Ainu have no history of their own outside of Japanese history. This chapter will briefly offer insights into ways that "the past" continues to have impact in the present and the future.

Nationalizing "the Past"

More than a decade after the Japanese government formally recognized the Ainu as "the Indigenous people of Japan," it passed the Act Promoting Measures to Achieve a Society in which the Pride of Ainu People is Respected (2019). This law further recognized the Ainu as an Indigenous people who have lived across the northern part of the Japanese archipelago, especially in Hokkaido.

This is troubling to many who continue to believe in the Japanese concept that there is a particular way of "being Japanese," known as Nihonjinron (see Habu and Fawcett 1999)—the idea that Japan was (and still is) a homogenous culture with a common origin. As Yoshio Sugimoto (1999, 82) explains:

> *Nihonjinron* defines the Japanese in racial terms with *nihonjin* comprising most members of the Yamato race and excludes, for example, indigenous Ainus and Okinawans as groups who are administratively Japanese, but not "genuinely" so. Furthermore, when Nihonjinron analysts refer to Japanese culture, they almost invariably mean Japanese ethnic culture and imply that the racially defined Japanese are its sole owners.

Junko Habu and Clare Fawcett (1999, 502) apply this concept to the manner in which archaeological sites in Japan have been used to promote the idea of a national history, concluding that

> use of Jomon sites such as Sannai Maruyama as models of Japanese ethnicity . . . may have to do with their role in the reification of the traditional ideology of Japanese linguistic, cultural and biological homogeneity by pushing the origins of Japanese *seishin* (spirit or essence) further into the prehistoric past. This is a conservative and reactionary position that upholds the political and social status quo of modern Japan.

As discussed in chapter 1, the use of archaeology for nationalistic endeavors is not new. The movement to recast the Jomon as "Japan's past" is an active attempt by the Japanese government to rewrite and rescribe the archaeological deep-time history of the Japanese archipelago. The inscription of "Jomon Prehistoric Sites in Northern Japan" onto the UNESCO World Cultural Heritage List on July 27, 2021, was celebrated by the issuance of postage stamps by the Japanese government (see figure 15). The UNESCO action has resulted in the reintroduction of this concept into Japanese thought as a point of national pride (and local tourism marketing) with the underlying idea that "We are all Jomon . . . unless some of us are Ainu."

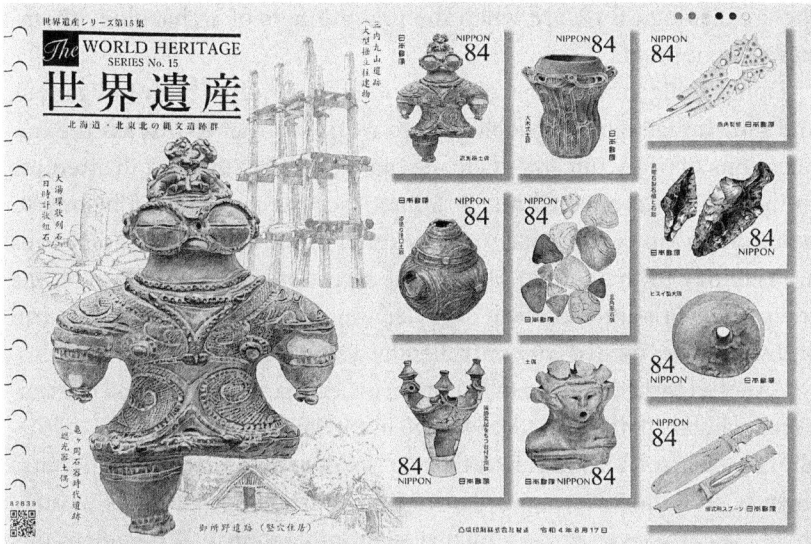

FIGURE 15 Postage stamps issued by the Japanese government celebrating the 2021 UNESCO World Heritage Convention Designation of Jomon Prehistoric Sites in Northern Japan.

Archaeology and the Ainu

As indicated in chapter 4, there is a rather strong correlation between the archaeological cultures of the Okhotsk, Satsumon, and Tobinitai and the development of the Ainu cultures of Hokkaido (and, to an extent, the Tsugaru Strait area of Honshu).

Indigenous archaeology, as George Nicholas (2008, 1660) writes, is "an expression of archaeological theory and practice in which the discipline intersects with indigenous values, knowledge, practices, ethics, and sensibilities, and through collaborative and community-originated or -directed projects and related critical perspectives." More recently, Nicholas and Lindsay M. Montgomery (2024) offer additional examples of ways that Indigenous archaeology has developed on a global scale.

One must ask, of what use is archaeology to the Ainu—an archaeology that ignores Ainu ideas about place, culture, and values? How are the Ainu expected to embrace ideas of archaeological heritage if contemporary cultures continue to lay claim to the deep historic time inherent in the archaeological record when the practitioners of archaeology themselves do nothing?

Doing Indigenous archaeology concretely requires both Indigenous and non-Indigenous archaeologists to work together to discuss the implications of pronouncements made that generalize the past in attempts to include "everyone" within it. Sometimes the past should belong to one group who can choose to allow others in if they wish. Indigenous archaeology in the United States is at a crossroads to an extent, some Indigenous practitioners feel, over deciding to what extent the past can and should be "owned" or controlled by a single group.

As noted earlier, the idea of Nihonjinron led many Japanese and international scholars to think that those who live in Japan are racially and culturally homogeneous. Their view is this: racism does not exist in Japan because there is no minority group in Japan. But, as Ishihara (2019) has written, there is racism, even if it is aimed at silent protagonists. Where does this homogeneity derive? Perhaps to some extent, "the Jomon" has been used to create an artificial base upon which to build the "Japanese persona."

"The Jomon," as Yoshida and Ertl (2016, 50) write, "is typically regarded as a hunter-gatherer culture that existed approximately from 16,000 B.P. to 3,000/2,500 B.P." Although there are six stages (Incipient, Initial, Early, Middle, Late, and Final) that span the emergence of pottery to the introduction of rice paddy agriculture, the idea that Jomon is a homogenous culture is believed by non-archaeologists. Some of the characteristics of the Jomon period include large-scale settlements, organized subsistence strategies such as storage pits and shell middens, ornamental clay figurines (dogū) and ritual objects, long-distance trade, and construction of large ceremonial features such as buildings and mound features (Habu 2008). However, as Habu (2008, 572) has suggested, because these characteristics are not uniform either temporally or geographically, "the Jomon should not be seen as a single entity characterized by a fixed set of cultural traits" the way that most/many archaeologists continue to imagine.

And yet "Jomon" so easily fills the bill as the foundation for a homogenous prehistory that meets the needs of those who still wish to push an idea of Nihonjinron into the twenty-first century. Why is this important, and how does it impact the Ainu?

Archaeologically, the Ainu have a different set of roots than the mainland Japanese. While the general Japanese population might embrace

"Jomon" as evidence of a fully shared past, the Ainu can make use of Hokkaido's archaeology to emphasize the actual differences that exist within the Japanese archaeological history as a way of reinforcing the idea that Hokkaido is Ainu Mosir, the Ainu world, that was subjected to colonization on a scale similar to other parts of the world.

The introduction of wet-rice agriculture from the Asian continent through what is now called the Korean peninsula forever changed the lifestyles and lives of those who lived in the islands of Kyushu, Shikoku, and Honshu. That culture—known archaeologically as the Yayoi—created a major disruption in the Jomon trajectory in the "mainland." But in Hokkaido and northeastern Honshu, the Jomon continued relatively unchanged, even with an overlay of rice agriculture in some areas.

And while the mainland more fully engaged in the Yayoi culture and its associated ceremonies and social complexities, on Hokkaido, the foundational population of the group of people who came to be historically known as the Ainu continued to live a Jomon lifestyle known (archaeologically) as "the Epi-Jomon." Even though they lived relatively isolated from the mainland cultures, they were indeed impacted by the changing mainland cultures. They traded with the Yayoi and interacted with cultures on the mainland as well. Metal made its way into the "proto-Ainu" cultures, and the existence of other economies and people were indeed known.

In northern and western Hokkaido, the Okhotsk archaeological culture (from about A.D. 500 to 1100) existed along the Sea of Okhotsk and Sea of Japan coastlines. This origin of this maritime-centered culture is complicated, being derived from Sakhalin and Epi-Jomon cultures and later groups from the East Asian lowlands of the Amur River basin and Sakhalin Island. This culture existed for about two hundred years or so before the onset of the Satsumon archaeological culture in southwestern Hokkaido and northern Honshu Island (ca. A.D. 700–1300). There is evidence that the Satsumon archaeological culture was derived from a postcontact group in southern Hokkaido that had trade networks with the Honshu-Shikoku-Kyushu islands (Siddle 1996, 26; B. Walker 2001, 22). Satsumon culture bearers eventually moved northwestward and subsumed Okhotsk. Some researchers, such as Richard Zgusta, believe that the Tobinitai culture of northern and eastern Hokkaido is a hybrid derived from this mixture of the Okhotsk and Satsumon cultures.

Even the genetics of the Ainu indicate that they are not the same as the Yayoi-derived Wajin of the HSK islands. The groups of people living on Hokkaido who eventually became known as the "Ainu" are economically, archaeologically, and genetically different from those people who imported/adopted wet-rice agriculture on the HSK islands. Noboru Adachi and colleagues (Adachi, Kakuda, et al. 2018, 143) note that "the genetic characteristics of the Ainu are based on the Hokkaido Jomon people and the subsequent input of Lower Amur region Siberian genes through the Okhotsk culture people" as well as "the presence of populations other than the Hokkaido Jomon and the Okhotsk culture people that contributed to the formation of the Ainu." They believe that mainland Japanese and native Siberians are the major candidates for the origin of these "other populations" that contributed to the genetic history of the Ainu because of their proximity to Hokkaido.

The contemporary argument that all Japanese derive from Jomon populations is true, so far as it goes. There is a shared genetic input from the Jomon populations that inhabited the archipelago from Upper Paleolithic times. It is during the influx of people with wet-rice agriculture (and associated rituals) about 2,300 B.P. that the separation becomes more acute. There were always regional differences among the Jomon, and the Jomon cultures of Hokkaido developed on a different trajectory than the local cultures on Honshu-Shikoku-Kyushu islands. The local differences, diverse histories, and complexities of identity have all combined to create the tapestry of Ainu history.

On Hokkaido, the local populations were able to maintain their existing economies and continued to rely heavily on hunting and gathering, supplemented by trade. Without the labor-intensive requirements of wet-rice agriculture, societies continued to practice seasonal rounds— they did not desire to develop cultural complexity because they did not need to control their social groups to have economic success. Intermittent trade allowed the Hokkaido groups to supplement their own economies with the items that technological advances in other groups had accomplished without the need to develop their own cultural complexity and social stratification.

After the Yayoi had fully integrated rice and its associated social structures into its culture, the difference between the Honshu-Shikoku-Kyushu and Hokkaido cultures grew more marked. The social complexities that developed out of the Yayoi created an "us" (i.e., mainland people) versus "them" (north Honshu and Hokkaido people) situation that developed more fully over time. The depiction of the Emishi of northern Honshu illustrated what might be seen as a transition zone between those who were "inside" the Japanese state and those who were "outsiders."

The hunting and gathering cultures in the north continued to exist with an increasing amount of "historic" overlay. These protohistoric cultures—the Okhotsk to the north, the Satsumon to the south, and the later Tobinitai to the north and east—were fully functional and self-aware groups. Genetically we can see that there was more isolation from the broader cultural expansions of the Jomon, with expanding ideas of "territory" over time. Eventually, the historical imprint of writing about "us" and the "others" strengthened artificial dichotomies that served to keep the power and wealth localized.

As noted in discussions of the origins of the bear-sending ceremony in chapter 4, Ainu populations continue to have relationships with the archaeological sites of the regions' previous inhabitants. The use of the pit-house depressions for bear-sending ceremonies (Takao Sato 2005; Takao Sato, Matsubayashi, and Yoneda 2022) indicates the continuing connection of contemporary Ainu populations with those from earlier times. Twenty years ago, Takao Sato (2005, 74) reported that there were more than fifteen sites known where Ainu people had used the depressions of the pit houses as locations for sending ceremonies.

Beginning with this premise that the Ainu continue to have relationships with archaeological sites, and hoping to publicize and reinforce those connections, Hirofumi Kato of Hokkaido University's Center for Ainu and Indigenous Studies invited the participation of Ainu cultural practitioners to his archaeological field schools beginning in 2008. In September of that year, Kato invited Ainu culture practitioner Koji Yuki to conduct a ceremony at a *chashi* site near the town of Utoro, on the Shiretoko peninsula.[1]

Yuki prepared *inaw* (straight tree branches shaved with a knife to create long wood curls) for the occasion, and he and a colleague offered

1. A *chashi* is a fortified site usually on an end of a peninsula of land with a fortification trench separating the site from the reminder of the peninsula.

FIGURE 16 *Inaw* carved by Koji Yuki and used in a ceremony at the beginning of
a field session at Utoro, Hokkaido, Japan, September 2008.

prayers and sake to the *kamuy* (spirits of deities) of the area in hopes
of good fortune for the excavations and the field crew (see figure 16).
This was one of the first purposeful involvements of contemporary Ainu
people with archaeological enterprises. The archaeology field school students, Kato, and my wife and I watched and participated as the ritual
place was created; the inaw blessed it with sake dripped onto it with the
ikupasuy (elaborately carved wands used by Ainu men to offer sake to
the gods—also known as "libation sticks") and then sipped some of the
sake from lacquerware cups.

The following year, the field school students returned to the Utoro site for more excavations. On September 21, 2009, as one part of the field school, the first Public Archaeology Day in Japan took place. Local people were invited to the site, where they viewed the excavations, took part in activities, and listened to students present the archaeological findings in relation to the local area. Many of the participants were children, but one individual, a teacher, talked about the lack of information about the Ainu in national history books.

Following the field session at Utoro, excavations moved to an archaeological pit-house village in Shari, a fishing village along the coast of the Okhotsk Sea, about twenty-four miles (39 kilometers) west of Utoro. During those excavations, more numerous situations occurred where bear skulls appeared to have been ritually placed within pit-house depressions. In addition, remnants of willow wands likely associated with Ainu inaw were found (see figure 17).

FIGURE 17 Kato photographs bear skull bones at the Ikushina-Kita Kaigan Site, Shari, September 2009. Note remnants of *inaw* (pointed ends of sticks) near the tree to the left.

FIGURE 18 Koji Yuki and colleagues preparing for a ceremony at the Ikushina-Kita Kaigan Site, Shari, September 2009.

Kato invited Ainu cultural practitioner Koji Yuki to the site. He and three other Ainu culture practitioners conducted a ceremony over one of the bear skulls before it was excavated (see figure 18). This continued the Ainu association with the site and the rituals of the bear skulls.

My wife and/or I have participated in archaeological excavations with the Hokkaido University field school almost yearly from 2008 until 2023, with a lag between 2013 and 2016. The Ainu have been involved in one form or another at most of the excavations run by Kato. His field school excavations on Rebun Island, begun in 2014, operate with an agreement in place relating to the field school's relationship with the Ainu, although there is no formal Ainu organization in place on the island; Kato was not the first to excavate at the site, but he is the first to invite the Ainu to participate there.

Kato (2009, 49) continues to work toward being more inclusive of Ainu people and Ainu sensibilities in his archaeological and cultural practices, as he recognizes that "although the Ainu people have lived as the original inhabitants of Hokkaido Island and have most of their archaeological and historical heritage, the Indigenous viewpoint is not sufficiently reflected in the museum exhibition and the historical interpretation on archeological collection." He rightly draws attention to the fact that Ainu involvement in the development of their deep-time histories is negligible; he has also created a more simplistic chronology of Hokkaido and Honshu as an aid in discussion for Ainu and scientific communities.

Kato has also written about the attempts by archaeologists and anthropologists to identify the "emergence" of Ainu culture. He notes (Kato 2018, 5) that such emergence is identified in archaeological deposit contexts as an archaeological culture based on material culture at around the thirteenth century. In general, the material that is generally associated with "Ainu" (as opposed to Satsumon cultures) is defined on the replacement of pottery by lacquerware and by the appearance of the bear ceremony (Iyomante).

Kato (2018, 5) discusses the cultural integration of the Satsumon culture bearers from the south with the Okhotsk culture bearers of northern Hokkaido that resulted in the creation of "the historical Ainu culture." Moving beyond the "formation" and into the periods of societal practice, Kato (2018, 9) writes that "the cultural shift from Satsumon culture to the archaeological 'Ainu culture' occurred within the same ethnic group, and it is a tautology to discuss the 'formation of Ainu culture' only by the appearance of materials related to the 'Ainu culture' after the eighteenth century" by mainland Japanese scientists.

Archaeologist Mark Hudson (2014b) also addresses this issue. On the ethnohistory and anthropology of the Ainu, he explains:

> There are two opposing approaches to this periodization and the problem of Ainu ethnogenesis. One argues that since a recognizably Ainu ethnicity did not develop until around AD 1200, it is technically incorrect to refer to Ainu culture before that date. . . . Supporters of this view do not deny the basic population continuities that gave rise to Ainu culture, but see the latter as something qualitatively different from what went before. (Hudson 2014b, 1056)

Archaeologist Harou Ohyi (2011, 90) agrees with this viewpoint: "because 'Ainu people' or 'Ainu culture' did not exist as such originally," it is improper to assign or ascribe archaeological sites to contemporary Ainu.

The second approach, Hudson (2014b, 1056) writes, "classifies the 'Ainu culture period' as simply one phase in the long history of the Ainu people in Hokkaido and neighbouring regions." Kato (2018, 9) argues that the phrase "Ainu culture period" is inappropriate since "there is no evidence of displacement by the pre-stage 'Satsumon culture' by the archaeological 'Ainu culture.'" "These two approaches," Hudson (2014b, 1056) notes, "clearly involve politically sensitive issues about Ainu indigeneity."

Hosanna Fukuzawa (2022, n.p.) writes that the "prevailing academic consensus is that Ainu ethnogenesis is understood as the mix of the Satsumon and the Okhotsk cultures up to the 12th century" and notes that Mark Hudson has written most convincingly on the origins of Ainu culture. Citing Hudson (1999, 209–10), he writes that the resultant "Ainu culture" is signified by four major changes in the archaeological record:

1. a shift to surface dwellings with a central hearth;
2. the replacement of locally produced ceramics with those obtained by trade;
3. a decline in plant cultivation (not entirely) and significant change in economic activities; and
4. the development of "sending-back" rituals, culminating in the famous Iyomante (bear ceremony). (Fukuzawa 2022, n.p.)

Even if archaeologists "create" the Ainu historically based on these changes to the archaeological material culture, there appears to be a continual cultural arc from Jomon times onward that can be seen as deep Ainu history: one cannot say, "This is 'pre-Ainu,' but this is Ainu" without hesitancy and unequivocally. Does one piece of metal make a culture "Ainu"? One piece of lacquerware? Does one have to have evidence of a bear ceremony to label a site "Ainu"? Does one have to have all four elements identified by Fukuzawa, or are three sufficient? Would two elements of the four in archaeological evidence be too little or enough— additionally, which two would be best?

Archaeologists can only artificially construct an Ainu origin in the archaeological record, but we can tease out its foundations in the deeper past with roots in the Jomon. Hokkaido has been a genetic and cultural crossroads with development of cultures within regional contexts. Hokkaido cultures retained a connection to the Jomon with a later overlay of

NATIONALIZING THE PAST AND HOMOGENIZING THE PRESENT   169

marine and terrestrial economics supplemented by trade with continental and mainland Japanese cultures.

Is there a future for "Indigenous archaeology" in Japan? Perhaps. If the Ainu (however defined by Ainu individuals, pan-Ainu organizations, or the Japanese government) choose, they can become more involved in the representation, interpretation, and education related to archaeological materials and have more of an impact on the materials that people encounter in museums and other displays. Their involvement in international and national repatriation issues has also increased their involvement with museums and other governments.

My visits to a variety of museums in Hokkaido in 2022 showed some different ways that the Ainu are depicted. In museums at Obihiro, Urahoro, and Kushiro, exhibits on the Ainu were often separated from the archaeological and historical exhibits, not-so-subtly implying that the Ainu are indeed separate from Japan's prehistory and perhaps a bit closer to nature than the "civilized" ethnic Japanese. Other museums, such as the Asahikawa Museum, crafted the Ainu story as a lead-in to its depiction of Japanese history, even though the "archaeology" section was on another floor. At Asahikawa, however, one had to walk through a reconstructed military barracks to enter an exhibit of "traditional" Ainu craft items, subtly reinforcing the role and dominance of the Japanese military in Hokkaido history.

Concluding Remarks

Proposing a single past for the entire archipelago of Japan erases regional and temporal variability in such a way that it masks local pasts and minimizes cultural variability and adaptation. Archaeologists recognize that there are often a variety of reasons for regional variability in archaeological cultures (climatic variability, ecological and biological variability, resource availability, and so forth). However, when politicians use archaeological information to create a national narrative of a common origin, history, or culture, the result is a generalized story that removes discussion of internal variability.

Attempts by right-wing politicians to prevent the Japanese government from providing services to Ainu individuals based on their status as

"Ainu" continues to push forward the idea that there are no "minorities" in Japanese society. Articles 13 and 14 of the Japanese Constitution enforce the idea of individual equality: "all of the people shall be respected as individuals" (Article 13) and "all of the people are equal under the law" (Article 14). From this perspective, some argue, providing services to one individual based on their background as an Ainu individual *discriminates against* an individual who is *not* an Ainu individual.

Creating generalized archaeological descriptions is an important part of crafting culture histories for large areas such as the Japanese mainland or the island of Hokkaido. Nonetheless, it is important to recognize that variability existed in the past, that various regions had their own cultural development similar to but different from other areas, and that there are possibilities of generalizing regional pasts. Such recognition should also come with the caveat that even the past is not without impact on the present and the future.

Further Reading

Readers interested in Indigenous archaeology should consult my 2000 volume *Indigenous Archaeology: American Indian Values and Scientific Practice*; George P. Nicholas and Lindsay M. Montgomery's 2024 article in the *Encyclopedia of Archaeology* (2nd ed.) titled "Indigenous Archaeology"; and Hirofumi Kato's 2017 article "The Ainu and Japanese Archaeology: A Change of Perspective" and his 2018 article in the *Encyclopedia of Global Archaeology* titled "Hokkaido Sequence and the Archaeology of the Ainu People."

CHAPTER 9

· · · · · · · · ·

Contemporary Ainu
and Their Issues

The contemporary Ainu of Japan, whether they reside in cities like Sapporo, smaller towns like Biratori, or in the larger cities of Honshu like Osaka and Tokyo, continue to live in a society that is not openly welcoming. Even though the government has officially declared that the Ainu are the "Indigenous population of Japan," there are still those who do not see the Ainu as separate, let alone "separate but equal." As noted by Mai Ishihara's discussion of the "Hidden Ainu," as explained in chapter 1, many Ainu people continue to experience prejudice and feel the need to hide their Ainu identity. Masaki Sashima, chairman emeritus of the Raporo Ainu Nation, in the statement he made before the District Court of Sapporo as part of the second argument for the Raporo Ainu Court Case on December 17, 2020, indicates how Sashima himself was a "hidden Ainu." The fact that he did not know for certain that he was Ainu until he graduated from high school indicates just one of the issues Ainu individuals face in terms of their Indigeneity and their identity.

It was when I graduated from high school that I first understood with certainty that I was Ainu. When I sent for the *koseki* [official family register] required for entrance into a university . . . When I entered into my forties, however, I decided to stop hiding my Ainu-ness and to declare, once and

for all, that I am Ainu. . . . And now my heart swells with pride to know
that I am genuinely Ainu. (Sashima 2021, 1)

Governmental Recognition and Access to Governmental Programs

The Japanese government has made attempts to provide program benefits for the Ainu despite complaints like those of Assemblyman Kaneko
(see chapter 1). However, there are jurisdictional and constitutional issues that hinder the programmatic application countrywide. Naohiro
Nakamura, in writing about the Dogai Ainu ("those Ainu living outside
Hokkaido"), calls attention to the fact that, even though the Working
Group for the Research on Living Conditions of the Dogai Ainu (WGDA)
suggested that the national government implement new ethnic policies
targeting the Dogai Ainu (e.g., WGDA 2011), "no comprehensive social
services have ever been offered" (Nakamura 2015, 661).

In some ways, the Ainu continue to be officially "invisible" even as they
are officially acknowledged. Ishihara (2019, 614) identifies how the Japanese census operates to homogenize the Japanese population, offering
"only two choices for ethnicity: Japanese or foreign. While foreigners are
asked to indicate their nationality, there is no place for Japanese nationals
to list race or ethnicity. Japanese nationals are thus presumed to be, and
officially recognized as, nationally, ethnically, and racially homogenous."
Thus, while the government's stated intent is to help alleviate the conditions of the Ainu, it is impossible at the time of this writing (2025) to
document the actual number of people of Ainu heritage living in Japan.

Anthropologist Mark Watson's work with the Ainu of Tokyo calls attention to the fact that some people, even though they are and have always been Ainu, do not have access to the governmental programs that
have been set aside for their benefit because they do not live within Hokkaido, the prefecture that has the budgetary set-asides for such programs.
He explains, "At the time of writing [2009], for example, Ainu do not
appear in the national census and as a result of the prefectural jurisdiction of social welfare budgets, non-Hokkaido Ainu are excluded from the
Hokkaido Utari Association's 'official' population statistic" (Watson 2010,
270) and are therefore unable to take advantage of prefectural programs.

Such research about the urban Ainu offers insights into the issues populations face in negotiating the complex societies of Japanese and Ainu lives. Ainu woman Kanako Uzawa (2018) writes about her life growing up in the Tokyo area and the needs of city Ainu. Stories such as hers reveal the true gaps in social and economic levels of urban Ainu compared to non-Ainu people. But why is it so difficult for the government to provide economic and social support to the Ainu in such large cities?

Such issues—uneven application of national laws, lack of access to economic programs, "invisibility" in national census counts, to name just three—reveal the fundamental inability of the Japanese Constitution to "recognize" the Ainu as an Indigenous population except in name. Teruki Tsunemoto, in discussing the significance of the Act Promoting Measures to Achieve a Society in which the Pride of the Ainu People is Respected (the Ainu Measures Promotion Act, or AMPA), notes that while the AMPA is "the first act to enshrine in law the recognition of the Ainu as an indigenous people, . . . it contains nothing that provides the indigenousness of the Ainu people with any legal effect: There is no definition of the Ainu people or a guarantee of their rights as an indigenous people" (2019a, 65). The consequence is that the act does not cover the Ainu as individuals or as groups but instead supports regional and local governments in "the adoption of regional promotion directed toward overall socioeconomic improvement in the region where the indigenous people, the Ainu, live" (Tsunemoto 2019a, 68).

While this program of state-backed subsidies avoids the difficulties of determining who is and who is not "Ainu," it falls short in providing direct support to the Ainu. Instead, it is "directed toward the socioeconomic improvement of the Ainu people in tandem with other people in the region based on the idea of harmonious co-existence" (Tsunemoto 2019, 9) and relies on local jurisdictions to apply for and implement the grants. As one colleague has noted, regions where the relationships between the Ainu and the local jurisdiction are problematic generally are lacking in programs for the benefit of the Ainu.

This has apparently been an issue in the past. As described in the 2022 report on Japan to the International Work Group for Indigenous Affairs (Uzawa, Gayman, and Nagai 2022, 224), "there are reports that local Ainu have been refused assistance to use the law as a means to achieve their local cultural aspirations." The authors relate a newspaper report that the town council of Honbetsu had denied a request from the Honbetsu Ainu Association to build a traditional *chise* dwelling in which to conduct Ainu ceremonies. The town objected to the Honbetsu Ainu Association's request, asserting that only the town could apply for financial subsidies, not private organizations such as the Ainu Association. The town government claimed that it first needed to "(hear) the opinions of local residents" (Uzawa, Gayman, and Nagai 2022, 224) and not just act on behalf of the Ainu.

This lack of "recognition" lies at the heart of many Ainu issues. Why should the national government expect local jurisdictions to enact national policies in the hopes that "regional promotion of Ainu culture" will meet the needs of individual or groups of Ainu? In Japan, there is no mechanism whereby an individual can "prove" Ainu identity. There were family registers in the past, beginning with the 1872 *Jinshin Koseki*, the oldest known family register created as a result of the 1871 Family Registration Law, but these do not carry sufficient legal standing today to be used in instances such as these. Even if they were given legal standing, many Ainu families converted their names to Japanese early as a means of trying to escape discrimination from non-Ainu people. And while Ainu are genetically different to some extent from the ethnic Japanese populations, genetics does not equate with culture and would be insufficient for determining eligibility for governmental programs.

In the United States, American Indian tribes are recognized to be "domestic, dependent nations" by the federal government as a result of several Supreme Court cases and based on the existence of treaties between the fledgling United States and European countries with the Indian tribes with which they came into contact. Indian Nations are also mentioned specifically in the U.S. Constitution. Some Ainu communities are looking at ways that American Indians are now exercising sovereignty in the United States to customize the intended results of government programs for their members and to provide alternative means of tribal income to expand such programs and economic impact. Tribes determine their members through various mechanisms, such as direct familial relationship (descendancy) with another recognized tribal member, percentage of "Indian blood," and other methods (see chapter 1). Additionally, each tribe has its own governance system that ensures that the tribes are free to develop programs that fit the needs of their members. The Ainu, however, currently have no such mechanism of determining who is and is not "eligible" to participate within their structures and eligible for any programs they might provide.

Yuko Osakada (2021, 1063) recognizes some of the challenges faced by Ainu individuals trying to trace back their ancestors' names through current family registers that do not refer to the ethnicity of residents. However, the Ainu Association of Hokkaido, the largest Ainu organization in Hokkaido, determines its membership by requiring Ainu individuals to trace back their ancestors' names through current family registers. Osakada realizes, as do many others, that this is an imperfect method because not all ancestors can be traced back in this way. Still, she notes that Article 33(1) of the UN Declaration recognizes it is Indigenous peoples, not national governments, that have the right to determine their own membership.

AN AMERICAN POSSIBILITY

There is one American Indian example that *might* work in Japan. In Alaska, the Alaska Native Claims Settlement Act (ANCSA) of 1971 established thirteen regional and more than two hundred village for-profit corporations to serve Alaska Native people. In addition to their normal corporate responsibilities, they have responsibilities for cultural and community efforts. Shares in corporations were issued to Alaska Natives born before December 18, 1971, and can be given away or inherited but not sold. Twelve of the thirteen regional corporations were given land in the area of their traditional cultural lands, but the thirteenth corporation oversees no land and is headquartered in Seattle, Washington. It was created for Alaska Natives who were no longer Alaskan residents and, as a result, don't have a primary cultural grouping.

There would still be problems in determining who would be eligible to participate under such a corporate system, but this might be a mechanism whereby the Ainu could develop more self-governance within a Japanese counterpart. Regional or village corporate structure and membership determinations could be problematic, but perhaps local Ainu organizations could begin to exercise their own self-determination outside of the Japanese government structures. However, these corporations would still not be operating as Indigenous corporations but rather as corporations run by individual Ainu.

In her discussion of her life as an urban Ainu in Tokyo, Kanako Uzawa (2018, 188) writes about the Tokyo Ainu Center (formally the Ainu Culture Center, Tokyo) as a place "used daily by Tokyo Ainu . . . [to] share many cultural practices, just like Hokkaidō Ainu, by using urban space and place to practise and revitalise Ainu culture." This in some ways mirrors situations in the United States where "urban Indians" (tribal people living in larger cities) use various centers that provide services to American Indian populations. These centers grew up in urban areas after disastrous federal government attempts to "assimilate" tribal people through the Indian Relocation Act of 1956, which moved Indians from rural to urban areas. Those who moved struggled and faced unemployment, low-end jobs, discrimination, homesickness, and the loss of traditional cultural support. Urban Indian centers served as intermediaries in helping tribal members adjust to the changes as well as provided social services that the tribal members needed. They also served as places where tribal members could go for emotional support, "pan-Indian/inter-tribal" cultural experiences, and access to some governmental programs.

There is one major difference between the Ainu and American Indian experiences. American Indian centers generally require those who take advantage of their programs to document their eligibility to access them. This usually takes place in the form of tribal membership cards or other documentation, such as a Bureau of Indian Affairs Certificate of Degree of Indian Blood (CDIB). At this point, there are no such membership criteria (or even a membership mechanism) for Ainu members. Still, urban centers offer places of comfort and support that can fulfill the needs of displaced Ainu in larger cities.

Many of the other issues faced by the Ainu of Japan, such as those outlined in the *Report on the 2008 Hokkaido Ainu Living Conditions Survey* (Onai 2011), could benefit from targeted programs *if* the Japanese national government were able to enact such programs. While American Indian populations in the United States still hover at or near the lowest rungs of the nation in terms of education attainment and health risk factors, directed government programs have alleviated much of the disparities over time in spite of claims by some that those programs create a perception of "discrimination" against those not eligible to receive them.

Return and Reburial of Ainu Human Remains

Like other global Indigenous groups, the Ainu are working toward the return of human remains taken either during archaeological excavations or, in some cases, directly from the graves of known individuals and families. Hirofumi Kato (2017) discusses some of the issues related to repatriation in Japan, such as those encountered during the handling of ancestral remains and grave goods excavated from graves of historical Ainu during rescue excavations in land development. The Ainu and institutions struggle to find common mechanisms within which to work for the return of the remains held in collections worldwide. He estimates that "over 1600 Ainu ancestral remains are stored in twelve Japanese universities. Ainu ancestral remains collected in this way are also stored in museums in UK, Germany, Russia and other western countries" (Kato 2017, 187).

Repatriation of ancestral remains from Japanese and international universities, medical schools, and museums still lags behind repatriation practices in the United States and Australia as Japanese institutions are struggling to accept and enact policies on a national scale. In July 2016, twelve Ainu ancestral remains were returned from Hokkaido University to one Ainu organization, Kotan no Kai, and reburied in a local graveyard after eighty-five years (Kato 2017, 185; N. Nakamura 2017, 2019; Shimizu 2018, 119). The Ainu ancestral remains that were returned included one known individual and eleven unidentified remains. This repatriation was the first formal Indigenous repatriation from a university to a local community in Japan. Naohiro Nakamura (2019) provides more details on the struggle and the process of repatriation of these and other Ainu human remains.

In 2013, the chief cabinet secretary set up a new national museum of Ainu people and a memorial facility to store unidentified Ainu ancestral remains in Shiraoi, Hokkaido, which opened in 2020 (see figure 19). The construction of the National Keeping Place for the temporary storage of returned human remains was meant to provide a solution so that Ainu ancestral remains would be away from institutions and available for reburial, but some Ainu are still concerned about storage (again) of human remains (Shimizu 2018, 120), out of fear that those items might never be reburied.

FIGURE 19 Upopoy Memorial Site, Shiraoi, Hokkaido (photograph courtesy of the Foundation for Ainu Culture).

Individuals working on the repatriation of Ainu remains (see figure 20) from international museums have seemingly had an easier time than those seeking Ainu human remains from domestic museums and institutions. For example, Kato worked on regaining Ainu human remains from Sakhalin Island, now a part of Russia, from an Australian museum. An article in a daily Japanese newspaper (Chiba 2023) outlines the proposed process to ease the return of the Ainu human remains from Australia. Ultimately, four sets of human skeletal remains, including the set from Sakhalin Island, were returned to Japan in May 2023.

In a 2021 report to the International Work Group for Indigenous Affairs on Japan's progress in terms of Indigenous issues, Kanako Uzawa, Jeffry Gayman, and Fuyima Nagai write about the Ainu's continued concerns about repatriation. They report that the human remains of "1,323 Ainu individuals and 287 boxes of aggregated remains" (Uzawa, Gayman, and Nagai 2021, 235) are housed in the Memorial Resting Place. They also note that "the challenge posed by the repatriation of Ainu human remains sheds lights on the highly problematic and unethical research conducted by researchers in the 19th and 20th centuries" (235).

FIGURE 20 The late Ryukichi Ogawa, a major leader of the repatriation movement in Sapporo (photograph by Carol J. Ellick).

In April 2024, after an ongoing process involving discussions between anthropologists and Ainu individuals, the Japanese Society of Cultural Anthropology issued a "Statement on Ainu Research" (JASCA 2024). The statement provides a brief history of anthropological research on Ainu human remains as well as its "1989 Statement on Ainu Studies by the Ethics Committee of the Japanese Society of Ethnology" ("the 1989 Statement"). The Society ultimately states,

> We, the members of the Japanese Society of Cultural Anthropology, acknowledge, and apologize for our past research orientation toward the Ainu people. We sincerely hope that this statement will serve as an expression of our responsibility towards the future, and that it will lead to

renewed communication with the Ainu people both within and outside of our Society. (JASCA 2024)

Repatriation of human remains continues to be an issue among the Ainu. The JASCA apology for the "past research orientation toward the Ainu people" doesn't acknowledge the excavation of Ainu human remains; rather, it merely apologizes for the study of Ainu in a broad sense. It remains to be seen whether this apology will create a more positive relationship between the Ainu and anthropologists in Japan.

The Raporo Ainu Nation Lawsuit over Indigenous Rights to Fish

In August 2020, the Raporo Ainu Nation (formerly Urahoro Ainu Association) filed lawsuit in the Sapporo District Court for the right to conduct commercial fishing for salmon in the Tokachi River. They argued that their right lies in Article 38 of the United Nations Declaration on the Rights of Indigenous Peoples (UNDRIP): "States . . . shall take the appropriate measures, including legislative measures, to achieve the ends of this Declaration." The plaintiffs maintain that, on this basis, the Japanese government has an obligation to recognize and protect their Indigenous rights as a member of the global community (Kayaba and Yoshikagi 2020).

Japan was one of 144 countries that voted in favor of the passage of UNDRIP on September 13, 2007. Shortly thereafter, in 2008, Japan recognized the Ainu as an Indigenous people of Japan. Ainu community members believed the support of the declaration by the Japanese government signaled a lessening of restrictions and the possibilities of stronger Ainu opportunities for self-governance and self-determination. Such has not been the case, however.

The Raporo Ainu Nation Court Case

The Raporo Ainu Nation is using the UNDRIP as part of its attempt to regain rights to net fish in the Urahoro-Tokachi River without having to seek permission from the Hokkaido government. It is also using American Indian methods as examples on ways to proceed. U.S. courts have held that, unless specific rights were signed away in treaties, those rights were retained by the tribe. The right to take fish is one of those rights retained by some Northwest Coast tribes, and those rights are among the examples the Raporo Ainu are using in their court case. American Indian tribes signed treaties with the United States on a nation-to-nation basis, and the Ainu have no such formal treaties (or similar instruments) to justify their claim of "retained rights" as exercised by Northwest Coast tribes.

UNDRIP STRUCTURE

UNDRIP has twenty-three preambular clauses and forty-six articles. In most of its articles, there are statements concerning aspirational ideals about how the state should promote and protect the rights of its Indigenous people. In this regard, many Indigenous people see this as a roadmap toward equality in their relationships with their countries' governments. However, UNDRIP was created specifically as an *aspiration* for how Indigenous individuals and peoples should be treated by states and not as a legally binding missive on how states *must* treat the Indigenous groups within their borders.

In May 2023, Masaki Sashima, the chairman emeritus of the Raporo Ainu Nation, hosted an international symposium as a representative of the Raporo Ainu Nation. The symposium, "The Right to Catch Salmon in Rivers as Indigenous Right: A Gathering of Indigenous People Who Live from the Sea (*i*), the Forest (*o*), and the Rivers (*ru*)," was sponsored by the Raporo Ainu Nation and cosponsored by the Hokkaido University Global Station for Indigenous Studies and Cultural Diversity (GSI) and the Hokkaido University Disclosure Documents Study Group.

The symposium brought Indigenous representatives from Taiwan, Australia, Finland, the United States, and Canada to Urahoro, Hokkaido, to offer stories and insights about fishing and other Indigenous rights. The event and the resultant international media coverage helped raise awareness of the Raporo Ainu Nation situation, and additional sponsorship from Patagonia allowed the Raporo Ainu Nation to publish *Sharing Story: Indigenous Struggles in the World* (International Symposium

Reports Editorial Committee 2024), a book composed of the various presentations published in both Japanese and English to further provide opportunities for international communities to experience what happened in Urahoro.

Following the symposium, the participants issued the Raporo Declaration on November 30, 2023. The declaration, signed by the seven Indigenous presenters of the symposium, a lawyer for Aboriginal peoples of Australia, and Raporo Ainu Nation chairman emeritus Masaki Sashima, espouses nine points:

1. Rights based on traditions and customs
2. Explicit stipulation of Indigenous rights in Constitutions and other laws
3. Implementation of the law respectful of Indigenous rights
4. The right to revitalize and develop
5. Natural resource management through the traditional knowledge of Indigenous peoples
6. The participation of Indigenous peoples in natural resources regulatory procedures
7. The recognition of the priority of Indigenous peoples' rights
8. Prohibition of deprivation of Indigenous rights on the grounds of resource protection, and
9. Exercise of sustainable Indigenous rights.

It closes with the following statement: "We confirm the above items as well as resolve to continue the struggle against the unfair invasion of our inherent rights, pledge to always share information, mutually contact one another, form a network of solidarity, and struggle in collaboration, as well as declare that we will further expand this struggle to the world" (International Symposium Reports Editorial Committee 2024, 240–44).

The Raporo continued to be involved in publicizing their push to regain the right to take fish from the Urahoro-Tokachi River for other than traditional uses, and in July Sashima gave a speech on Ainu rights in Geneva for the UN Expert Mechanism for the Rights of Indigenous Peoples (EMRIP) conference. He testified as a witness in the salmon-capture rights trial on November 30, 2023. On February 1, 2024, the trial was concluded. Sashima, the primary plaintiff of the court case against the Japanese government, passed away on February 6, 2024.

The Sapporo District Court verdict for the salmon-capture trial was issued on April 18, 2024 (Kyodo News 2024; Osaka 2024). It rejected the Ainu claim for Indigenous rights to catch salmon in the river based on the idea that the current laws forbidding the taking of salmon were justifiable since they were aimed at all individuals and regulated from the perspective of public welfare.

Morihiro Ichikawa, the attorney for the Raporo Ainu Nation, provided a "Report on the ruling in the Ainu fishing rights case" (Ichikawa 2024) via email within which he summarized the court decision. Ichikawa (2024) writes that the court believed that gillnet fishing in the mouth of the Urahoro-Tokachi River and the right to process and sell the salmon they caught was an exercise of property rights because it exceeded "the scope of traditional ceremonies, the transmission of fishing methods, and the dissemination of knowledge regarding preservation." The court held that this placed the action as an economic activity in exercise of a property right and therefore denied the Raporo Ainu Nation's claim.

Ichikawa indicates the Raporo Ainu Nation has decided to appeal the case. Perhaps more importantly, Ichikawa explains that he had hoped to clarify the historical pre-state rights of Ainu kotans as sovereign entities to show that Japanese control over the Ainu was illegal. The fact that there are no treaties or formal agreements between the Ainu and the Japanese state (or Hokkaido government) could draw into question whether Ainu autonomy was ever extinguished through any internationally recognized legal instruments. Ichikawa (2024) notes that "we hope to clarify Japan's acts of aggression since the Meiji era, and in contesting the existence of pre-constitutional and pre-state authority of each Ainu group."

If the Raporo Ainu Nation were victorious in the Sapporo District Court, the implications would be monumental. The recognition of Ainu sovereignty would immediately change interactions between Ainu governing structures and the Japanese state in a manner similar to the shift that occurred in the United States between American Indian tribal governments and the U.S. federal government. The arc of Ainu futures would certainly swing in a different direction.

Economic Development: Tourism and Otherwise

Ainu groups in Hokkaido are creating and/or continuing economic development programs in order to gain income. Many communities rely on some aspects of tourism for income, and other communities rely on regional programs and resources. Ainu individuals in the bigger cities like Sapporo and Asahikawa have numerous opportunities for employment perhaps directly or indirectly tied to tourism.

As I mentioned in the introduction, during our first visit to Hokkaido in 2007, my wife and I were visitors to the Ainu Museum and Porotokotan in Shiraoi, south of Sapporo. We enjoyed the hospitality of the Ainu performers, museum employees, and staff and toured the museum and shops. That museum no longer exists. In its place, the Japanese government created a new facility in 2020. Upopoy (meaning "singing in a large group," symbolizing the facility's mission to provide a place for people to gather and learn as a community) is a large complex with a performing area, the National Ainu Museum, a craft studio that offers demonstrations of Ainu crafts, and a traditional Ainu village.

The National Ainu Museum at Upopoy is just about everything the Japanese government wants you to know about the Ainu (see figure 21). The permanent exhibition encompasses six themes related to Ainu people and culture: language, universe (spirituality and customs), lives, history, work, and exchange (Ainu interactions with other ethnic groups) and features information about notable Ainu individuals. However, Upopoy has been criticized by some Ainu activists over a variety of shortcomings (Uzawa, Gayman, and Nagai 2021, 235).

Another tourism-dependent town is at Lake Akan in east-central Hokkaido (see figure 22). An Ainu village was created in the 1950s to cater to tourists, and Ainu artists were invited to live there and sell their crafts. Since that time, the Ainu kotan has expanded to include shops lining both sides of a street that sell Ainu crafts and carvings. The "village" also has an auditorium where Ainu performers demonstrate Ainu dances and songs and play the *tonkori* (a distinctive Ainu stringed instrument) and the *mukkuri* (bamboo mouth harp), traditional Ainu instruments.

Nibutani, along the Saru River in the Hidaka region of Hokkaido about sixty-five miles by road (109 kilometers) southeast of Sapporo, also relies on tourism, but its draw is Ainu arts and crafts. The Nibutani Ainu Cul-

FIGURE 21 National Ainu Museum in Upopoy (photograph courtesy of the Foundation for Ainu Culture).

FIGURE 22 Entryway to Lake Akan's Ainu village (photograph by Carol J. Ellick).

ture Museum highlights traditional crafts as well as craftwork of contemporary artists. The Biratori Ainu Crafts and Heritage Center is an artist's cooperative named "Urespa" (meaning "growing together") that offers workshop facilities as well as sales opportunities for Ainu craftspeople. Another notable facility in Nibutani is the Kayano Shigeru Nibutani Ainu Museum, whose collections were started by Shigeru Kayano in the 1950s as a means of preserving traditional Ainu craft and cultural materials.

Hidehiko Kimura, the present chairman of the Biratori Ainu Association, emphasizes the importance of educational possibilities for Ainu students. The Hidaka area, within which Biratori and Nibutani are situated, has one of the largest densities of Ainu people, yet the educational opportunities for them are insufficient. Advanced education requires that Ainu students move away from home in order to pursue college degrees. The idea of a community college was raised at a conference with Kimura and Mayor Keiichi Endoh of Biratori. Such a college would allow local students to receive educational benefits in a local area and would not require that they move away from their family support system. It would be less financially demanding if the students could continue to live at home and continue to use their social networks. Such a local college is not common in Hokkaido, but there are private colleges that could serve as models. In the United States, tribal colleges such as the College of the Muscogee Nation in Oklahoma or Blackfeet Community College in Montana provide opportunities for students to further their careers, attain an advanced degree, or better support their communities.

At the moment, the idea of an Ainu Community College in Biratori is a dream, but if the Raporo were successful in their case, it might become a reality. If the kotans were seen as sovereign governments, their ability to create funding resources for such enterprises would be expanded. Hokkaido University is already offering classes to local students virtually. Hirofumi Kato, as the immediate past director of the Center for Ainu and Indigenous Studies at Hokkaido University, is willing to act as a go-between for the Ainu in trying to make portions of Hokkaido University facilities in the Biratori area (such as the Dr. Munro House in Nibutani) available for archives, classrooms, or other uses once the Munro House is remodeled.

The Raporo Ainu situation is another one that is not reliant on tourism. The recent death of Masaki Sashima has struck the community, but the organization is continuing to move forward. The leaders of the Raporo Ainu Nation continue to discuss developing an Ainu fishing enterprise, but currently the organization does not have any standing to create a business or obtain fishing permits outside of the already-cumbersome system. The Sapporo District Court's ruling against the Raporo Ainu Nation in the fishing case is a setback, but the Raporo Ainu Nation still has hopes of influencing the views of the Japanese judicial system toward reinstating Ainu sovereignty.

Not all communities rely on tourism, and not all Ainu communities rely on craftwork for a living, but tourism is nonetheless an important part of Ainu economy. Smaller communities across Hokkaido compete with the larger metropolitan museums and struggle to keep their facilities open and updated.

Cultural Revitalization

In 1956, American anthropologist Anthony F. C. Wallace (1956, 264) wrote about the tendencies for cultures to attempt or achieve innovations of cultural systems, proposing "revitalization" as a term to describe "uniformly-found processual dimensions" of such movements. To him, the "revitalization movement" is defined as "a deliberate, organized, conscious effort by members of a society to construct a more satisfying culture" (265). In this sense, one can posit that the contemporary Ainu of Japan are initiating purposeful change through the process of reintroducing, reinventing, and/or reinvigorating aspects of traditional Ainu cultural systems, such as language, dance, and ceremony, through local culture organizations.

The idea of Ainu cultural revitalization is not new. Ainu scholar Kanako Uzawa, an assistant professor for the Global Station for Indigenous Studies and Cultural Diversity at Hokkaido University in Japan, writes about what Ainu cultural revitalization means in the twenty-first century for both Ainu and Wajin youth (Uzawa 2019). She contextualizes Ainu cultural revitalization within Japan as "most often connected to cultural preservation—keeping what remains—or restoration—recovering what has been lost" (2019, 168).

These programs of cultural preservation and/or restoration are some-what reliant on various Ainu associations in local communities (Ainu Association of Hokkaido n.d.). These organizations mainly focus on Ainu traditional dance and song, and participation is generally open to both Ainu and Wajin individuals. Many of these local municipal organiza-tions perform dances or songs at the Annual Shakushain Festival. Out-side Hokkaido (mainly around the capital), there are other Ainu cultural preservation groups that have similar functions. Nowhere is the result of these local organizations' practice seen as openly and happily as at the annual Shakushain Festival, when groups of dancers, singers, and others perform for the crowd (see figure 23).

But cultural revitalization is about more than just practicing dances and songs of the past; it is, at least, as much about the future. In the United States, Haley Shea and other researchers from the University of Miami in Ohio examined the impact of cultural revitalization on a tribal commu-nity and a sample of its college-aged members. Their research supports the idea that "when a people reclaim their cultural context, an awakening

FIGURE 23 Assembled Ainu dancers and non-Ainu participants at the Shaku-shain Festival (photograph by Carol J. Ellick).

occurs. . . . A strengthening of cultural ties refreshes the self and the community, offering an alternative path to healing" (Shea et al. 2019, 564). Such positive results are likely to occur among other Indigenous people, including the Ainu, as they move toward restrengthening their cultures.

The first Ainu ceremony I attended—other than during the field school in Otaru—was at an archaeological site on the Hokkaido University campus in 2010 (see figure 24). The event was organized by the Sapporo Ainu Association, held with support of the Center for Ainu and Indigenous Studies, and led by Koji Yuki. The event involved many Sapporo Ainu individuals and served to invoke safety and healing from the kamuy (deities) of the area. The rights to conduct this ceremony on the Hokkaido University campus were won through the negotiation of the Ainu activist Ryukichi Ogawa and have been granted to the Sapporo Ainu Association.

While I was in Hokkaido from July 2022 through August 2023, I was able to participate in two Ainu ceremonies with specific aims toward revitalization of cultural practices and ceremonies of the Raporo Ainu Nation

FIGURE 24 Kamuynomi held at an archaeological site on the Hokkaido University campus.

and the Biratori Ainu Association. There were similarities to each ceremony, but I was not easily able to recognize the differences. Similarities in hand movements, prayer offerings and the use of the ceremonial "libation sticks" (ikupasuy), and offerings of sake were common to both ceremonies, but the recitations and processes were different in terms of the language spoken, the recitations made, and the actions of the participants.

In August 2022, the Raporo Ainu Nation held a Kamuynomi—a religious ceremony performed for the sake of communicating with the kamuy (deities), such as delivering prayers, calling for favors, and expressing gratitude to and maintaining connections with one's ancestors through the *icharpa*, which is often performed as part of the Kamuynomi (see figure 25).

The ceremony, conducted in the Ainu language, enforces Ainu ideas toward traditional ways as well as strengthens Ainu communities. The 2022 ceremony relied on someone from outside the local Raporo Ainu Nation community to lead the ceremony, and the locals primarily read from pages prepared to guide them through the ceremony. Belarusian researcher Tatsiana Tsagelnik (2022, 1078), herself married to an Ainu man,

FIGURE 25 Altar of the Raporo Ainu Nation Kamuynomi.

recounts the work Mitsuru Ota undertook to reestablish the Kamuynomi (*kamuy* = deity; *nomi* = ritual). In concluding, Tsagelnik (2022, 113) notes that the "Kamuynomi can provide a feeling of security and acceptance from the community, becoming places of healing and salvation for adult individuals (most of whom have been openly or indirectly exposed to discrimination or biased behavior)."

In October 2022, the Nibutani Ainu Community held an Asircep-nomi (*asir* = new; *cep* = fish; *nomi* = ritual)—the ritual to receive the first salmon of the season as they return upriver to spawn (see figure 26). The Ainu used traditional Ainu fishing implements to harvest the salmon obtained from the Saru River for the ceremony and then conducted the ceremony itself. Ainu and non-Ainu people attended the ceremony and participated in the harvesting of the salmon.

These ceremonies and the others I have seen in Hokkaido serve to unite the Ainu community in a pan-community manner, but, in a similar vein, tourism has also served to provide impetus for cultural revitalization. Joyce Hsui-yen Yeh and other researchers (Yeh et al. 2021, n.p.), working in Taiwan, write of "heritagization" as "the renewal of cultural heritage by strengthening and promoting the roots of indigenous traditions of knowledge and practice (which are themselves changing), towards social and economic development options that are culturally appropriate." They also note that, in Taiwan, "cultural revitalization is an essential part of heritagization, and the context for understanding social, cultural, economic, and political action in indigenous communities."

Among the Ainu, as among the Taiwanese communities, heritage-based tourism is continuing to grow as an acceptable and somewhat sustainable means of economic development. The Ainu kotan (tourist village) at Lake Akan sells Ainu crafts and artwork, and many of the shops act as "mini museums" and display old Ainu materials. The owner of one such shop on the plaza insisted that my wife and I put on traditional Ainu clothing and accessories and then have our photo taken as a memento of our visit (see figure 27). Other members of our group (a young Swiss woman and a Danish couple) were subjected to the same routine, and we all were depicted as what might be best described as "non-Ainu Ainu."

The National Ainu Museum at Upopoy, as described earlier in this chapter, also proposes to strengthen Ainu culture and cultural revitalization. However, the situation with the museum is complicated by the

FIGURE 26 Nibutani Ainu Community Asircepnomi (First Salmon Ceremony).

Japanese government's inability to transfer control over the museum to the Ainu people. The Japanese government is also reluctant to pursue a path that might be seen by the general Japanese population as providing rights to the Ainu beyond those afforded to *all* Japanese as provided for by Article 14 of the Japanese Constitution.

FIGURE 27 The author and Carol Ellick dressed in Ainu finery (photograph by anonymous shop owner).

Museum professional Gwyneira Isaac (curator of North American ethnology at the National Museum of Natural History, Smithsonian Institution, in Washington, D.C.), along with other researchers (Isaac et al. 2023, 18), notes that "revitalization programs have encouraged a fundamental transformation of museums" into organizations that can serve to regenerate Indigenous knowledge. I hope that, as Upopoy matures, the Ainu will be able to interact in such a way with their "national museum" so that their knowledge is continually regenerated.

Concluding Remarks

There are, of course, other issues that Ainu groups are concerned about, although many of them are regional in scope. Access to natural resources such as forestry and plant products and fish and other game animals stands high on the list. In terms of education and educational achievement, Japanese public universities currently have no way of officially recognizing who is and who is not Ainu within their records: administration officials are not allowed to ask for ethnic or racial information of their students or student applicants. Generally, professors become aware of their students' ethnic backgrounds only if the student provides that information directly and voluntarily. Thus, the information on attainment of Ainu individuals at higher education levels is officially "unknown," and perhaps unknowable.

Further Reading

Information about contemporary Ainu issues can be found in anthropologist Mark K. Watson's 2014 work with the Ainu of Tokyo, *Japan's Ainu Minority in Tokyo: Diasporic Indigeneity and Urban Politics*; Ainu woman Kanako Uzawa writes about her life growing up in the Tokyo area in her chapter "Everyday Acts of Resurgence and Diasporic Indigeneity Among the Ainu of Tokyo," which can be found in the 2018 volume *Indigenous Efflorescence: Beyond Revitalization in Sapmi and Ainu Mosir*, edited by Gerald Roche, Hiroshi Maruyama, and Åsa Virdi Kroik.

In addition, many topics related to contemporary and current Ainu issues are now being covered in Japanese and international newspapers as well as in specialized magazines such as *Cultural Survival*, and information on the new museum at Upopoy is available on the internet.

Also, interested readers should watch the 2020 film *Ainu Mosir*, by Takeshi Fukunaga. The fictional story offers insights into contemporary Ainu issues as seen through the eyes of a coming-of-age Ainu boy. It not only makes the Ainu central to the story but also casts nonactors of Ainu ancestry to play the leading Ainu roles.

CHAPTER 10
· · · · · · · · ·
Looking Back
and Moving Forward

It seems odd that I no longer feel it is necessary to get up each morning, log onto my computer, and search the internet for publications that I have not seen and for articles that are new but unavailable (researchers will understand what I mean). I continue to search for ways to refine my thoughts and to think about new avenues. Still, there comes a time when it is necessary to finalize one's thoughts on paper.

Many have written about the Ainu and their cultures from the perspectives of ministers and travelers such as John Batchelor (1892, 1901) and A. H. Savage Landor (1893); historians such as Richard Siddle (1996) and Brett Walker (2001); doctors such as Neil Gordon Munro (1963); and, of course, anthropologists Romyn Hitchcock (1892), Takakura Shinichiro (1960), Hitoshi Watanabe (1973), and Kaori Tahara (2006). All these have offered insights into the Ainu they encountered. Additionally, a dated but useful presentation of some major researchers on the Ainu can be gained from Takao Yamada's (2003) article on anthropological studies on the Ainu in Japan.

Still, even much of the historical information is dated and depicts the Ainu as "savage," "hairy," "barbaric," and other culturally loaded terms that have contributed to the historic perceptions of these people as less than human or worthy of contempt, tropes common in colonial discourses on the Indigenous peoples they sought to displace. In this regard, I have tried not to repeat too much of those interpretations of Ainu information since they are culturally biased toward the Ainu. Even though some of the volumes mentioned were written at a time of Western contempt for non-Western people, reading some of the descriptions and interpretations of the Ainu made my skin crawl and my hackles rise.

In this final chapter, I propose some not-so-rhetorical questions about the Ainu and then provide some answers based on my understandings of the situations as they exist in Japan today. I try not to let stories I have been told about things color my opinions too vividly, and I have tried to approach experts with questions about specific issues I have seen as problematic. In this way, the chapter will offer a summation of some of the academic approaches to the Ainu and their culture(s) as I discuss the questions I have explored. I still have many such questions, and I look forward to continuing to work with Ainu people to try to find answers.

Who Are the Ainu?

I opened this book with the question "Who are the Ainu?," and I hope in some way(s) I have answered it. The Ainu *are* the governmentally recognized Indigenous people of Japan. They are one of the newest groups of Indigenous peoples *in the world* to be so recognized by their dominant government, even though they still have a long way to go to gain educational, social, and economic equality with their non-Ainu Japanese countrymen.

It is important once more to emphasize that there is not a single Ainu group or a single Ainu identity; rather, the Ainu communities across Hokkaido—and the Ainu individuals who live in major urban centers in places such as Tokyo, Sapporo, and elsewhere—are descended from Ainu individuals who suffered the consequences in one form or another of that recognition. Historically, there were regional differences among the groups lumped together as "Ainu," with groups in southwestern Hokkaido culturally distinct from those on the southeastern (Pacific) side. Groups in the north and in the central mountains had different economies and cultures from those to the south, and it is possible that their languages might have been mutually unintelligible to each other, as was the case between the northern and southern Kurils and on Sakhalin. We also know that the consequences of exposure to the Yayoi and later cultures of the Japanese mainland had impacts on the Ainu groups in direct relation to their distance from the mainland core area, with the groups along the Tsugaru Strait in Hokkaido the first to encounter the purposeful push of the Wajin toward colonization.

Even today, it is inadvisable to lump "the Ainu" into one group, much as it is impossible to consider the label "American Indian" as sufficiently explanatory to try to describe each of the 574 Native entities of the United States. Even in places where the Indigenous group is considered singular, such as the Māori in New Zealand, regional differences exist. Still, until such time as the group further defines itself within the international community, the term will likely remain as a singular appellation. And, in spite of my complaints, in the following discussion I will allow use of "the Ainu" as a convenient explanatory term, in spite of its limitations.

What Does the Archaeology of the Japanese Archipelago Tell About the Ainu?

As illustrated in chapters 3, 4, and to an extent in chapter 8, the archaeology of the Japanese archipelago gives insights into not only how the people who first settled the island adapted to their environments but also information on the divergence of archaeological cultures of mainland Japan and Hokkaido Island. The migration of people from the continent through what is now the Korean peninsula, and the different economies they brought with them in the form of wet-rice agriculture, created two trajectories that forever altered the original people of the islands.

The political system (i.e., the "Japanese state") that developed from the Yayoi culture created the "us versus them" differentiation between the "Japanese" and "the Others." People who were on the periphery of the nascent Japanese state were excluded until colonization became a major part of the state's response to protect resources and goods from Russian and European desires. As the Japanese state developed, it borrowed political models and practices from the mainland governments. The distinction between "Japanese" (Wajin) and "Indigenous" (non-Wajin) was unwavering at times, and some "Indigenous groups" (such as the Emishi) ultimately became subsumed in the broader category "Ainu."

For various reasons of history, geography, resistance, and persever-
ance, the Ainu continue to reassert their Indigeneity in the context of international support and changing political trends. Their identity as Ainu
is shaped by this history and the variable impacts local communities
faced at the hands of the Japanese colonial government, and these groups
could have as easily generated several different Indigenous groups in the
past, as has happened to American Indian groups in the United States.

Looking at the archaeological histories that have been identified, the
Late Paleolithic cultures of the archipelago were well adapted to local
environments and used a wide variety of local plants and animals. Local
populations interacted with other groups, and trade networks began expanding, uniting some regions with others. Obsidian and other resources
were traded across the archipelago, as were other commodities of use.

The Neolithic lifeways of the Jomon were shared across the archipelago as well, with the greatest expression of these in the northern Honshu / southern Hokkaido areas. Local populations continued their adaptation to local environments, and trade increased with communities
outside the local realms. Religious life expanded, and there appears to
have been some sort of governance organization in place to regulate (or
initiate) community projects that resulted in the construction of large local structures that might have served community functions of some sort
or another, such as a so-called tower structure at the Sannai Maruyama
Site in Aomori City (see figure 28).

However, with the migration of new peoples from the west, the resultant Yayoi culture created lasting differences in cultural organization
that impacted the groups that are now known as Ainu. Even if "Ainu" did
not exist as a named entity prior to historical times, this was the point
at which it appears that cultural (and genetic) separation of the nascent
"Japanese" populations began. One can trace in the archaeological record
the new cultural and economic differences that arose concomitant with
the development of wet-rice agriculture in the Japanese "mainland" (the
Honshu-Shikoku-Kyushu islands).

At the end of the Yayoi period, history and archaeology compete for
the information on local development that they can provide. Relations
with Chinese officials begin the insertion of "history" into the archipelago, and the people of Honshu-Sikoku-Kyushu enter world history as
"the people of Wa"—the Wajin. The trajectory of the Japanese mainland

FIGURE 28 Reconstructed tower at Sannai Maruyama Site, Aomori City, Honshu.

changed forever, and the development of internal Japanese cultures and society is documented in historical chronicles as well as within archaeological excavations.

In northern Honshu and Hokkaido, the Jomon continues its cultural march onward. As the Yayoi people enter the historical period, the archaeological cultures in the north maintain their economies, even though interaction between the groups begins and increases over time. Trade indicates awareness of each other, and subsequently artifacts from the continent begin to show up more frequently in Hokkaido and northern Honshu cultures.

Based on interpretations of archaeological material by archaeologists such as Junko Habu (2004), Koji Mizoguchi (2017), and others, the separation of groups arises out of wet-rice agriculture and the associated religious and social functions that were needed to carry out the internal political and social structures required of that economy. On Hokkaido, where wet-rice agriculture was not feasible, the local populations continued their established trajectories. Trade increased, and, ultimately, the desire for specific artifacts and materials resulted in economic relationships that had far-reaching impacts on the people of the region. Additionally, toward the end of this period, the Emishi and other "barbarians" of northern Honshu and Hokkaido entered into historical chronicles of the Chinese and the mainland Japanese culture.

The practice of Indigenous archaeology on Hokkaido and its interactions with local Ainu communities offer opportunities to tell us about lasting relationships between the archaeological cultures foundational to "the Ainu" and the cultures that became known historically as "the Ainu." Hirofumi Kato and others note the use of depressions of Tobinitai pit houses as ritual bear-sending ceremonies, indicating that the Ainu did not avoid such habitations of previous cultures but continued to integrate those places as part of contemporary rituals.

What Does Genetics Tell About the Ainu and the Mainland Japanese?

Genetics—both ancient and modern—continues to offer explanation and insights into the composition of contemporary Japanese people. However, it is important to remember that genetics does not equal culture, nor can it explain cultural differences. For some researchers, it is important to know the genetic differences between groups that have contributed to the original populations and resultant people of the Japanese archipelago; to others, genetics is peripheral to the understanding of cultural influences from other regions more so than any genetic differences.

Ever since Kazuro Hanihara (1991) proposed the dual structure hypothesis for Japanese origins (that physical and cultural differences in Japan can be explained based on the amount of admixture between the original Paleolithic populations and the more recent Yayoi peoples), scientists have tried to refine further and further the genetic structure of the original inhabitants of what is now Japan, the people who can be identified as having moved into the islands over time, and the genetic makeup of contemporary populations. Some ask why such questions continue to drive genetic research, and others continue to push the idea that such research will provide insights into how Japanese culture has developed through time. Whether such ideas are awash in a sea of genetic determinism, or whether such information will be used to support ideas of Japanese exclusion/inclusion, remains to be seen.

In the United States, American Indian groups are concerned about genetic determinism, as mentioned in chapter 1. While some tribal groups *might* use DNA to test whether a tribal applicant is related to known enrolled tribal members, there is no singular or specific "American Indian DNA" that could be used to automatically "prove" an individual is "American Indian."

Indigenous groups globally are concerned about the unfettered practice of genomic research on Indigenous materials. As a means of ensuring the presence of qualified Indigenous scientists, the Summer Institute for INdigenous [sic] peoples in Genomics (SING) was created in 2011 in Illinois, although now SING workshops have been held in the United States, Canada, Australia, and New Zealand.

Through a weeklong workshop, Indigenous students and community members learn about genomics through hands-on experience, integrative lectures, and discussion about the ethical, legal, and social implications of doing genomics with Indigenous communities. The goal of the workshops is to train Indigenous students and community members in next-generation genomic and bioinformatics analyses, to build capacity for scientific research involving Indigenous communities (SING), and to use a framework for enhancing ethical genomic research with Indigenous communities (Claw et al. 2018).

Additionally, as I said in chapter 2, genetics does not equal culture. Culture is learned, and historically non-American Indians were adopted into American Indian cultures. Cynthia Ann Parker, a German immigrant child, was captured by a Comanche raiding party in Texas in 1836. She lived most of her life as a Comanche woman until she was recaptured by Texas Rangers and returned to her Anglo-American family in 1860. She was the mother of the last great war chief of the Comanches, Quanah Parker. Even though she was genetically non-Indian, she was culturally Comanche (Hacker 2018).

However, there is genetic evidence (although based on limited sample sizes) that the people now known as Ainu are genetically different from the people who are known as the "ethnic Japanese." Those genetic differences arise mostly as a result of the genetic makeup of the people from the continent who migrated into the Japanese mainland and have become known archaeologically as Yayoi. It appears likely that the migrants intermarried (or at least interbred) with the local Jomon people, thus resulting in genetic differences between the two original populations and the resultant population derived from the merger of the two. Other genetic differences probably relate to migration of people from mainland Sakhalin into Hokkaido, both in the late Pleistocene and again with the Okhotsk. More research is needed to strengthen population-wide statements with confidence.

As the Yayoi culture and culture-bearing people spread across the region, and as the wet-rice economy and associated social and religious structures were accepted by people, the genetic makeup of the Honshu-Shikoku-Kyushu islands became more homogenized; at the same time, the Jomon cultures on Northern Honshu and Hokkaido, somewhat insulated by the Tsugaru Strait, received less genetic material from the Yayoi people. These genetic differences are recognizable both in human remains from archaeological cultures that have had their DNA analyzed as well as analyses done on contemporary populations.

Even though the two populations are genetically different from each other, the early people of the archipelago are still considered the foundation populations of both contemporary Japanese and Ainu people. It is evident that there is a genetic difference between the Yayoi and the Jomon, but what does the difference mean? While some Japanese have argued, "We are all Jomon," it is naïve to believe that genetics determines culture and cultural expression. Ultimately, it might be said that all humanity is "African," but that is homogenizing and antithetical to a functional explanation of human cultural development.

Perhaps the important thing to remember is that there is some biological relationship between the mainland Japanese and the Ainu but that their genetic makeup is different enough to indicate a common but fragmented linear relationship. The Yayoi are different from the Jomon and the Ainu; the Ainu are not "Jomon," but much of the genetic material is derived from genetic material that was widespread during the Jomon archaeological culture period, with other contributions of genetic material from populations in the Lower Amur River area of East Asia in what is now known as Russia.

What Does History Tell About Ainu Relationships with the Wajin and the Rest of the World?

Wajin–Ainu history is awash with evidence of the initial and continuing Wajin biases against the Ainu and other Indigenous cultures. The "Emishi" and other northern peoples were considered "barbarians" by the people who became historically known as the Wajin. Such terms of exclusion were based on social and religious perspectives rather than anything else, although the appearances of the northern peoples were startling in contrast to those of the Wajin and were outward reminders of the differences that were perceived as distinctive cultural and social markers.

Historical relationships between the two populations seem to have worsened over time, as the barbarian populations were deemed to be less human in the eyes of the Wajin. Whether these perspectives were the result of religious teachings, social perceptions, political actions, economic intentions, actual interactions, or a growing form of "nationalistic pride," the gulf grew to the point that the inequality between the groups was obvious.

Eventually, as the Japanese ideas of empire developed more fully, the Ainu became nothing more than tools for economic development or obstacles in the way of "progress." Much as the Indigenous populations of the United States, Canada, Great Britain, and other settler countries were seen as problems to be solved or swept away, the Ainu were a problem that needed to be solved.

The annexation of Hokkaido and the assimilation of the Ainu people therein was in line with other countries; indeed, Japan's policies toward the Ainu of Hokkaido were modeled on the policies used by Western governments in response to Indigenous people within their countries. The assimilation policies continued to emphasize the separateness and differences between the Ainu communities and the colonist farmers, but the Ainu quietly continued on. Like American Indians, First Nations, Aboriginal Australians, and the Māori, the Ainu have refused to quietly fade away.

What Does the Development of the Ainu as an Indigenous People Tell About the Situation of Indigenous People / Colonized People in Contemporary Society Today?

An examination of the Ainu as the only officially recognized Indigenous population of Japan can serve as a case study for students and researchers in university Indigenous studies programs as they look at unequal relationships between colonizing and colonized populations. Ainu resilience has been obvious, and their struggles should not be forgotten or erased. In many ways, the recent chapter of the Ainu story is the result of civil rights struggles across the world during the social unrest of the 1960s and 1970s. It is also the result of increased availability of international communication between existing cultures of Indigenous peoples on a global scale and the rising political savvy that was exchanged from one group to another.

The struggle is not over by any means, but it is an important addition to examples of operating within the system to initiate change. There are still Indigenous groups who do not have the same level of recognition— the Ryukyuan people, as noted previously—but who are taking more active roles in trying to develop their own level of self-governance and self-determination options.

The Ainu are not finished in their struggles with the Japanese government for full recognition of their rights yet, either. Contemporary Ainu populations are trying to find ways to fit their perspectives within the international guidelines established within the United Nations Declaration on the Rights of Indigenous People in terms of self-governance, self-determination, access to natural resources, and their ability to provide levels of services to their community members. As noted in chapter 7, the idea of membership within an organization that has the overall benefit of the Ainu community as its foremost goal needs to be addressed and developed.

Beyond this, the Ainu are taking beginning steps in their journey toward some version of nationhood, but it takes work beyond just declaring oneself a nation. It will require a commitment from Ainu people across the Japanese state, and it will require expansion of Ainu education, economies, and Ainu persistence. There are numerous examples for the Ainu to draw from, and some examples will work better than others. In the United States, tribal governments have developed strong programs that provide economic support to their members; in New Zealand, the Māori continue to work within the dominant governance system to strengthen representation of Māori issues in federal and local systems.

The Raporo Ainu Nation court case discussed in chapter 9 could have far-reaching impact on the future of the Ainu people. If the Raporo were to win their appeal of the recent defeat and convince the Sapporo District Court that the Ainu never ceded their autonomy through any internationally recognized instrument, the relationships between the contemporary Ainu and the state government would likely shift. The status of the Ainu as a fully functioning Indigenous people with sovereignty and the right to self-determination would certainly become more possible, and the government funding mechanism that hinders Ainu economic development might ease its control over Ainu finances in a broad sense. Local Ainu groups would not have to rely on local governments to apply for funding to be used to benefit the entire region of which the Ainu are a part. The Ainu themselves could apply for programs of benefit to the Ainu, and such economic development would likely benefit the economies of the local jurisdiction as well. Such a reversal of roles would strengthen the role of the Ainu in regional economies rather than continuing to force the Ainu to remain a lesser organization.

How Can the Information Be Used to Help Better Understand Indigenous People and the Struggles They Have Faced?

It is easy to assume that every Indigenous person shares and understands the struggles of every other Indigenous person. The idea of pan-Indianism was rampant in the United States during the Red Power movement amid the civil unrest in the 1960s and 1970s. Pan-Indianism worked in the United States as a mechanism to draw together American Indian people from urban areas who had been lured away from reservations in the 1950s in response to federal government programs toward assimilating them and thus doing away with the "Indian problem." Pan-Indianism gave disparate groups of people common goals, common structure, and common "contextual background" of understanding and sharing.

For members of the dominant society, the stories of "being Indigenous" might be unheard or ignored; the Indigenous might be seen as a minor part of a homogenized national past that is inclusive of everyone. For some, the idea that there are still people who have different identities, different histories, and different cultural experiences might be foreign. This idea of "Indigenous" is easy for some to comprehend but often difficult to explain or quantify.

Likewise, it is also difficult for many members of the dominant society to perceive of "Indigenous rights" outside of the rights provided by the dominant culture. In the United States, some people complain about tribal sovereignty and the idea that tribal people should not have rights that other U.S. citizens don't have, regardless of the historical reasons that have created the differences.

Some members of the dominant society see this as another type of "reverse discrimination," where groups of people receive access to programs that specifically exclude others. The response of Yasuyuki Kaneko declaring that "by identifying themselves as 'Ainu,' people benefit from government welfare, including low-interest housing loans, scholarships, and support for obtaining driving licenses, as well as subsidies to the Ainu Association of Hokkaidō" (Ishihara 2019, 613), as detailed in chapter 1, continues to inflame distrust of Ainu people and the programs created for them by the Japanese government.

Government programs created to minimize discrimination suffered historically by specific groups are intended to help alleviate the impacts suffered by members of that group in the past. However, these programs are not intended to financially repay those historic wrongs. Restitution programs have been proposed in the United States to provide reparations for "black Americans whose ancestors were enslaved in the United States for government policies that allowed centuries of chattel slavery and legal race discrimination" (Darity et al. 2024, 1) to be initiated in addition to the antidiscrimination programs available to *all* citizens of the United States.

What Can Be Done to Help Improve the Ainu Situation?

During my time in Hokkaido, I was asked by Ainu communities for information about how American Indians exercise their sovereignty, economic development, self-determination, and other rights in the contemporary United States. I tried to offer general insights but generally focused on providing examples from my own tribe, the Choctaw Nation of Oklahoma, since it is the one that I am the most familiar with. The examples I provided related to four themes: (1) self-governance as demonstration of the ability of a group to work within existing national governments to govern its tribal members, (2) tribal economic development programs as a means to support group members, (3) the idea of tribal membership programs to determine qualified group members, and (4) the types and range of services provided by the Choctaw Nation to its enrolled tribal members as a way of bypassing or supplementing government programs for greater self-reliance and self-governance.

Ainu communities are trying to find examples to follow in their struggles to gain self-sufficiency as a means of controlling their own destinies. Reliance on the Japanese government to help them reach self-sufficiency is likely misplaced, in that the government does not seem to see itself as able to focus programs on any ethnic group to the exclusion (perceived or real) of all/any individuals regardless of ethnicity or cultural background. Teruki Tsunemoto (2023) and other experts have written that Article 14 of the Japanese Constitution prevented the government from creating specifically focused programs for the Ainu. Article 14 states that "all of the people are equal under the law and there shall be no discrimination in political, economic or social relations because of race, creed, sex, social status or family origin."[1]

Tsunemoto (2023) argues, however, that the Constitution allowed the passage of the Ainu Policy Promotion Act of 2019 because Article 14 has generally been interpreted to allow differential treatment for a portion of the population if the treatment is based on rational reasons in accordance with the nature of things. He writes that the Advisory Council decided that "deriving policies from the indigenousness of the Ainu would satisfy the condition of a rational reason in accordance with the nature of things" (2019a, 68).

Indigenous archaeology might have something to offer Hokkaido Ainu groups. Currently, the recognition of Ainu culture on Hokkaido begins at historical times, or about A.D. 1300 to 1500. Would further recognition of the time depth of the Ainu and their tenure on Hokkaido influence how others see the annexation of Hokkaido? Would such evidence of Ainu heritage further back in time indicate a stronger claim to the territory, or is the current historical depth enough to draw into question the "legality" of the mainland annexation of Hokkaido? Kato is hoping his research will provide more evidence of cultures in the archaeological past that can be equated with "Ainu" as a means of strengthening Ainu claims to the history and their past and to help them be more in control of (or at least a part of) scientific interpretations of their culture. His attempts at involving the Ainu in archaeological research "with, for, and by Indigenous peoples" (Nicholas and Andrews 1997, 3) is a nascent form of Indigenous archaeology, but it is a start in trying to make archaeology more useful to the local communities (see Nicholas and Montgomery 2024 for a current discussion of Indigenous archaeology on a more global scale).

Ultimately, I think it will be up to the Ainu—however they choose to define themselves and however they set themselves up to exist in the contemporary world—to determine how they would like external help. It should not be up to outsiders to second-guess their needs, but rather

---

1. Constitution of Japan, May 3, 1947, https://japan.kantei.go.jp/constitution_and _government_of_japan/constitution_e.html.

the Ainu communities should be in charge of their destinies. Researchers should not be working *on* the Ainu but rather *with* them.

This book is an attempt at offering something that might be of use to them in the days forward. To me, it is a first step, and in no way is it meant to be the last word on Ainu issues. I hope that it will provide some information for people who are not aware of Ainu history and contemporary Ainu issues in Japan.

REFERENCES

Abe, Ai. 2023. "An Outstanding Claim: The Ryukyu/Okinawa Peoples' Right to Self-Determination Under International Human Rights Law." *Asian Journal of International Law* 13 (1): 22–45.

Abe, Chiharu, Christian Leipe, Pavel E. Tarasov, Stefanie Müller, and Mayke Wagner. 2016. "Spatio-temporal Distribution of Hunter–Gatherer Archaeological Sites in the Hokkaido Region (Northern Japan): An Overview." *The Holocene* 26 (10): 1627–45.

Adachi, Noboru, Tsuneo Kakuda, Ryohei Takahashi, Hideaki Kanzawa-Kiriyama, and Ken-ichi Shinoda. 2018. "Ethnic Derivation of the Ainu Inferred from Ancient Mitochondrial DNA Data." *American Journal of Biological Anthropology* 165 (1): 139–48.

Adachi, Noboru, Hideaki Kanzawa-Kiriyama, Takashi Nara, Tsuneo Kakuda, Iwao Nishida, and Ken-ichi Shinoda. 2021. "Ancient Genomes from the Initial Jomon Period: New Insights into the Genetic History of the Japanese Archipelago." *Anthropological Science* 129 (1): 13–22.

Aikens, C. Melvin, and Takayasu Higuchi. 1982. *Prehistory of Japan.* Studies in Archaeology. Academic Press.

Ainu Association of Hokkaido. n.d. "Ainu Historical Events." Accessed November 29, 2024. https://www.ainu-assn.or.jp/english/history.html.

Alford, Katrina. 2005. "Comparing Australian with Canadian and New Zealand Primary Care Health Systems in Relation to Indigenous Populations: Literature Review and Analysis." Onemda VicHealth Koori Health Unit Discussion Paper No. 13.

Amano, Tetsuya. 2003. "Ohôtsuku bunka to wa nanika" [What is the Okhotsk culture?]. In *Shin Hokkaidô no Kodai 2: Zoku-Jômon, Ohôtsuku Bunka* [New ancient

Hokkaido 2: The post-Jomon and Okhotsk cultures], edited by Takashi Nomura and Hiroshi Utagawa. Sapporo, Hokkaido.

Amano, Tetsuya, Hideo Akanuma, and Artur V. Kharinskiy. 2013. "Study on the Production Region of Iron Goods and the Roots of Forging Technology of the Okhotsk Culture." [In Japanese.] *Bulletin of the Hokkaido University Museum* 6:1–17.

Amemiya, Mizuki. 1994. "Minamikyushu Jomonjidai sosoki doki hennen—Futome no ryutaimondoki kara entokikagaramonkei doki heno hensen" [The chronology of the Incipient Jomon: From thick Ryutaimon pottery to Entokikagaramonkei pottery]. *Newsletter of Jomon Study in South Kyushu* 8:1–12.

Anguita-Ruiz, Augusto, Concepción Aguilera, and Ángel Gil. 2020. "Genetics of Lactose Intolerance: An Updated Review and Online Interactive World Maps of Phenotype and Genotype Frequencies." *Nutrients* 12 (9): 1–20.

Aqil, Alber, Stephanie Gill, Omer Gokcumen, Ripan S. Malhi, Esther Aaltséen Reese, Jane L. Smith, Timothy T. Heaton, and Charlotte Lindqvis. 2023. "A Paleogenome from a Holocene Individual Supports Genetic Continuity in Southeast Alaska." *iScience* 26 (5): 1–23.

Aquash, Mark. 2013. "First Nations in Canada: Decolonization and Self-Determination." *In Education* 19 (2): 120–37.

Arnold, Bettina. 1990. "The Past as Propaganda: Totalitarian Archaeology in Nazi Germany." *Antiquity* 64 (244): 464–78.

Asch, Michael. 2014. *On Being Here to Stay: Treaties and Aboriginal Rights in Canada.* University of Toronto Press.

Bae, Christopher J. 2017. "Late Pleistocene Human Evolution in Eastern Asia: Behavioral Perspectives." *Current Anthropology* 58 (S17): 514–26.

Bailey, Douglas. 2009. "The Chobonaino Dogū: Understanding a Late Jomon Figure from Hakodate." In *The Power of Dogū*, edited by Simon Kaner. British Museum Press.

Bannai, Makoto, Jun-ya Ohashi, Shinji Harihara, Yuji Takahashi, Takeo Juji, Keiichi Omoto, and Katsushi Tokunaga. 2000. "Analysis of HLA Genes and Haplotypes in Ainu (from Hokkaido, Northern Japan) Supports the Premise That They Descent from Upper Paleolithic Populations of East Asia." *Tissue Antigens* 55 (2): 128–39.

Batchelor, John. 1892. *The Ainu of Japan: The Religions, Superstitions, and General History of the Hairy Aborigines of Japan.* Religious Tract Society.

Batchelor, John. (1901) 2006. *The Ainu and Their Folklore.* Religious Tract Society.

Broeker, Wallace S. 2001. "Was the Medieval Warm Period Global?" *Science* 291 (5508): 1497–99.

Browning, Zachary. 2019. "A Comparative Analysis: Legal and Historical Analysis of Protecting Indigenous Cultural Rights Involving Land Disputes in Japan, New Zealand, and Hawai'i." *Washington International Law Journal* 28 (1): 207–42.

Bullfinch, Chris. 2017. "'Freakshow': The Treatment of Ainu at Japanese World's Fair Exhibits of 1893 and 1904." Trinity College Digital Repository.

Burden, Conrad J. 2019. "Population Genetics." In *Encyclopedia of Bioinformatics and Computational Biology*, edited by Shoba Ranganathan, Michael Gribskov, Kenta Nakai, and Christian Schönbach. Academic Press.

Buvit, Ian, Masami Izuho, Karisa Terry, Yorinao Shitaoka, Tsutomu Soda, and Dai Kunikita. 2014. "Late Pleistocene Geology and Paleolithic Archaeology of the Shimaki Site, Hokkaido, Japan." *Geoarchaeology: An International Journal* 29 (3): 221–37.

Caldwell, Joseph R. 1958. *Trend and Tradition in the Prehistory of the Eastern United States*. Scientific Papers 10. Illinois State Museum and American Anthropological Association.

Canadian Department of Justice / Ministère de la Justice. 2018. "Principles: Respecting the Government of Canada's Relationship with Indigenous Peoples." https://www.justice.gc.ca/eng/csj-sjc/principles.pdf.

Cartwright, Mark. 2017a. "Buddhism in Ancient Japan." *World History Encyclopedia*, June 19. https://www.worldhistory.org/article/1080/buddhism-in-ancient-japan/.

Cartwright, Mark. 2017b. "Queen Himiko." *World History Encyclopedia*, May 1. https://www.worldhistory.org/Queen_Himiko/.

Cartwright, Mark. 2017c. "Shinto." *World History Encyclopedia*, April 3. https://www.worldhistory.org/Shinto/.

Cassidy, Jim, Irina Ponkratova, and Ben Fitzhugh, eds. *Maritime Prehistory of Northeast Asia*. Springer.

CBC-Radio Canada. 2022. "Indigenous Archaeologist Argues Humans May Have Arrived Here 130,000 Years Ago." *Ideas*, January 13. https://www.cbc.ca/radio/ideas/indigenous-archaeologist-argues-humans-may-have-arrived-here-130-000-years-ago-1.6313892.

Centers for Disease Control and Prevention. 2013. "CDC Health Disparities and Inequalities Report—United States, 2013." MMWR 2013;62(Suppl 3). U.S. Government Printing Office: 2013-623-210; Region IV. https://www.cdc.gov/mmwr/pdf/other/su6203.pdf.

Chen, Jianhui, Fahu Chen, Song Feng, Wei Huang, Jianbao Liu, and Aifeng Zhou. 2015. "Hydroclimatic Changes in China and Surroundings During the Medieval Climate Anomaly and Little Ice Age: Spatial Patterns and Possible Mechanisms." *Quaternary Science Reviews* 107:98–111.

Cheung, Sidney C. H. 2003. "Ainu Culture in Transition." In "Futures of Indigenous Cultures," edited by V. M. Razak. Special issue, *Futures: The Journal of Policy, Planning, and Futures Studies* 35 (9): 951–59.

Chiba, Norikazu. 2023. "Remains of Sakhalin Ainu, Who Faced Troubled History, Set to Return to Japan for 1st Time." *The Mainichi*, March 12. https://mainichi.jp/english/articles/20230309/p2a/00m/0na/027000c.

Clavell, James. 1975. *Shōgun*. Delacorte.

Claw, Katrina G., Matthew Z. Anderson, Rene L. Begay, Krystal S. Tosie, Keolu Fox, Nanibaa' A. Garrison, and the Summer Internship for Indigenous Peoples in Genomics (SING) Consortium. 2018. "A Framework for Enhancing Ethical Genomic Research with Indigenous Communities." *Nature Communications* 9:2957.

Coates, Ken S. 2004. *A Global History of Indigenous Peoples: Struggle and Survival.* Palgrave Macmillan.

Cole, Wade. 2011. *Uncommon Schools: The Global Rise of Postsecondary Institutions for Indigenous Peoples.* Stanford University Press.

Commonwealth of Australia. 1997. *Bringing Them Home: National Inquiry into the Separation of Aboriginal and Torres Strait Islander Children from Their Families.* https://humanrights.gov.au/sites/default/files/content/pdf/social_justice /bringing_them_home_report.pdf.

Cooke, Martin, Francis Mitrou, David Lawrence, Eric Guimond, and Dan Beavon. 2007. "Indigenous Well-Being in Four Countries: An Application of the UN-DP'S Human Development Index to Indigenous Peoples in Australia, Canada, New Zealand, and the United States." *BMC International Health and Human Rights* 7:9.

Cooke, Niall P., Valeria Mattiangeli, Lara M. Cassidy, et al. 2021. "Ancient Genomics Reveals Tripartite Origins of Japanese Populations." *Science Advances* 7 (38).

Cornell, John B. 1964. "Ainu Assimilation and Cultural Extinction: Acculturation Policy in Hokkaido." *Ethnology* 3 (3): 287–304.

Cornell, Stephen. 2005. "Indigenous Peoples, Poverty and Self-Determination in Australia, New Zealand, Canada and the United States." In *Indigenous Peoples and Poverty: An International Perspective,* edited by Robyn Eversole, John-Andrew McNeish, and Alberto D. Cimadamore. CROP International Studies in Poverty Research and Zed Books.

Cotterill, Simon. 2011. "Ainu Success: The Political and Cultural Achievements of Japan's Indigenous Minority." *Asian-Pacific Journal* 9 (2): 1–26.

Crawford, Gary W. 1983. *Paleoethnobotany of the Kameda Peninsula Jomon.* Museum of Anthropology, University of Michigan.

Crawford, Gary W. 1987. "Plant Seeds Excavated from the K135 Site." [In Japanese.] In *The K135 Site, Sapporo, Japan.* Sapporo-shi Kyoiku Iinkai.

Crawford, Gary W. 2008. "The Jomon in Early Agriculture Discourse: Issues Arising from Matsui, Kanehara and Pearson." *World Archaeology* 40 (4): 445–65.

Crawford, Gary W. 2011. "Advances in Understanding Early Agriculture in Japan." *Current Anthropology* 52 (S4): 331–45.

Crawford, Michael H. 2006. *Anthropological Genetics: Theory, Methods, and Applications.* Cambridge University Press.

Crawford, Michael H., and Kristine G. Beaty. 2013. "DNA Fingerprinting in Anthropological Genetics: Past, Present, and Future." *Investigative Genetics* 4:23.

Crema, Enrico R., Junko Habu, Kenichi Kobayashi, and Marco Madella. 2016. "Summed Probability Distribution of 14C Dates Suggests Regional Divergences in the Population Dynamics of the Jomon Period in Eastern Japan." *PLOS ONE* 11 (4): e0154809.

D'Andrea, A. Catherine. 1995. "Archaeobotanical Evidence for Zoku-Jomon Subsistence at the Mochiyazawa Site, Hokkaido, Japan." *Journal of Archaeological Science* 22 (5): 583–95.

Darity, William, Jr., Thomas Craemer, Daina Ramey Berry, and Dania V. Francis. 2024. "Black Reparations in the United States, 2024: An Introduction." *RSF: The Russell Sage Foundation Journal of the Social Sciences* 10 (2): 1–28.

Davenport, Charles. 1911. *Heredity in Relation to Eugenics*. Henry Holt.

Deloria, Vine, Jr. 1995. *Red Earth, White Lies: Native Americans and the Myth of Scientific Fact*. Scribner and Sons.

Derby, Mark. 2012. "Ngā Take Māori—Government Policy and Māori." *Te Ara—The Encyclopedia of New Zealand*. https://teara.govt.nz/en/nga-take-maori-govern ment-policy-and-maori.

Dubreuil, Chisato O. 2004. *From the Playground of the Gods: The Life & Art of Bikky Sunazawa*. Arctic Studies Center, National Museum of Natural History, Smithsonian Institution.

Durham, William H. 1991. *Coevolution: Genes, Culture, and Human Diversity*. Stanford University Press.

Dye, David H., and Patty Jo Watson. 2010. "Primary Forest Efficiency in the Eastern Woodlands of North America." *Early Georgia* 38 (2): 159–67.

Ens, Gerhard J., and Joe Sawchuck. 2016. *From New Peoples to New Nations: Aspects of Métis History and Identity from the Eighteenth to the Twenty-First Centuries*. University of Toronto Press.

Falls, Thomas, and Joel Anderson. 2022. "Attitudes Towards Aboriginal and Torres Strait Islander Peoples in Australia: A Systematic Review." *Australian Journal of Psychology* 74 (1): e2039043.

Fawcett, Clare. 2009. "Nationalism and Postwar Japanese Archaeology." In *Nationalism, Politics, and the Practice of Archaeology*, edited by Philip L. Kohl and Clare Fawcett. Cambridge University Press.

Fitzhugh, Ben, Valery O. Shubin, Kaoru Tezuka, Yoshihiro Ishizuka, and Carole A. S. Mandryk. 2002. "Archaeology in the Kuril Islands: Advances in the Study of Human Paleobiogeography and Northwest Pacific Prehistory." *Arctic Anthropology* 39 (1–2): 69–94.

Fitzhugh, William, and Chisato O. Dubreuil, eds. 1999. *Ainu: Spirit of a Northern People*. Arctic Studies Center, National Museum of Natural History, Smithsonian Institution, in association with the University of Washington Press.

Foundation for Ainu Culture. n.d. "Basic Policies." Accessed November 29, 2024. https://www.ff-ainu.or.jp/web/english/project.html.

Fowler, Don D. 1987. "Uses of the Past: Archaeology in the Service of the State." *American Antiquity* 52 (2): 229–48.

Foxhall, Lin. 2018. "Introduction: Rethinking Protohistories: Texts, Material Culture and New Methodologies." *World Archaeology* 50 (5): 677–89.

Freeman, Milton M. R. 2011. "Looking Back—and Looking Ahead—35 Years After the Inuit Land Use and Occupancy Project." *The Canadian Geographer / Le Géographe Canadien* 55 (1): 20–31.

Fukuzawa, Hosanna. 2022. "Ainu Ethnogenesis and State Evasion (12th–17th Centuries)." *Asia-Pacific Journal* 20 (2).

Gao, Xing, and Christopher J. Norton. 2002. "A Critique of the Chinese 'Middle Paleolithic.'" *Antiquity* 76 (292): 397–412.

Gayman, Jeffry, Kanako Uzawa, and Ryoko Nakamura. 2023. "Japan." In *The Indigenous World 2023*, edited by Dwayne Mamo. IWGIA.

Gayman, Jeffry, Kanako Uzawa, Ryoko Nakamura, and Risako Sakai. 2024. "Japan." In *The Indigenous World 2024*, edited by Dwayne Mamo. IWGIA.

Graber, Robert Bates. 2010. "Social Evolution." In *21st Century Anthropology: A Reference Handbook*, vol. 1, edited by H. James Birx. SAGE Reference.

Grant, Madison. 1916. *The Passing of the Great Race, or The Racial Basis of European History*. Charles Scribner's Sons.

Grunow, Tristan R., Fuyubi Nakamura, Katsuya Hirano, Mai Ishihara, ann-elise lewallen, Sheryl Lightfoot, et al., eds. 2019. "Hokkaidō 150: Settler Colonialism and Indigeneity in Modern Japan and Beyond." Special issue, *Critical Asian Studies* 51 (4): 597–636.

Gustafsson, Anders, and Håkan Karlsson. 2012. "Changing of the Guards." In *The Oxford Handbook of Public Archaeology*, edited by J. Carman, Carol McDavid, and Robin Skeates. Oxford University Press.

Habu, Junko. 2004. *Ancient Jomon of Japan*. Cambridge University Press.

Habu, Junko. 2008. "Growth and Decline in Complex Hunter-Gatherer Societies: A Case Study from the Jomon Period Sannai Maruyama Site, Japan." *Antiquity* 82 (317): 571–84.

Habu, Junko, and Clare Fawcett. 1999. "Jomon Archaeology and the Representation of Japanese Origins." *Antiquity* 73 (281): 587–93.

Habu, Junko, Peter V. Lape, and John W. Olsen, eds. 2018. *Handbook of East and Southeast Asian Archaeology*. Springer.

Habu, Junko, Akira Matsui, Naoto Yamamoto, and Tomonori Kanno. 2011. "Shell Midden Archaeology in Japan: Aquatic Food Acquisition and Long-Term Change in the Jomon Culture." *Quaternary International* 239 (1–2): 19–27.

Hacker, Margaret Schmidt. 2018. "Parker, Cynthia Ann. (ca. 1825–ca. 1871)." *Handbook of Texas*. Texas State Historical Association, September 18. https://www.tshaonline.org/handbook/entries/parker-cynthia-ann.

Hammer, Michael F., Tatiana M. Karafet, Hwayong Park, Keiichi Omoto, Shinji Harihara, Mark Stoneking, and Satoshi Horai. 2006. "Dual Origins of the Japanese: Common Ground for Hunter-Gatherer and Farmer Y Chromosomes." *Journal of Human Genetics* 51:47–58.

Hanazaki, Kohei. 2001. "Ainu Moshir and Yaponesia: Ainu and Okinawan Identities in Contemporary Japan." Translated by Mark Hudson. In *Multicultural Japan: Palaeolithic to Postmodern*, edited by Donald Denoon, Mark Hudson, Gavan McCormack, and Tessa Morris-Suzuki. Cambridge University Press.

Hanihara, Kazuro. 1990. "Emishi, Ezo and Ainu: An Anthropological Perspective." *Japan Review*, no. 1, 35–48.

Hanihara, Kazuro. 1991. "Dual Structure Model for the Population History of the Japanese." *Japan Review*, no. 2, 1–33.

Hasebe, Kotondo. 1940. "The Ancient Japanese." [In Japanese.] *Journal of the Anthropological Society of Nippon* 55:27–34.

Heiss, Anita. n.d. "Government Policy in Relation to Aboriginal People." Sydney Barani. Accessed November 29, 2024. http://www.sydneybarani.com.au/sites/government-policy-in-relation-to-aboriginal-people/.

Henderson, William B. 2006. "Indian Act." Updated by Zach Parrott, 2022. *The Canadian Encyclopedia*. Accessed November 29, 2024. https://www.thecanadianencyclopedia.ca/en/article/indian-act.

Hendry, Joy. 2013. *Understanding Japanese Society*. 4th ed. Nissan Institute/Routledge Japanese Studies Series. Routledge.

Hennessey, John L. 2020. "A Colonial Trans-Pacific Partnership: William Smith Clark, David Pearce Penhallow and Japanese Settler Colonialism in Hokkaido." *Settler Colonial Studies* 10 (1): 54–73.

Heyes, Cressida. 2024. "Identity Politics." *Stanford Encyclopedia of Philosophy*. https://plato.stanford.edu/entries/identity-politics/.

Hill, Richard S. 2009. *Māori and the State: Crown–Māori Relations in New Zealand/Aotearoa, 1950–2000*. Victoria University Press.

Hirano, Katsuya. 2019. "Terra Nullius and the Modern Settler Colonization of Ainu Mosir." In "Hokkaidō 150: Settler Colonialism and Indigeneity in Modern Japan and Beyond," edited by Tristan R. Grunow, Fuyubi Nakamura, Katsuya Hirano, Mai Ishihara, ann-elise lewallen, Sheryl Lightfoot, et al. Special issue, *Critical Asian Studies* 51: (4): 600–606.

Hitchcock, Romyn. 1892. *The Ainos of Yezo, Japan*. Smithsonian Institution.

Hnin, Nang Thet Hsu, and Nang Khin Mya. 2021. "Comparison of the International Health Care Systems Through the Consideration of Population Health and Performance Indicators in Canada, Australia and New Zealand: A Systematic Literature Review." *International Journal of Scientific and Research Publications* 11 (2): 199–205.

Hodgson, Jason A., and Todd R. Disotell. 2010. "Anthropological Genetics: Inferring the History of Our Species Through the Analysis of DNA." *Evolution: Education and Outreach* 3:387–98.

Howell, David L. 1994. "Ainu Ethnicity and the Boundaries of the Early Modern Japanese State." *Past and Present*, no. 142, 69–93.

Howell, David L. 2005. *Geographies of Identity in Nineteenth-Century Japan*. University of California Press.

Howell, David L. 2014. "Is Ainu History Japanese History?" In *Beyond Ainu Studies: Changing Academic and Public Perspectives*, edited by Mark J. Hudson, ann-elise lewallen, and Mark K. Watson. University of Hawai'i Press.

Howells, William W. 1966. "The Jomon Population of Japan: A Study by Discriminant Analysis of Japanese and Ainu Crania." *Papers of the Peabody Museum of Archaeology and Ethnology, Harvard University* 57:1–43.

Hudson, Mark J. 1996. "Sannai Maruyama: A New View of Prehistoric Japan." *Asia-Pacific Magazine*, no. 2, 47–48.

Hudson, Mark J. 1999. *Ruins of Identity: Ethnogenesis in the Japanese Islands*. University of Hawai'i Press.

Hudson, Mark J. 2004. "The Perverse Realities of Change: World System Incorporation and the Okhotsk Culture of Hokkaido." *Journal of Anthropological Archaeology* 23 (3): 290–308.

Hudson, Mark J. 2014a. "Ainu and Hunter-Gatherer Studies." In *Beyond Ainu Studies: Changing Academic and Public Perspectives*, edited by Mark J. Hudson, ann-elise lewallen, and Mark K. Watson. University of Hawai'i Press.

Hudson, Mark J. 2014b. "The Ethnohistory and Anthropology of 'Modern' Hunter-Gatherers: North Japan (Ainu)." In *The Oxford Handbook of the Archaeology and Anthropology of Hunter-Gatherers*, edited by Vicki Cummings, Peter Jordan, and Marek Zvelebil. Oxford University Press.

Hudson, Mark J. 2017. "The Historical Ecology of Colonialism and Violence in Hokkaido, Sakhalin, and the Kuril Islands, AD 1200–1900." In *Handbook of East and Southeast Asian Archaeology*, edited by Junko Habu, Peter V. Lape, and John W. Olsen. Springer.

Hudson, Mark J., Shigeki Nakagome, and John B. Whitman. 2020. "The Evolving Japanese: The Dual Structure Hypothesis at 30." *Evolutionary Human Science* 2:e6.

Ichikawa, Morihiro. 2024. "Report on the Ruling in the Ainu Fishing Rights Case." Email pdf document in possession of the author.

Iizuka, Fumie, and Masami Izuho. 2017. "Late Upper Paleolithic-Initial Jomon Transitions, Southern Kyushu, Japan: Regional Scale to Macro Processes a Close Look." *Quaternary International* 441 (B): 102–12.

Imamura, Keiji. 1996. *Prehistoric Japan: New Perspectives on Insular East Asia*. University of Hawai'i Press.

International Symposium Reports Editorial Committee. 2024. *Sharing Story: Indigenous Struggles in the World*. Report of the International Symposium 2023: The Right to Catch Salmon in Rivers as Indigenous Right: A Gathering of Indigenous People Who Live from the Sea (*i*), the Forest (*o*), and the Rivers (*ru*). Raporo Ainu Nation.

Isaac, Gwyneira, Ingrid Ahlgren, Alan Ojiig Corbiere, and Judith Andrews. 2023. "Being Present and Bearing Witness: Talking About Cultural Revitalization Programming in Museums." *Museum Management and Curatorship* 38 (1): 18–42.

Ishihara, Mai. 2019. "The Silent History of Ainu Liminars." In "Hokkaidō 150: Settler Colonialism and Indigeneity in Modern Japan and Beyond," edited by Tristan R. Grunow, Fuyubi Nakamura, Katsuya Hirano, Mai Ishihara, ann-elise lewallen, Sheryl Lightfoot, et al. Special issue, *Critical Asian Studies* 51 (4): 597–636.

Ishikawa, Hideshi. 2000. "Tohoku-Nihon no hitobito no kuashi" [The life of the people of northeastern Japan]. In *Wajin o torimaku sekai* [The worlds surrounding the domain of the Wa people]. National Museum of Japanese History. Yamakawa Shuppan.

Izumi, Takura. 1985. "Jomon shuraku no chiiki-teki tokushitsu: Kinki Chiho no jirei kenkyu" [Regional characteristics of Jomon settlements: Case studies from the

Kinki region]. In *Chiri-gaku* [Lectures in archaeo-geography], vol. 4, edited by K. Koko. Gakusei-sha.

Japanese Society of Cultural Anthropology (JASCA). 2024. "Statement on Ainu Research." April 1. https://www.jasca.org/onjasca-e/JASCA%20Statement%20%20 20240401.pdf.

Jeong, Choongwon, Shigeki Nakagome, and Anna Di Rienzo. 2016. "Deep History of East Asian Populations Revealed Through Genetic Analysis of the Ainu." *Genetics* 202 (1): 261–72.

Jinam, Timothy A., Yosuke Kawai, and Naruya Saitou. 2021. "Modern Human DNA Analyses with Special Reference to the Inner Dual-Structure Model of Yaponesian." *Anthropological Science* 129 (1): 3–11.

Johnson, Rhiannon. 2019. "Exploring Identity: Who Are the Métis and What Are Their Rights?" CBC News, April 28. https://www.cbc.ca/news/indigenous/metis -identity-history-rights-explainer-1.5098585.

Jordon, Peter, Irina Y. Ponkratova, Viktor M. Dyakonov, Elena A. Solovyova, Toshiro Yamahara, Hirofumi Kato, and Marjolein Admiraal. 2022. "Tracking the Adoption of Early Pottery Traditions into Maritime Northeast Asia: Emerging Insights and New Questions." In *Maritime Prehistory of Northeast Asia*, edited by Jim Cassidy, Irina Ponkratova, and Ben Fitzhugh. Springer.

Kaner, Simon, and Yasuhiro Taniguchi. 2017. "The Development of Pottery and Associated Technological Developments in Japan, Korea, and the Russian Far East." In *Handbook of East and Southeast Asian Archaeology*, edited by Junko Habu, Peter V. Lape, and John W. Olsen, 321–45. Springer.

Kato, Hirofumi. 2009. "Whose Archaeology? Decolonizing Archaeological Perspective in Hokkaido Island." *Journal of the Graduate School of Letters* 4:47–55.

Kato, Hirofumi. 2017. "The Ainu and Japanese Archaeology: A Change of Perspective." *Japanese Journal of Archaeology* 4:185–90.

Kato, Hirofumi. 2018. "Hokkaido Sequence and the Archaeology of the Ainu People." In *Encyclopedia of Global Archaeology*, edited by Claire Smith.

Kayaba, Yuta, and Fumiko Yoshigaki. 2020. "Ainu Lawsuit over Fishing Rights Test Case for Much Larger Issues." *The Asahi Shimbun*, August 18. https://www.asahi .com/ajw/articles/13646254.

Kayano, Shigeru. 1994. *Our Land Was a Forest: An Ainu Memoir*. Westview Press.

Kiedrowski, John. 2013. *Trends in Indigenous Policing Models: An International Comparison*. Compliance Strategy Group, Ottawa. https://www.publicsafety.gc.ca/cnt /rsrcs/pblctns/trnds-ndgns-plc-mdl/.

Kikuchi, Toshihiko. 1986. "Continental Culture and Hokkaido." In *Windows on the Japanese Past*, edited by Richard Pearson. Center for Japanese Studies, Ann Arbor.

Kiyono, Kenji. 1943. *Studies on the Japanese Natives*. [In Japanese.] Ogiwara Seibunkan.

Kiyono, Kenji. 1949. *The Origin of Japanese as Viewed from Skeletal Morphology of the Early Populations*. [In Japanese.] Iwanami-shoten.

Kobayashi, Audrey. 2020. "Identity Politics." In *International Encyclopedia of Human Geography*, vol. 7, edited by Audrey Kobayashi. Elsevier.

Kobayashi, Seiji. 2001. "Eastern Japanese Pottery During the Jomon-Yayoi Transition: A Study in Forager-Farmer Interaction." *Bulletin of the Indo-Pacific Prehistory Association* 21:37–42.

Kodama, Daisei. 2003. "Komakino Stone Circle and Its Significance for the Study of Jomon Social Structure." In *Hunter-Gatherers of the North Pacific Rim*, edited by Junko Habu, James M. Savelle, Shuzo Koyama, and Hitomi Hongo. Senri Ethnological Studies 63. National Museum of Ethnology, Osaka.

Kohl, Philip L. 1998. "Nationalism and Archaeology: On the Constructions of Nations and the Reconstructions of the Remote Past." *Annual Review of Anthropology* 27:223–46. https://www.jstor.org/stable/223370.

Kojima, Kyōko. 2014. "The Making of Ainu Citizenship from the Viewpoint of Gender and Ethnicity." In *Gender, Nation and State in Modern Japan*, edited by Andrea Germer, Vera Mackie, and Ulrike Wöhr. Routledge.

Kudo, Yuichiro. 2012. *Environment and Culture History of the Upper Paleolithic and the Jomon Period: High-Precision Radiocarbon Dating and Archaeology.* [In Japanese.] Senshensha.

Kunitake, Sadakatsu. 2016. "Settlement Behavior in the Kanto Plain During the Japanese Paleolithic Based on Lithic Raw Material Procurement and Consumption." *Quaternary International* 425:158–72.

Kyodo News. 2024. "Ainu Lose Legal Battle over Right to Catch Salmon in Northern Japan." April 18. https://english.kyodonews.net/news/2024/04/288d6c42499c-ainu-loses-legal-battle-over-right-to-catch-salmon-in-northern-japan.html.

Lamb, Hubert H. 1965. "The Early Medieval Warm Epoch and Its Sequel." *Palaeogeography, Palaeoclimatology, Palaeoecology* 1:13–37.

Landor, A. H. Savage. 1893. *Alone with the Hairy Ainu: Or, 3800 Miles on a Pack Saddle in Yezo and a Cruise to the Kurile Islands.* John Murray.

Leach, Colin Wayne, Lisa M. Brown, and Ross E. Worden. 2008. "Ethnicity and Identity Politics." In *Encyclopedia of Violence, Peace & Conflict*, edited by Lester Kurtz. Academic Press.

Leslie, John. 1982. "The Bagot Commission: Developing a Corporate Memory for the Indian Department." *The Canadian Historical Association / La Société historique du Canada* 17 (1): 31–52.

Levin, Mark A. 2001. "Essential Commodities and Racial Justice: Using Constitutional Protection of Japan's Indigenous Ainu People to Inform Understandings of the United States and Japan." *International Law and Politics* 33:419–526.

lewallen, ann-elise. 2008. "Indigenous at Last! Ainu Grassroots Organizing and the Indigenous Peoples Summit in Ainu Mosir." *Asia-Pacific Journal* 6 (11): 1–22.

lewallen, ann-elise. 2015. "Human Rights and Cyber Hate Speech: The Case of the Ainu." *Focus Asia-Pacific* 81:9–12.

lewallen, ann-elise. 2016. *The Fabric of Indigeneity: Ainu Identity, Gender, and Settler Colonialism in Japan.* SAR Press.

Lightfoot, Sheryl. 2019. "New Perspectives on Indigeneity and Settler Colonialism: Implications from Japan's Colonial Rule on the Ainu and Hokkaidō." In "Hokkaidō

150: Settler Colonialism and Indigeneity in Modern Japan and Beyond," edited by Tristan R. Grunow, Fuyubi Nakamura, Katsuya Hirano, Mai Ishihara, annelise lewallen, Sheryl Lightfoot, Mayunkiki, Danika Medak-Saltzman, Terri-Lynn Williams-Davidson, and Tomoe Yahata. Special issue, *Critical Asian Studies* 51 (4): 617–21.

Loy, Christopher D. 2010. "The Ainu of Northern Japan: Indigeneity, Post-national Politics, Territoriality." PhD diss., Binghamton University, State University of New York.

MacCharles, Tonda. 2014. "Supreme Court Grants Land Title to B.C. First Nation in Landmark Case." *Toronto Star*, June 26.

Mann, Michael E., Zhihua Zhang, Scott Rutherford, et al. 2009. "Global Signatures and Dynamical Origins of the Little Ice Age and Medieval Climate Anomaly." *Science* 326 (5957): 1256–60.

Manning, Daniel. 2023. "Hokkaido from Edo Samurai to Reiwa Japan: The Challenge of Preserving History." *JAPAN Forward*, August 8. https://japan-forward.com /hokkaido-from-edo-samurai-to-reiwa-japan-the-challenge-of-preserving-history/.

Marks, Jonathan. 2012. "Origins of Anthropological Genetics." *Current Anthropology* 53 (S5): 161–72.

Mastana, Sarabjit. 2007. "Molecular Anthropology: Population and Forensic Genetic Applications." *The Anthropologist*, special vol., no. 3, 373–83.

Matsumoto, Naoko, Junko Habu, and Akira Matsui. 2017. "Subsistence, Sedentism, and Social Complexity Among Jomon Hunter-Gatherers of the Japanese Archipelago." In *Handbook of East and Southeast Asian Archaeology*, edited by Junko Habu, Peter V. Lape, and John W. Olsen. Springer.

Matsumura, Hirofumi, Mark J. Hudson, Kenichiro Koshida, and Yoichi Minakawa. 2006. "Embodying Okhotsk Ethnicity: Human Skeletal Remains from the Aonae Dune Site, Okushiri Island, Hokkaido." *Asian Perspectives* 45 (1): 1–23.

Matsu'ura, Taheshiro. 2002. *Ainu Jinbutsu-shi* [The Ainu people]. Hebonsha.

McKee, Jessie O., and Steve Murray. 1986. "Economic Progress and Development in the Mississippi Band of Choctaw Indians Since 1945." In *After Removal: The Choctaw in Mississippi*, edited by Samuel J. Wells and Roseanna Tubby. University Press of Mississippi.

Merlan, Francesca. 2009. "Indigeneity: Global and Local, with CA Comments." *Current Anthropology* 50 (3): 303–33.

Minamikayabe Buried Cultural Properties Research Team. 2002. *The Kakinoshima B Site*. [In Japanese.] Minamikayabe Buried Cultural Properties Research Team.

Miyazawa, Eiji, and Mary Inez Hilger. 1967. "Japan's 'Sky People,' the Vanishing Ainu." *National Geographic* 131 (2): 268–96.

Mizoguchi, Koji. 2017. "The Yayoi and Kofun Periods of Japan." In *Handbook of East and Southeast Asian Archaeology*, edited by Junko Habu, Peter V. Lape, and John W. Olsen. Springer.

Morris-Suzuki, Tessa. 2018. "Performing Ethnic Harmony: The Japanese Government's Plans for a New Ainu Law." *Asia-Pacific Journal* 16 (2): 1–18.

Morse, Edward S. 1879. *Shell Mounds of Omori*. Memoirs of the Science Department, University of Tokyo 1, pt. 1. University of Tokyo.

Munro, Neil Gordon. 1963. *Ainu Creed and Cult*. Columbia University.

Murakami, Noboru. 2008. "The Chronology of Early Jomon Pottery in the Western Japanese Archipelago: Especially Focused on the South Kyushu Region." [In Japanese.] *Journal of the Japanese Archaeological Association* 14 (24): 1–20. https://doi.org/10.11215/nihonkokogaku1994.14.24_1.

Nakama, Kenji. 1987. "Shogikuri-gata jukyo" [The Shogikuri-type pit-dwelling]. In *Higashi-Ajia no koko to rekishi* [Archaeology and history in East Asia,], vol. 2, edited by Committee for the Celebration of the Retirement of Professor Takashi Okazaki. Dohosha.

Nakamura, Keiko. 2022. *The Edo Shogunate's Northern Defense: How the Samurai Defended the "Japan Territory."* [In Japanese.] Heart Publishing.

Nakamura, Naohiro. 2008. "An 'Effective' Involvement of Indigenous People in Environmental Impact Assessment: The Cultural Impact Assessment of the Saru River Region, Japan." *Australian Geographer* 39 (4): 427–44.

Nakamura, Naohiro. 2015. "Being Indigenous in a Non-Indigenous Environment: Identity Politics of the Dogai Ainu and New Indigenous Policies of Japan." *Environment and Planning A* 47 (3): 660–75.

Nakamura, Naohiro. 2017. "Cultural Affiliation Is Not Enough: The Repatriation of Ainu Human Remains." *Polar Record* 53 (2): 220–24.

Nakamura, Naohiro. 2019. "Redressing Injustice of the Past: The Repatriation of Ainu Human Remains." *Japan Forum* 31 (3): 358–377.

Nakamura, Oki. 1999. "Social Stratification in Jomon Society on the Basis of Burial Analysis." [In Japanese.] In *The World of Jomon Archaeology*, edited by Tatsuo Kobayashi. Asahi Shinbun-sha.

Nakazawa, Yuichi. 2017. "On the Pleistocene Population History in the Japanese Archipelago." *Current Anthropology* 58 (S17): 539–52.

Nakazawa, Yuichi, and Christopher J. Bae. 2018. "Quaternary Paleoenvironmental Variation and Its Impact on Initial Human Dispersals into the Japanese Archipelago." *Palaeogeography, Palaeoclimatology, Palaeoecology* 512:145–55.

Nicholas, George P. 2008. "Native Peoples and Archaeology." In *Encyclopedia of Archaeology*, edited by Deborah M. Pearsall. Academic Press.

Nicholas, George P., and Thomas D. Andrews, eds. 1997. *At a Crossroads: Archaeology and First Peoples of Canada*. Publication no. 24. Archaeology Press.

Nicholas, George P., and Lindsay M. Montgomery. 2024. "Indigenous Archaeology." In *Encyclopedia of Archaeology*, vol. 1, edited by Peter F. Biehl and Maria-Luz Endere. 2nd ed. Elsevier.

Niklasson, Elisabeth, and Herdis Hølleland. 2018. "The Scandinavian far-right and the new politicisation of heritage." *Journal of Social Archaeology* 18 (2): 121–48.

Nishida, Masaki. 1983. "The Emergence of Food Production in Neolithic Japan." *Journal of Anthropological Archaeology* 2 (4): 305–22.

Noda, Satoru. 2014. *Golden Kamuy*. Shueisha Publishing.

Ohyi, Haruo. 2011. "Questions about 'Indigenous Archaeology,' or Current Situation and Problems of 'Ainu Archaeology.'" [In Japanese.] *Hokkaido Archaeology* 47:87–96.

Oikawa, Sarasa, and Tomoko Yoshida. 2007. "An Identity Based on Being Different: A Focus on Biethnic Individuals in Japan." *International Journal of Intercultural Relations* 31 (6): 633–53.

Okada, Hiroaki. 1998. "Maritime Adaptations in Hokkaido." *Arctic Anthropology* 35 (1): 340–49.

Okasha, Samir. 2022. "Population Genetics." *Stanford Encyclopedia of Philosophy.* https://plato.stanford.edu/entries/population-genetics/.

Onai, Toru, ed. 2011. *Living Conditions and Consciousness of Present-Day Ainu: Report on the 2008 Hokkaido Ainu Living Conditions Survey, Part 1.* Center for Ainu and Indigenous Studies, Hokkaido University.

Osaka, Tomohiro. 2024. "Japan Court Denies Fishing Rights to Ainu People." *The Japan Times*, April 19.

Osakada, Yuko. 2021. "An Examination of Arguments over the Ainu Policy Promotion Act of Japan Based on the UN Declaration on the Rights of Indigenous Peoples." *International Journal of Human Rights* 25 (6): 1053–69.

O'Sullivan, Dominic. 2017. *Indigeneity: A Politics of Potential: Australia, Fiji and New Zealand.* Bristol University Press.

Pai, Hyung Il. 2013. *Heritage Management in Korea and Japan: The Politics of Antiquity and Identity.* University of Washington Press.

Parata, Hekia. 1994. "Mainstreaming: A Maori Affairs Policy?" *Social Policy Journal of New Zealand*, no. 3.

Parezo, Nancy J., and Donald D. Fowler. 2007. *Anthropology Goes to the Fair: The 1904 Louisiana Purchase Exposition.* University of Nebraska Press.

Peltier, Shanna, and Jeffrey Ansloos. 2021. "Indigeneity: Critical Implications of Indigenous Identity on Indigenous Child and Youth Mental Health." In *The Palgrave Encyclopedia of Critical Perspectives on Mental Health*, edited by Jessica Nina Lester and Michelle O'Reilly. Palgrave Macmillan.

Pratt, Richard Henry. (1892) 1973. "The Advantages of Mingling Indians with Whites." In *Americanizing the American Indians: Writings by the "Friends of the Indian,"* *1880–1900*, edited by Francis Paul Prucha. Harvard University Press.

Pulver, Lisa Jackson, Melissa R. Haswell, Ian Ring, John Waldon, Wayne Clark, Valoria Whetung, et al. 2010. "Indigenous Health—Australia, Canada, Aotearoa New Zealand, and the United States—Laying Claim to a Future That Embraces Health for Us All." Background paper no. 33. World Health Organization, Geneva, Switzerland.

Reynolds, Henry. 1999. *Why Weren't We Told? A Personal Search for the Truth Behind Our History.* Penguin Books Australia.

Riedl, Karin. 2014. "Beyond Numbers: The Participation of Indigenous Peoples in Parliament." Survey report. Inter-Parliamentary Union, Geneva.

Sakahira, Fumihiro, and Takao Terano. 2016. "Revisiting the Dynamics Between Two Ancient Japanese Descent Groups: What Happened from the Jomon to the Yayoi

Periods in Japan." In *Simulating Prehistoric and Ancient Worlds*, edited by Juan A. Barceló and Florencia Del Castillo. Computational Social Sciences. Springer.

Sashima, Masaki. 2021. "Lawsuit for Declaratory Judgment on Salmon Fishing Rights." English translation by Michael J. Ioannides. *Utaspano Uoupekare*, no. 25, 1–3. http://shimingaikou.org/wp-content/uploads/2022/07/Newsletter-25_MI _June-26.pdf.

Sato, Takao. 2005. "Brown Bear Cranium Excavated from Ikushina-Kita Kaigan Site." [In Japanese.] *Bulletin of the Shiretoko Museum* 26:71–76.

Sato, Takao. 2019. "A Zooarchaeological Study of the Formation Process of the Ainu Bear-Sending Ceremony." In *Animals and Their Relation to Gods, Humans and Things in the Ancient World*, edited by Raija Mattila, Sanae Ito, and Sebastian Fink. Springer VS.

Sato, Takao, Jun Matsubayashi, and Minoru Yoneda. 2022. "Rausu-chō otafuku iwa dōkutsu to Kitami-shi Nakanoshima iseki kara shutsudo shita higuma itai no hō-shasei tanso nendai — 'kuma okuri' girei no kigen to zen kindai no kyokō keitai o megutte" [Radiocarbon dates estimated from brown bear remains unearthed from the Otafukuiwa Cave in Rausu Town and the Nakanoshima site in Kitami City, with special reference to the origin and pre-modern style of bear-sending rituals of the Ainu]. *Zooarchaeology* 39:31–43.

Sato, Takehiro, Tetsuya Amano, Hiroko Ono, Hajime Ishida, Haruto Kodera, Hirofumi Matsumura, et al. 2007. "Origins and Genetic Features of the Okhotsk People, Revealed by Ancient Mitochondrial DNA Analysis." *Journal of Human Genetics* 52 (7): 618–27.

Segawa, Takuro. 2005. *Ainu ekoshisutemu no kokogaku: Ibunka koryu to shizen riyo kara mita Ainu shakai seiritsushi* [The archaeology of the Ainu ecosystem: Intercultural exchange and natural resource use in the formation of Ainu society]. Hokkaido Shuppan Kikaku Senta.

Segawa, Takuro. 2011. *Ainu no sekai* [The world of the Ainu]. Kodansha.

Shea, Haley, G. Susan Mosley-Howard, Daryl Baldwin, George Ironstrack, Kate Rousmaniere, and Joseph E. Schroer. 2019. "Cultural Revitalization as a Restorative Process to Combat Racial and Cultural Trauma and Promote Living Well." *Cultural Diversity & Ethnic Minority Psychology* 25 (4): 553–65.

Shimizu, Yuji. 2018. "Towards a Respectful Repatriation of Stolen Ainu Ancestral Remains." Translated by Jeff Gayman. In *Indigenous Efflorescence: Beyond Revitalization in Sapmi and Ainu Mosir*, edited by Gerald Roche, Hiroshi Maruyama, and Åsa Virdi Kroik. Monographs in Anthropology Series. Australia National University Press.

Shinichiro, Takakura. 1960. "The Ainu of Northern Japan: A Study in Conquest and Acculturation." Translated and annotated by John A. Harrison. *Transactions of the American Philosophical Society*, n.s. 50 (4): 1–88.

Siddle, Richard. 1996. *Race, Resistance and the Ainu of Japan*. Routledge.

Siddle, Richard. 2003. "The Limits to Citizenship in Japan: Multiculturalism, Indigenous Rights and the Ainu." *Citizenship Studies* 7 (4): 447–62.

Siebold, Philipp F. von. 1897. *Nippon*. Vols. 1 and 2. 2nd ed. L. Woerl.

Smith, Anna V. 2020. "Trump's Impact on Indian Country over Four Years." *High Country News*, December 16. https://www.hcn.org/articles/indigenous-affairs-trumps-impact-on-indian-country-over-four-years.

Sommer, Ulrike. 2017. "Archaeology and Nationalism." In *Key Concepts in Public Archaeology*, edited by Gabriel Moshenska. University of British Columbia Press.

Steeves, Paulette. 2018. "Indigeneity." *Oxford Bibliographies*. https://doi.org/10.1093/obo/9780199766567-0199.

Steeves, Paulette. 2021. *The Indigenous Paleolithic of the Western Hemisphere*. University of Nebraska Press.

Stevens, Georgina. 2014. "The Ainu, Law, and Legal Mobilization, 1984–2009." In *Beyond Ainu Studies: Changing Academic and Public Perspectives*, edited by Mark J. Hudson, ann-elise lewallen, and Mark K. Watson. University of Hawai'i Press.

Strout, Benjamin. 1982. "A New Era." In *Tribal Government: A New Era*, edited by William Brescia. Choctaw Heritage Press, Mississippi Band of Choctaw Indians.

Sugimoto, Yoshio. 1999. "Making Sense of Nihonjinron." *Thesis Eleven* 57 (1): 81–96.

Tahara, Kaori. 1999. "Asia & Pacific: Nibutani Dam Case." *Indigenous Law Bulletin* 70. https://classic.austlii.edu.au/au/journals/IndigLawB/1999/70.html.

Tahara, Kaori. 2006. *Senjuminzoku Ainu* [The Indigenous Ainu]. Ningenshupan.

Tajima, Atushi, Masanori Hayami, Katsushi Tokunaga, Takeo Juji, Masafumi Matsuo, Sangkot Marzuki, et al. 2004. "Genetic Origins of the Ainu Inferred from Combined DNA Analyses of Maternal and Paternal Lineages." *Journal of Human Genetics* 49:187–93.

Takase, Katsunori. 2020. "Long-Term Marine Resource Use in Hokkaido, Northern Japan: New Insights into Sea Mammal Hunting and Fishing." *World Archaeology* 51 (3): 408–28.

TallBear, Kim. 2013. "Genomic Articulations of Indigeneity." *Social Studies of Science* 43 (4): 509–33.

Tanaka, Sakurako. 2000. "The Ainu of Tsugaru: The Indigenous History and Shamanism of Northern Japan." PhD diss., University of British Columbia.

Tani, Kazutaka. 2007. "Transition of Pre-ceramic Age Assemblages of Stone Tools in Nojiri-ko Archaeological Sites." [In Japanese.] *Bulletin of the Nagano Prefectural Museum of History* 13:3–21.

Taylor, John Leonard. 2006. "Indigenous Peoples and Government Policy in Canada." Last updated by Gretchen Albers in 2020. *The Canadian Encyclopedia*. https://www.thecanadianencyclopedia.ca/en/article/aboriginal-people-government-policy.

Trigger, Bruce. 1984. "Alternative Archaeologies: Nationalist, Colonialist, Imperialist." *Man*, n.s. 19 (3): 355–70.

Truth and Reconciliation Commission (TRCC). 2015. *Canada's Residential Schools: The Métis Experience; The Final Report of the Truth and Reconciliation Commission of Canada*. Vol. 3. McGill-Queen's University Press.

Tsagelnik, Tatsiana. 2022. "In Search of Indigenous Identity Through Re-creation of Ainu Self-Sustaining Community: Praxis and Learning in Action." In *Discourses of*

Identity: Language Learning, Teaching, and Reclamation Perspectives in Japan, edited by Martin Mielick, Ryuko Kubota, and Luke Lawrence. Palgrave Macmillan.

Tsunemoto, Teruki. 2019a. "Ainu Shisaku Suishin Ho: Ainu to Nihon ni Tekigou Shita Senjumin Seisaku wo Mezashite" [The significance of the 2019 Ainu Measure Promotion Act: An Indigenous people's policy that suits the current conditions of Japan]. *Hogaku Kyoshitsu* 468:65–71.

Tsunemoto, Teruki. 2019b. "Overview of the Ainu Policy Promotion Act of 2019." https://fpcj.jp/wp/wp-content/uploads/2019/11/b8102b519c7b7c4a4e129763f23 ed690.pdf.

Tsunemoto, Teruki. 2023. "The Significance of the 2019 Ainu Measure Promotion Act: An Indigenous People's Policy That Suits the Current Conditions of Japan." [In Japanese.] Partial translation with revision of Teruki Tsunemoto, "Ainu Shisaku Suishin Ho: Ainu to Nihon ni Tekigou Shita Senjumin Seisaku wo Mezashite," *Hogaku Kyoshitsu* 468 (2019): 63–69.

Uribe, Julieta. 2006. "A Study on the Relationship Between Canadian Aboriginal Peoples and the Canadian State." Focal Policy Paper 06-04. Canadian Foundation for the Americas (FOCAL). https://canadacommons.ca/artifacts/1216330/a-study -on-the-relationship-between-canadian-aboriginal-peoples-and-the-canadian -state/1769432/.

Utagawa, Hiroshi. 2002. "The World of the Okhotsk 'Bear Festival.'" [In Japanese.] In *Another World of the North*, edited by Yoshihiro Nishiaki and Hiroshi Utagawa. University of Tokyo Press.

Uzawa, Kanako. 2018. "Everyday Acts of Resurgence and Diasporic Indigeneity Among the Ainu of Tokyo." In *Indigenous Efflorescence: Beyond Revitalization in Sapmi and Ainu Mosir*, edited by Gerald Roche, Hiroshi Maruyama, and Åsa Virdi Kroik. Monographs in Anthropology Series. Australia National University Press.

Uzawa, Kanako. 2019. "Japan." In *The Indigenous World 2019*, edited by David Nathaniel Berger. IWGIA.

Uzawa, Kanako, and Jeffry Gayman. 2020. "Japan." In *The Indigenous World 2020*, edited by Dwayne Mamo. IWGIA.

Uzawa, Kanako, Jeffry Gayman, and Fumiya Nagai. 2021. "Japan." In *The Indigenous World 2021*, edited by Dwayne Mamo. IWGIA.

Uzawa, Kanako, Jeffry Gayman, and Fumiya Nagai. 2022. "Japan." In *The Indigenous World 2022*, edited by Dwayne Mamo. IWGIA.

Walker, Alexa, Brian Egan, and George Nicholas, eds. 2016. *DNA and Indigeneity: The Changing Role of Genetics in Indigenous Rights, Tribal Belonging, and Repatriation*. Symposium Proceedings. Intellectual Property Issues in Cultural Heritage (IPinCH) Project, Simon Fraser University.

Walker, Brett. 2001. *The Conquest of Ainu Lands: Ecology and Culture in Japanese Expansion, 1590–1800*. University of California Press.

Wallace, Anthony F. C. 1956. "Revitalization Movements." *American Anthropologist*, n.s. 58 (2): 264–81.

Watanabe, Hitoshi. 1973. *The Ainu Ecosystem: Environment and Group Structure.* University of Washington Press.

Watkins, Joe. 2000. *Indigenous Archaeology: American Indian Values and Scientific Practice.* AltaMira Press.

Watson, Mark K. 2010. "Diasporic Indigeneity: Place and the Articulation of Ainu Identity in Tokyo, Japan." *Environment and Planning A* 42 (2): 268–84.

Watson, Mark K. 2014. *Japan's Ainu Minority in Tokyo: Diasporic Indigeneity and Urban Politics.* Routledge.

Weber, Andrzej W., Peter Jordan, and Hirofumi Kato. 2013. "Environmental Change and Cultural Dynamics of Holocene Hunter–Gatherers in Northeast Asia: Comparative Analyses and Research Potentials in Cis-Baikal (Siberia, Russia) and Hokkaido (Japan)." *Quaternary International* 290–91:3–20.

Wilkins, David. 2011. "A History of Federal Indian Policy." In *American Indian Politics and the American Political System*, edited by David E. Wilkins and Heidi Kiiwetinepinesilk Stark. 3rd ed. Rowman & Littlefield.

Working Group for the Research on Living Conditions of the Dogai Ainu (WGDA). 2011. *Hokkaido Gai Ainu no Seikatsu Jittai Chosa' Sagyo Bukai Hokokusho* [Final report of the Working Group for the Research on Living Conditions of the Dogai Ainu]. Working Group for the Research on Living Conditions of the Dogai Ainu.

Yamada, Goro, and Sachiko Shibauchi. 1997. "Nuts Excavated from Jomon Sites of Hokkaido." [In Japanese.] *Bulletin of the Historical Museum of Hokkaido* 25:17–30.

Yamada, Takao. 2003. "Anthropological Studies of the Ainu in Japan: Past and Present." *Japanese Review of Cultural Anthropology* 4:75–106.

Yamanouchi, Sugao. 1964. "Nihon senshi jidai gaisetsu" [The outline of Japanese history]. In *Nihon genshi bijutsu I: Jomon-shiki doki* [Primitive art in Japan, vol. 1, Jomon pottery]. Kodansha.

Yamaura, Kiyoshi. 1998. "The Sea Mammal Hunting Cultures of the Okhotsk Sea with Special Reference to Hokkaido Prehistory." *Arctic Anthropology* 35 (1): 321–34.

Yanagida, Yasuo. 1986. "Shudan-bochi kara obo e" [From communal cemeteries to kingly burials]. In *Hakkutsu ga kataru Nihon-shi* [Japanese history as seen from excavations], vol. 6, edited by K. Yokoyama. Shin-Jinbutsuoraisha.

Yeh, Joyce Hsiu-yen, Su-chen Lin, Shu-chuan Lai, Ying-hao Huang, Chen Yi-fong, Yi-tze Lee, and Fikret Berkes. 2021. "Taiwanese Indigenous Cultural Heritage and Revitalization: Community Practices and Local Development." *Sustainability* 13 (4): 1799.

Yoshida, Akira. 1998. *Wa-oken no jidai* [The age of the Wa kingship]. Shin'nihon Shuppan.

Yoshida, Yasuyuki, and John Ertl. 2016. "Archaeological Practice and Social Movements: Ethnography of Jomon Archaeology and the Public." *Journal of the International Center for Cultural Resource Studies* 2:47–71.

Yoshihara, Hideki, and Noriko Inoue. 2018. "The Sacred Landscape of Ainu Culture and Its Cultural Landscapes: Case Study on the Conservation Strategy in Biratori City, Hokkaido." *Almatourism* 9 (8): 107–28.

Zellen, Barry. 2010. "The Inuit, the State, and the Battle for the Arctic." *Georgetown Journal of International Affairs* 11 (11): 57–64.

Zgusta, Richard. 2015. *The Peoples of Northeast Asia Through Time: Precolonial Ethnic and Cultural Processes Along the Coast Between Hokkaido and the Bering Strait.* Brill.

INDEX

Aboriginal Australians, 120, 121, 122*t*7, 123, 133, 182, 204; land rights, 123–24; "stolen generations," 121–23, 122*t*7. *See also* Torres Strait Islanders

Aboriginal Canadians, 114, 115, 116, 117, 118*t*6, 119, 120. *See also* First Nations of Canada; Inuit; Métis

aboriginal title, in Canada, 118*t*6, 120. *See also* Native title

Advisory Council for Future Ainu Policy, 105*t*4, 149, 150, 208

Ainu: allotment of land, 106, 136, 138; and archaeology, 88–89, 159–69, 198, 200, 208; assimilation of, 8, 9, 20, 21, 33, 97, 99, 100, 101, 103, 104, 106, 136, 137, 139, 140, 142, 152, 204; colonization of, 9, 21, 33; cultural practices banned, 99, 100, 131; Dogai Ainu ("those Ainu living outside of Hokkaido"), 172; economic and social disparities, 23; economic development, 11, 184–87, 191, 203, 205, 206; ethnogenesis of, 90, 93, 95, 106, 167, 168; genetics, 5, 7, 27, 29, 35, 43, 44, 47, 48, 162, 174, 200, 203; "hidden Ainu," 26, 171; history, 7, 19–22, 92, 96–104, 105–6*t*4, 139, 150, 157, 162, 167, 168, 184, 203, 208, 209; homeland, 15, 95; identity, 33; interest in American Indian governance, 7, 174, 175, 176, 181, 207; international festivals, 21–22; Japan's Indigenous population, 5, 11, 12, 13, 15; origins of, 41–46, 92, 95, 167, 168; population statistics, 22–23; proto-Ainu culture, 161; protohistoric, 88–89; relationship to Okhotsk culture, 44, 88, 89, 159, 162, 167, 168; relationship to Satsumon culture, 83, 88, 167, 168; relationship to Tobinitai culture, 88, 158, 163, 200; relationship with Wajin, 21, 22, 33, 96–100, 106*t*4, 203–4; "Silent Ainu," 26; urban Ainu, 11, 23–24, 31, 34, 172–73, 176, 194, 196

Ainu: Spirit of a Northern People, 15, 33

Ainu Association of Hokkaido, 12, 22, 137–41, 137*n*1, 152, 153, 175, 188, 206. *See also* Hokkaido Ainu Association; Hokkaido Ainu Kyokai; Hokkaido Utari Kyokai

Ainu Mosir ("world, or land of the Ainu"), 102, 102*n*1, 161, 194

Ainu Mosir (World of the Ainu), film, 31
allotment of land, 106, 111*t*5, 112, 130,
    136, 138; in Japan, 106, 136, 138; in the
    United States, 111*t*5, 112, 130
America/ns, 8, 14, 21, 22, 28, 36, 40, 41,
    99, 101, 102, 103, 106, 110, 111*t*5, 112,
    113, 137, 146, 175, 187, 202, 207. *See
    also* United States
American Indian, 3, 4, 6, 7, 8, 14, 15, 22,
    23, 25, 26, 27, 28, 29, 30, 36, 37*n*1, 41,
    93, 99, 101, 103, 104, 110–14, 111*t*5,
    130, 131, 132, 136, 170, 174, 175, 176,
    181, 183, 197, 198, 201, 202, 204, 206,
    207; Ainu interest in governance, 7,
    174, 175, 176, 181, 207; allotment of
    land, 111*t*5, 112, 130; ancestry, 27–28;
    assimilation of, 7, 99, 106, 112, 130,
    131; economic development, 207;
    relationships with United States
    government, 22, 26, 27, 99, 101, 104,
    110–14, 111*t*5, 131, 132, 136, 174, 175,
    183; tribal blood quantum, 27; urban
    Indians, 113, 176. *See also* Native
    American
American Indian Movement (AIM), 111*t*5,
    113–14, 114*n*1; and Alcatraz Island
    (1969), 111*t*5, 114; and Trail of Broken
    Treaties 1972, 111*t*5, 114
Amur River region, 43, 47, 49, 85, 88, 96,
    161, 162, 203; genetic contribution to
    Okhotsk culture, 85, 162, 203
Aotearoa. *See* New Zealand.
ascribed versus *achieved* status, 69*t*3,
    72–73
asircepnomi ceremony, 191, 192*f*26
assimilation, 7, 8, 9, 20, 21, 33, 97, 99,
    100, 101, 103, 104, 106, 112, 117, 121,
    126*t*8, 129, 130, 131, 132, 136, 137, 139,
    140, 142, 152, 204; of Ainu, 8, 9, 20,
    21, 33, 97, 99, 100, 101, 103, 104, 106,
    136, 137, 139, 140, 142, 152, 204; of
    American Indians, 7, 99, 106, 112, 130,
    131; of Australian Aboriginals, 121; of

First Nations of Canada, 117, 130, 131;
    of Māori 126*t*8, 129, 131, 132
Australia, 101, 103, 120, 121, 122*t*7, 123,
    124, 129, 130, 131, 133, 134, 146, 177,
    178, 181, 182, 201; assimilation of
    Aboriginal Peoples, 121; relationships
    with Aboriginal Peoples, 120–24;
    support for UNDRIP, 122*t*7, 124. *See
    also* Australia, Commonwealth of; *see
    specific states by name*
Australia, Commonwealth of, 121, 122*t*7,
    123, 124; Aboriginal and Torres Strait
    Islander Heritage Protection Act 1984,
    122*t*7, 123. *See also* Australia; *see spe-
    cific states by name*
authenticity, 29–31

bakufu (military government), 20
basho (trading zone), 20, 97, 130
Batchelor, John, 36, 195
Biratori, town of, 4, 13, 147, 148, 171, 186
Biratori Dam Project, 147–48; Biratori
    Dam Area Cultural Conservation
    Measures Study Group, 148
blood quantum, 27–28; versus hypodes-
    cent, 28. *See also* hypodescent
Buddhism, 74–75

Canada, 8, 37, 101, 107, 109, 114, 115, 116,
    117, 119, 118–19*t*6, 120, 121, 129, 130,
    131, 133, 146, 181, 201, 203; aboriginal
    title, 129; assimilation of First Nations,
    117, 130, 131; ratification of UNDRIP,
    118*t*6, 119; Truth and Reconciliation
    Commission of Canada (TRCC),
    115–16
Canadian legislation related to First Na-
    tions, 117–19, 118–19*t*6; Constitution
    Act 1867, 117, 118*t*6; Constitution Act
    1982, 118*t*6; Gradual Civilization Act
    1857, 117, 119*t*6; Gradual Enfranchise-
    ment Act 1869, 117, 118*t*6; Indian Act
    1876, 117, 118*t*6; Indian Act Amend-

ment 1884, 118t6; Indian Act Amendment 1894, 118t6; Indian Act 1951,
117, 118t6; Indian Lands Act 1860, 117,
118t6.
Capron, Horace, 102
Carlisle Indian Industrial School, 111t5,
112
Center for Ainu and Indigenous Studies,
3, 4, 12, 22, 163, 186, 189
chashi (fortified site), 163, 163n1
chise (traditional Ainu dwelling), 174
Choctaw Nation of Oklahoma, 6, 111t5,
207
Clark, William Smith, 102; President, Sapporo Agricultural College / Hokkaido
University, 102
Council for Ainu Policy Promotion,
137n1, 150
cultural revitalization, 187–93; Ainu
ceremonies, 189f24, 190–91, 190f25,
192f26; Shakushain Festival, 4, 188,
188f23

daimyo (vassals to shoguns), 19, 21
Dawes Severalty Act 1887. See General
Allotment Act 1887
Dogai Ainu ("those Ainu living outside of
Hokkaido"), 172
dogū (ceramic figurines), 55, 56–57t2, 58–
59, 59f5, 61, 64
dotaku (bronze bells), 69t3
dual structure model, 42–43, 48. See also
genetics; Hanihara, Kazuro

Edo, 11, 20, 21, 93, 97, 98, 99, 106t4
Ellick, Carol J., 3, 45f3, 50f4, 78f10,
84f13, 86f14, 179f20, 185f22, 188f23,
193f27
Emishi, 19, 35, 92, 92–93, 94–96, 100,
104, 106t4, 163, 197, 200, 203. See also
Watarishima Emishi
Epi-Jomon, 77, 77n1, 83, 84f13, 91, 94. See
also Zuko-Jomon

ethnicity, 25
ethnic Japanese, 12, 15, 27, 33. See also
Wajin
Ezo, 11, 19, 20, 21, 96, 97, 98, 99, 105–6t4.
See also Hokkaido

First Nations of Canada, 37n1, 114, 117,
130, 131; assimilation of by Canada,
117, 130, 131; comprised of First
Nations, Métis, and Inuit, 37n1, 114;
relationships with British Columbia,
119–20; relationships with Canada,
114–20, 118–19t6. See also Inuit;
Métis
Foundation for Ainu Culture, 105t4,
137n1, 145, 145t10
Foundation for Research and Promotion
of Ainu Culture (FRPAC), 105t4, 145,
145t10

General Allotment Act 1887, 111t5, 112
genetics, 38–40, 40–41, 42–43, 41–45,
46–47, 48, 66, 162, 201, 202; misuse,
40–41; and the dual structure model,
42–43; population admixtures, 46–
47, 66; and the population history of
Japanese archipelago, 41–45, 48; and
Yayoi, 43, 66, 162, 201, 202
Global Station for Indigenous Studies and
Cultural Diversity, 6, 148, 181, 187
Golden Kamuy, The (Japanese manga,
graphic novel), 30, 34

Habu, Junko, 48, 53, 58, 61, 75, 76, 80,
158, 160, 200
Hanihara, Kazuro, 42–43, 48. See also
dual structure model; genetics
haniwa (funerary pottery sculptures), 73
heritage, 22, 23, 26, 42, 43, 122t7, 123,
148, 159; Ainu heritage, 22, 23, 26, 167,
172, 186, 208; in Taiwan, 191
heritage-based tourism, 191. See also
cultural revitalization

"heritagization," defined 191
Hokkai Ainu Kyokai, 137
Hokkaido Ainu Association, 23, 105*t*4, 137*n*1, 155. *See also* Ainu Association of Hokkaido; Hokkaido Ainu Kyokai; Hokkaido Utari Kyokai
Hokkaido Ainu Kyokai, 139, 140
Hokkaido Colonization Office, 100. *See also* Hokkaido Development Commission; Kaitakushi
Hokkaido Development Commission, 99, 102, 104*t*4. *See also* Hokkaido Colonization Office; Kaitakushi
Hokkaido Island, 3, 4, 7, 8, 11, 12, 13, 14, 15, 16, 20, 21, 22, 23, 24, 30, 31, 33, 41, 43, 44, 45*f*3, 46, 49, 50*f*4, 92, 93, 94, 95, 96, 110, 136, 137, 138, 139, 144, 147, 148, 151, 154, 172, 175, 176, 177, 178*f*19, 181, 184, 186, 187, 189, 191, 196, 197, 198, 199, 200, 207, 208; archaeology of, 51, 54, 58, 61, 71, 75, 77–90, 78*f*10, 82*f*11, 82*f*12, 86*f*14, 91, 96, 104, 157, 158, 159–69, 164*f*16, 166*f*18, 170, 202; chronology, 78*f*10, 84*f*13, 167; climate, 19; colonization of, 21, 33, 99–104, 106, 107, 135, 204; geography of, 17–19; government, 22, 23, 145, 181, 183; history, 11, 19, 91, 92, 96–104, 105*t*4, 140. *See also* Ezo
Hokkaido University, 3, 6, 12, 22, 102, 137*n*1, 148, 163, 166, 177, 181, 186, 187, 189, 189*f*24. *See also* Sapporo Agricultural College
Hokkaido Utari Kyokai, 105*t*4, 139, 140
Honshu Island, 13, 15, 16, 17, 19, 24, 33, 44, 45, 45*f*3, 46, 49, 50*f*4, 52, 54, 55, 60*f*6, 61, 65*f*8, 66, 70*f*9, 71, 77, 81, 83, 84*f*13, 85, 87, 92, 95, 96, 97, 104, 159, 161, 163, 167, 171, 198, 199, 199*f*28, 200, 202. *See also* Honshu–Shikoku–Kyushu Islands; HSK islands
Honshu–Shikoku–Kyushu Islands, 49, 64, 66, 75, 91, 161, 162, 198, 202; as

Japanese mainland, 49, 64, 75, 91. *See also* HSK islands
Howell, David, 92, 97, 98, 100, 104, 106
HSK islands, 91, 157, 162; as Japanese mainland, 91, 157
Hudson, Mark J., 35, 85, 91, 92, 95, 167, 168
Hunn Report on the Department of Māori Affairs, 126*t*8, 127–28
Hypodescent, 28, 28*n*1

Ichikawa, Morihiro, 154, 183
identity, 24–29; and authenticity, 29–31; and ethnicity, 24; biethnic identity, 25–26; and DNA, 28–29
identity politics, 24, 31–32; defined 31
ikupasuy ("libation sticks"), 164, 190; defined, 164
inaw (ritually prepared tree branches), 163, 164, 164*f*16, 165, 165*f*17
indigeneity, 28, 32
Indigenous Archaeology, 4, 6, 159, 160, 169, 170, 200, 208; and the Ainu, 4, 169, 200, 208
Initial Kofun Package (IKP), composition of 73
International Work Group for Indigenous Affairs (IWGIA), 140, 151, 153, 173, 178
Inuit, 37*n*1, 114, 115
Ishihara, Mai, 12, 26, 132, 160, 171, 172
Iyomante, 88, 168, 179. *See also* sending ceremonies

Japan, climate of, 17, 18*t*1, 19; geography of, 16–19; map of, 16*f*2; ratifies UN-DRIP, 12, 105*t*4
Japanese legislation related to Ainu, 12, 13; Act for the Promotion of Ainu Culture and Dissemination of Knowledge Regarding Ainu Traditions, etc. 1997 / Ainu Culture Promotion Act 1997, 105*t*4, 137, 140, 142, 143–46, 147;

Act Promoting Measures to Achieve a Society in which the Pride of Ainu People is Respected 2019, 13, 105*t*4; Ainu Measures Promotion Act / Ainu Policy Promotion Act / Ainu Policy Measures Promotion Act 2019, 105*t*4, 150–54, 155; Ainu Shinpo / Ainu New Law, 140; Family Registry Law 1871, 100, 105*t*4, 174; Former Aborigines Protection Act 1899, 21, 105*t*4, 136–37, 140, 142; Hakodate Edict 1802, 99, 106*t*4; Land Reform Ordinance 1948, 138; Law for the Promotion of Ainu Culture and for the Dissemination and Advocacy for the Traditions of the Ainu and Ainu Culture 2006, 4, 105*t*4; Regulations for Sale and Lease of Hokkaido Lands 1872, 105*t*4; Resolution calling for the Recognition of the Ainu People as an Indigenous People of Japan 2008, 12, 105*t*4, 148–50

Jinshin Koseki (Family Registry) 1872, 174

Jomon, 13, 14, 41, 42, 43, 44, 53, 56–57*t*2, 65, 66, 67, 71, 75, 80, 81, 83, 84*f*13, 92, 158, 159*f*15, 160, 161, 163, 168, 198, 202, 203; burials and burial placement, 57*t*2, 61, 63–64, 67; chronology, 53, 56–57*t*2, 78f10, 80, 84f11; Early Jomon, 58–59, 56*t*2; economy and daily life, 54, 56–57*t*2, 63–64; Final Jomon, 62–63, 57*t*2; food resources, 53, 54, 55, 56–57*t*2, 59, 60, 61, 63, 80, 81; of Hokkaido, 75, 78*f*10, 80–82, 84*f*13, 84, 85, 87, 88, 89, 161, 162, 199; house styles, 54, 55, 56–57*t*2, 58, 63; Incipient Jomon, 54–55, 56*t*2; Initial Jomon, 55–58, 56*t*2; of the Japanese mainland, 53–64; Jomon Prehistoric Sites in Northern Japan inscription, 13, 158, 159*f*15; lacquerware, 59, 61, 64; Late Jomon 61, 57*t*2; Middle Jomon, 60–61, 57*t*2; pottery, 54, 55, 56–57*t*2, 58, 61, 65, 80

Kaitakushi, 99, 100, 103, 104*t*4

Kato, Hirofumi, 1, 90, 163, 164, 165*f*17, 166, 167, 168, 170, 177, 178, 186, 200, 208; on formation of Ainu culture, 167, 168

Kakizaki clan, 97, 106*t*4. *See also* Matsumae clan

Kamchatka Peninsula, 43, 44, 45*f*3, 95

kamuy (Ainu deity), 164, 189, 190, 191

kamuynomi ceremony, at Hokkaido University, 189*f*24; at Raporo Ainu Nation, 190–91, 190*f*25; defined, 191

Kayano, Shigeru, 29, 142, 143, 186

Kofun, 43, 67, 72, 73–75, 83, 86, 87, 89, 91; burials and burial placement, 73, 74; chronology, 73; Early Kofun, 73; *haniwa*, 73; Kinki-core Region/Horizon, 73, 74; Late Kofun, 73, 74; metalworking, 73, 74; Middle Kofun, 73, 74. *See also* Initial Kofun Package (IKP)

Korean peninsula, 16, 44, 45*f*3, 46, 59, 74, 89, 161, 197; and Yayoi, 66, 67, 68–69*t*3, 71

koseki (household registers) 100, 171, 174. See also *Jinshin Koseki* 1872

Koshamain's War 1457, 97, 106*t*4

kotan (Ainu village or town), 102, 155, 183, 184, 186, 191

Kuril Islands, 15, 29, 45*f*3, 49, 50*f*4, 85, 87, 89, 92, 95, 96, 99, 196

kyudojin ("former aborigines"), 100

Kyushu Island, 16, 44, 45, 45*f*3, 46, 49, 55, 59, 63, 64, 66, 67, 69*t*3, 71, 72, 75, 91, 161, 162, 198, 202. *See also* Honshu–Shikoku–Kyushu Islands; HSK islands

lacquerware, 19, 57*t*2, 59, 60*f*6, 61, 64, 97, 164, 167, 168

Lake Akan, 4, 184, 191; Ainu village at, 4, 185*f*22, 191

lewallen, ann-elise, 11, 12*n*1, 28

Loy, Christopher, 34, 100, 106, 137*n*1, 139, 140, 141, 155

Māori, 124, 125, 126, 127, 128, 129, 130,
    131, 132, 134, 197, 204, 205; assimila-
    tion of, 126t8, 129, 131, 132; economic
    development, 127; Kīngitanga (King
    movement) 1858, 125; relationship
    with New Zealand government, 124–
    29, 126t8, 130, 131; *rūnanga*, 125, 126;
    Treaty of Waitangi 1840, 125, 126t8,
    128; urbanization, 127, 128. *See also*
    New Zealand legislation regarding
    Māori
marae (Māori central meeting ground),
    126
Matsumae clan 11, 20, 97–99, 106t4. *See
    also* Kakizaki clan
Meiji era, 21, 99–104, 183; government, 8,
    21, 33, 96, 99–104, 106, 135
Meiji Restoration of 1868, 21, 33, 96, 106t4
Métis, 37n1, 114, 115, 118t6; defined, 115–
    16. *See also* First Nations of Canada
minzoku ("ethnic group;" "nation;" "race;"
    "separate people"), 12, 151
Mizoguchi, Koji, 66, 67, 69t3, 70, 71, 72,
    73, 74, 76, 200
Menashi-Kunashir rebellion, 98, 106t4
Munro, Neil Gordon, 195; Munro House,
    186

nationalist archaeology, 13–14, 158
National Keeping Place (Japan), 177,
    178f19
Native American, 26, 28, 37n1. *See also*
    American Indian
Native title, 122t7, 123, 124. *See also*
    aboriginal title
nettu uyoku (net far right), 12
Neolithic, 41, 42, 43; characteristics, 51,
    52–53; lifeways, 54, 198
New South Wales (Australia), 122t7, 123;
    Aboriginal Protection Amending Act
    1915, 122t7; Board for Protection of
    Aborigines 1883, 122t7; penal colony
    at Port Jackson 1788, 122t7

New Zealand, 8, 101, 109, 120, 124–29,
    126t8, 130, 131, 132, 133, 134, 146, 197,
    201, 205; assimilation of Māori, 126t8,
    129, 131, 132; Hunn Report 1960,
    126t8, 127–28; Native Department,
    125, 126, 127; Native Land Court 1865,
    126; relationship with Māori, 124–29,
    126t8, 130, 131; and UNDRIP, 126t8.
    See also Māori; New Zealand legisla-
    tion regarding Māori
New Zealand legislation regarding Māori,
    126t8; Māori Affairs Act 1953, 126t8,
    127; Māori Affairs Amendment
    Act 1967, 126t8, 127; Māori Affairs
    Restructuring Act 1989, 126t8, 128;
    Māori Councils Act 1900, 126, 126t8;
    Māori Representation Act 1867, 126t8;
    New Zealand Constitution Act 1852,
    125, 126t8
Nibutani Dam court case, 105t4, 141, 142–
    43, 144, 147, 155
Nicholas, George P., 6, 159, 170, 208
Nihonjinron, 13, 158, 160
Nihon Shoki, 19, 92, 94, 106t6
Nivkh/Nivkhi culture, 43, 88, 95
North America/n, 17, 29, 37, 37n1, 93, 116,
    146, 193
Northern Territory (Australia), 122t7,
    123; Aboriginal Land Rights Act 1976,
    122t7; *Millirrpum v Nabalco Pty Ltd*
    1971, 122t7, 123

obsidian, as raw material source, 18, 55,
    63, 64, 198; as trade item, 55, 64, 198;
Okinawa Island, 16, 36, 46, 146. *See also*
    Ryukyu Islands
Okhotsk culture, 44, 83, 85–86, 87, 88, 91,
    92, 95, 96, 159, 161, 163, 202; economy,
    87; geographical extent, 44; genetics, 44;
    house styles, 86f14; iyomante, 88, 89;
    pottery, 87; relationship to Ainu culture,
    44, 88, 89, 159, 162, 167, 168; relation-
    ship to Satsumon culture, 88, 89, 161,

168; relationship to Tobinitai culture, 88, 161; trade 86. *See also* Ainu culture; Satsumon culture; Tobinitai culture

Okhotsk, Sea of, 16, 45*f*3, 83, 161, 166

Oshima Peninsula, 19, 33, 87, 97

Pākehā ("White person"), 125, 128

Paleo-Honshu Island, 49, 50*f*4, 51

Paleolithic, dates, 51; Early versus Late, 51; on Hokkaido, 78*f*10, 79–80; on Japanese mainland, 52, 54

Paleo-Sakhalin-Hokkaido-Kurile Peninsula (Paleo-SHK Peninsula), 49, 50*f*4

Pan-Indianism, 206

Parker, Cynthia Ann, 202

Penhallow, David, 102, 103, 110

Porotokotan, Ainu Museum, 3, 4*f*1, 184

Queensland (Australia), 122*t*7, 123; Native Title Act 1993, 122*t*7, 124; *Mabo v Queensland* 1988, 122*t*7, 123; *Mabo v Queensland 2* 1992, 122*t*7, 123

Raporo Ainu Nation, 32, 154, 171, 180, 181, 182, 183, 186, 187, 189, 190, 190*f*25, 205; Lawsuit on Indigenous Rights to Fish, 154, 171, 180–83, 186, 187, 205; and UNDRIP, 32, 180–81

reburial, 72, 177–79

repatriation, 28, 29, 154, 169, 177–80, 179*f*20

Report on the 2008 Hokkaido Ainu Living Conditions Survey, 22–24, 176

rice 46, 47, 54, 63, 64, 66, 67, 68*t*3, 70*f*9, 71, 75, 77, 85, 160, 161, 162, 197, 198, 200, 202; introduction of, 47, 63, 68*t*3, 161; irrigation-based / wet rice agriculture, 46, 47, 64, 66, 67, 68*t*3, 70*f*9, 75, 77, 160, 161, 162, 197, 198, 200, 202

ronin (masterless, wandering samurai), 20

rūnanga (Māori tribal councils), 125

Ryukyu Islands, 36, 45*f*3, 76; conquered by Japan, 36

Sakhalin Island, 15, 29, 43, 44, 45*f*3, 47, 49, 50*f*4, 85, 88, 92, 95, 96, 99, 101, 105*t*4, 161, 178, 196, 202

Sapporo, 3, 4, 6, 13, 18, 18*t*1, 19, 137, 171, 179*f*20, 184, 189, 196; Ainu Association of, 189; District Court, 141, 149, 154, 171, 180, 183, 187, 205

Sapporo Agricultural College, 102

Sashima, Masaki, 171, 172, 181, 182, 183, 186; chairman emeritus of Raporo Ainu Nation, 171, 181, 182; death of, 183; as "hidden Ainu", 171

Saru River, 142, 143, 147, 148, 184, 191

Saru River Development Project and Flood Control Plan, 147

Saru River System Improvement Plan, 147

Sato, Takao, 88, 163

samurai, 11, 12*n*2, 20

Sannai Maruyama, 63, 65*f*8, 198, 199*f*28

Satsumon culture, 83, 86–87, 88, 89, 91, 96, 97, 100, 159, 161, 163, 167, 168; economy, 87; geographical extent, 161; house styles, 87; bear veneration, 88; relationship to Ainu culture, 83, 88, 167, 168; relationship to Okhotsk culture, 88, 89, 161, 168; relationship to Tobinitai culture, 87, 161. *See also* Ainu culture; Okhotsk culture; Tobinitai culture

seishin, 158

self-determination, 31, 111*t*5, 113, 119, 124, 133, 140, 151, 152, 175, 180, 204, 205, 207

sending ceremonies, 88, 95, 163, 168, 200. *See also* Iyomante

Shakushain, Ainu chieftain, 4, 20, 21, 98, 106*t*4

Shakushain Festival, 4, 188, 188*f*23

Shakushain Revolt, 20–21, 98, 106*t*4

Shikoku Island, 16, 45*f*3, 46, 49, 55, 64, 66, 71, 75, 91, 161, 162, 198, 202. *See also* Honshu–Shikoku–Kyushu Islands; HSK islands

Shintoism, 73, 74

shogun, 19, 20, 21

Shogun, book by James Clavell 1975, 19–20; television miniseries 1980, 19; television miniseries 2024, 20

shogunate, 11, 99

Siddle, Richard, 33, 94, 95, 100, 106, 136, 137*n*1, 146, 195

Social Darwinism, 101

South Australia (Australia), 122*t*7, 123; Aboriginal Land Trust Act 1966, 122*t*7, 123

Sushen, 92, 94, 106*t*4

Symbolic Space for Ethnic Harmony. *See* Upopoy

Tasmania (Australia), 123

terra nullius, 102, 119, 120, 131, 137; defined, 102; in Australia, 120; in British Columbia, 119; in Japan, 102, 137. *See also* aboriginal title; Native title

Tobinitai culture, 83, 87–88, 92, 159, 161, 163, 200; bear veneration, 88; geographical extent, 87; pottery, 87; as hybrid, 161; pithouse depressions for bear sending ceremonies, 200; relationship to Ainu culture, 88, 158, 163, 200; relationship to Okhotsk culture, 88, 161; relationship to Satsumon culture, 87, 161. *See also* Ainu culture; Okhotsk culture; Satsumon culture

Tohoku, region of Honshu, 17, 33, 58, 61, 71, 77, 81, 83, 87, 92, 94; immigrants from, 87; Emishi, 94

Tokugawa period, government, 20–21, 93, 97, 104, 130; shogunate, 99. *See also* Edo Period

Tokyo, 17, 18, 18*t*1, 19, 23, 24, 31, 34, 65, 97, 154, 171, 172, 176, 194, 196; climate, 18, 18*t*1, 19; Ainu Center, 176; National Museum, 67*f*7

Torres Strait Islanders, 122*t*7, 123, 133; Aboriginal and Torres Strait Islander

Heritage Protection Act 1984, 122*t*7, 123

tourism, 13, 30, 150, 151, 158, 184–87, 191

Treaty of St. Petersburg 1875, 96, 101, 105*t*4

Tsugaru Strait, 16, 17, 96, 159, 197, 202

Tsunemoto, Teruki, 137*n*1, 150, 151, 152, 153, 154, 155, 173, 207, 208

UNESCO World Cultural Heritage list, Jomon Prehistoric Sites in Northern Japan inscription, 13, 158, 159*f*15

United Nations Declaration on the Rights of Indigenous Peoples (UNDRIP) 12, 32, 105*t*4, 111*t*5, 118*t*6, 119, 122*t*7, 124, 126*t*8, 129, 149, 150, 152, 153, 175, 180, 181, 182, 205; supported by Australia, 122*t*7, 124; ratified by Canada, 118*t*6; ratified by Japan, 105*t*4, 149, 180; supported by New Zealand, 126*t*8; supported by the United States, 111*t*5; UNDRIP structure, 181; and the Raporo Ainu Nation, 32, 180–81

United States legislation related to American Indians, 111*t*5, 112–13, 176; Alaska Native Claims Settlement Act 1971, 111*t*5, 113; House Concurrent Resolution 108 1953, 111*t*5, 113; Indian Civil Rights Act 1968, 111*t*5, 113, Indian New Deal, 111*t*5, 112; Indian Relocation Act 1956, 111*t*5, 113, 176; Indian Reorganization Act 1934, 111*t*5, 112; Indian Self-Determination and Education Assistance Act 1975, 111*t*5, 113. *See also* American Indian relationships with United States.

Upopoy National Symbolic Space and Museum, 105*t*4, 184

Uzawa, Kanako, 24, 173, 176, 178, 187, 194

Victoria (Australia), 122*t*7; Aboriginal Lands Act 1970, 122*t*7, 123; Aboriginal Protection Act 1869, 122*t*7

Wajin, 12, 19, 20, 21, 22, 29, 32, 33, 35, 47, 96, 97, 98, 100, 104, 106*t*4, 136, 139, 150, 162, 187, 188, 197, 198, 203; as ethnic Japanese, 12, 15, 27, 33; "People of Wa", 19, 47, 106*t*4, 198; relationships with Ainu, 21, 22, 33, 96–100, 106*t*4, 203–4. *See also* ethnic Japanese

Walker, Brett, 34, 104, 106, 195

Watarishima Emishi, 94

Western Australia (Australia), 122*t*7, 123; Land (Titles and Traditional Usage) Act 1993, 124; *Western Australia v Commonwealth* 1995, 122*t*7, 124

Wheeler, William, 102

Yamato, 73, 94, 158; clan, 73; Kingdom, 73, 94; race, 158

Yayoi, 43, 64–74, 76, 77, 83, 84*f*13, 89, 91, 94, 161, 162, 163, 197, 198, 199, 201, 202; burials and burial placement, 67, 68–69*t*3; chronology, 66–67, 68–69*t*3, 84*f*13; derivation of name, 65; *dotaku* (bronze bells), 69*t*3; *Eastern Horizon*, 69*t*3, 71, 73; economies, 63, 64, 66, 68–69*t*3,70; genetics, 43, 66, 162, 201, 202; house styles, 67, 68–69*t*3,70; Initial Yayoi and Yayoi I, 67–70, 68*t*3; *Kyushu Horizon*, 68*t*3, 71, 73; Late Yayoi (Yayoi V), 69*t*3; metal use, 66, 84; Middle Yayoi (Yayoi II-IV), 71–72, 68*t*3; pottery of, 65–66; relation to China, 72, 73; relation to Jomon, 66, 68*t*3; relation to Korean peninsula, 66, 67, 68–69*t*3, 71; rice cultivation, 63, 64, 66, 67, 70*f*9, 77, 161, 202; transition to Kofun, 72–73; *Western Horizon*, 69*t*3, 71, 73

Yuki, Koji, 163, 164*f*16, 166, 166*f*18, 189

Zuko-Jomon, 77*n*1. *See* Epi-Jomon

ABOUT THE AUTHOR

Joe Watkins, a member of the Choctaw Nation of Oklahoma, currently works as a senior consultant for Archaeological and Cultural Education Consultants (ACE Consultants) and is an affiliated faculty member in the School of Anthropology at the University of Arizona. He was president of the Society for American Archaeology during 2019–21 and received its Lifetime Achievement Award in 2025. His study interests concern the ethical practice of anthropology and anthropology's relationships with descendant communities and populations on a global scale.